DANIEL DEFOE (1660–173...   ...ers including
hosiery merchant, owner of...   ...pantile works, soldier,
secret agent and political pam...   ...teer. He was also a prolific and
versatile writer and produced several hundred publications on a
wide variety of topics ranging from economics, politics and history,
to biography and crime, but it is for his novels, such as *Robinson
Crusoe* (1719), *Moll Flanders* (1722) and *Roxana* (1724), that he
remains best known.

RICHARD HAMBLYN is the author of *The Invention of Clouds:
How An Amateur Meteorologist Forged the Language of the Skies*,
which was shortlisted for the Samuel Johnson Prize 2002, and the
editor of *Earthly Powers*, an anthology of eighteenth-century earth
science writing. He is currently completing a collection of stories
about natural disasters in history.

DANIEL DEFOE

The Storm

Edited with an Introduction and Notes by
RICHARD HAMBLYN

PENGUIN BOOKS

PENGUIN BOOKS

Published by the Penguin Group
Penguin Books Ltd, 80 Strand, London WC2R ORL, England
Penguin Group (USA) Inc., 375 Hudson Street, New York, New York 10014, USA
Penguin Books Australia Ltd, 250 Camberwell Road, Camberwell, Victoria 3124, Australia
Penguin Books Canada Ltd, 10 Alcorn Avenue, Toronto, Ontario, Canada M4V 3B2
Penguin Books India (P) Ltd, 11 Community Centre, Panchsheel Park, New Delhi – 110 017, India
Penguin Group (NZ), cnr Airborne and Rosedale Roads, Albany, Auckland 1310, New Zealand
Penguin Books (South Africa) (Pty) Ltd, 24 Sturdee Avenue, Rosebank 2196, South Africa

Penguin Books Ltd, Registered Offices: 80 Strand, London WC2R ORL, England

www.penguin.com

First published 1704
This edition first published by Allen Lane 2003
Published in Penguin Books 2005
1

Introduction and editorial matter copyright © Richard Hamblyn, 2003
All rights reserved

Typeset by Rowland Phototypesetting Ltd, Bury St Edmunds, Suffolk
Printed in England by Clays Ltd, St Ives plc

Contents

Acknowledgements

First and foremost, many thanks to Laura Barber for commissioning and overseeing this edition, and to Peter Straus for paving its way.

Thanks also to Markman Ellis, Chris Reid and the members of the Eighteenth-Century Disasters Reading Group at Queen Mary, University of London, for the opportunity to discuss *The Storm*, and for their generosity in sharing their insights into it. I have also enjoyed enlightening conversations about Defoe and the weather with Giles Bergel, Gregory Dart, William Fiennes, Charlotte Grant, Judith Hawley, Megan Hiatt, Gavin Jones, Joanna Lynch, Michael Newton, John Shaw and Nicholas Webb.

I would also like to thank the staff of the British Library, the Guildhall Library, the National Meteorological Library and Archive, and the Beinecke Library, Yale University, who were uniformly helpful and efficient, as were Judith Doré and the Deal Maritime Museum, and Michael Hunt of the Ramsgate Maritime Museum.

Chronology

1660 Daniel Foe born in London (exact date unknown), son of James Foe and Alice Foe.

1662 Act of Uniformity passed. The Foes follow the lead of their minister, Samuel Annesley, and leave the Church of England to become Presbyterian Dissenters.

1665–6 The Plague and the Great Fire, the first two disasters to hit London in Defoe's lifetime.

c.1671–9 Attends the Revd James Fisher's school at Dorking, Surrey, then the Revd Charles Morton's Dissenting Academy in Newington Green, London. Plans to become a Presbyterian minister.

c.1683 Abandons the ministry and establishes himself instead as a hosiery merchant in London, living in Cornhill, near the Royal Exchange.

1684 Marries Mary Tuffley, whose dowry is worth £3,700.

1685–92 Fights in the rebellion against James II led by the Duke of Monmouth, then becomes a successful merchant dealing in wine, tobacco, hosiery and other goods. Travels on business throughout England and Europe.

1688 James II forced to abdicate; William of Orange becomes William III of England.

1692 Declared bankrupt for £17,000 and imprisoned for debt in the Fleet.

1694 With William III's help, establishes a brick and pantile works at Tilbury, Essex.

1695 Begins to refer to himself as De Foe.

1697 Publishes *An Essay on Projects*, a socio-economic treatise written in prison. Becomes an agent for William III in England and Scotland.

1701 Publishes *The True-Born Englishman*, a poetic satire on xenophobia written in defence of the Dutch-born William III.

1702 Death of William III and accession of Queen Anne. Publishes *Reformation of Manners*, an attack on moral hypocrisy, and, in December, *The Shortest-Way with the Dissenters*, an attack on High Church extremists. A warrant is issued for his arrest in response to the latter.

1703   Goes into hiding in January, but is arrested in May, charged with
       sedition and sentenced to three days in the pillory and an indefinite
       stay in Newgate Prison. Publishes *A Hymn to the Pillory* in defiance.
       His brick and pantile works collapses and he is bankrupt once
       more. Released in November through the intervention of the Tory
       politician Robert Harley. Witnesses the 26–7 November storm and
       begins to write his first full-length work, *The Storm*.

1704–14 Becomes secret agent and political journalist for Harley and
       other ministers; travels widely in England and Scotland promoting
       the union of the two countries. Single-handedly writes the *Review*,
       a pro-government newspaper which appeared as often as three
       times a week. Publishes *The Storm* in July 1704.

1707   Union of England and Scotland.

1710   Tories in power.

1713–14 Arrested several times for debt and for political writings but
       released each time through government influence.

1714   Death of Queen Anne and accession of George I, Elector of Hanover;
       fall of Robert Harley and the Tory government.

1715   *The Family Instructor*, the first of Defoe's conduct books.

1719   *Robinson Crusoe*, *The Farther Adventures of Robinson Crusoe*.

1720   *Memoirs of a Cavalier*, *Captain Singleton*, *Serious Reflections* . . .
       of Robinson Crusoe.

1722   *Moll Flanders*, *Religious Courtship*, *A Journal of the Plague Year*,
       Colonel Jack.

1724   *Roxana*, *A General History of the Pyrates*, *A Tour thro' the Whole
       Island of Great Britain* (3 vols., 1724–6).

1725   *The Complete English Tradesman* (vol. II in 1727).

1726   *The Political History of the Devil*.

1727   *Conjugal Lewdness*, *An Essay on the History and Reality of Appar-
       itions*, *A New Family Instructor*.

1728   *Augusta Triumphans*, *A Plan of the English Commerce*.

1729   *The Compleat English Gentleman* (not published until 1890).

1731   24 April: dies in Ropemaker's Alley, London, in debt, hiding from
       creditors. 26 April: buried in Bunhill Fields.

Introduction

The storm of 26–7 November 1703 remains the worst storm in British history. An extratropical cyclone of unusual ferocity, it hammered into Britain from the North Atlantic at over seventy miles per hour, cutting a 300-mile-wide swathe of destruction across southern and central England and Wales, before moving on to Scandinavia and out across the Baltic Sea. It raged without pause between midnight and 6 a.m., during which time it claimed the lives of more than 8,000 people on land and unbelievable sea. It was, as Queen Anne described it in a public proclamation made at St James's Palace on 12 December, 'a Calamity so Dreadful and Astonishing, that the like hath not been Seen or Felt, in the Memory of any Person Living in this Our Kingdom.'[1]

Her words were no overstatement: a fifth of the seamen of the sovereign fleet were drowned that night, as were the crews of the dozens of merchant and fishing vessels that were lost amid the violence of the storm at sea. On land, the cities of London and Bristol were hit particularly hard, their streets left scattered with the debris from thousands of damaged buildings, while the rural landscape of southern Britain as a whole was reshaped overnight by the loss of millions of trees, uprooted by the strength and insistence of the wind.

The damage was terrible to behold, and the storm, both in its timing and its temper, was quickly claimed by many to have been a judgement from on high, a warning to those who had survived, and a punishment on those who had not. As Daniel Defoe suggested in the opening words of his *Lay-Man's Sermon upon the Late Storm* (1704), a short tract written soon after the event, God chose the storm to be the vehicle of his wrath, the means by which to chastise London, 'a Powerful, Populous, Wealthy and most reprobate City', in an attempt to direct its forgetful inhabitants towards the path of godliness and repentance (p. 183).

In fact London, in common with much of the rest of the country, was already in the throes of meteorological introspection, and had been for some time. The weather, always a cause for complaint among the long-suffering British islanders, had been particularly bad that year, with what seemed endless bouts of rain and strong winds gusting in from the south and southwest. On 26 May 1703 Richard Chapman, the vicar of Cheshunt, preached a sermon on 'the present War, and Strange Unseasonableness of the Weather at Present', in which he interpreted the prevailing weather conditions as evidence of divine displeasure, and predicted that there would be worse to come should the country not turn wholeheartedly towards a renewed contemplation of God.[2]

Chapman's warnings seem to have gone unheeded, however, for the days leading up to the arrival of the storm saw a sequence of deep lows and frontal wave depressions advance towards the British Isles from south and south-westerly directions. Depressions, or lows, are areas of low pressure which begin as small waves on polar fronts, as the boundaries between warm and cold air are known; such depressions are usually associated with cyclonic or unstable weather conditions. During the week before the storm, as many as five or six separate depressions, with their origins in the Atlantic waters off the coasts of France and Spain, coalesced over the British Isles, forming what the historical meteorologist Hubert Lamb described as 'an increasingly vigorous cyclonic situation focussed over Britain'.[3] Contemporary reports, including Defoe's The Storm (1704), confirm that increasingly strong squally winds and rain buffeted the country for ten days or more, veering around the compass as the unstable moving air-masses collided and changed direction during their tempestuous wanderings north. These winds were already strong enough to cause some structural damage on land: Defoe describes a lucky escape on the evening of the 24th when, as he was walking past a neighbour's house in the North London suburb of Newington Green, part of it suddenly collapsed due to the 'unusual Violence' of the wind (p. 26). But the damage caused by these late November gales was only a taste of what was just about to come in from the west: an entirely separate cyclonic system, a severe storm depression which almost certainly originated in the West Indies or off the coast of Florida, was rapidly making its way over the Atlantic. It would take three or four days for it to arrive in Britain from the coast of North America, but when it did, late on Friday night, 26 November, it would proceed to make its presence felt as it battered its way through the darkness in an east-north-easterly direction.

It was only when the sun rose on the morning of the 27th that the scale of the devastation became apparent. When Defoe, who hadn't slept all night, ventured outside to inspect 'the Havock the Storm had made', he could hardly believe his eyes. He saw 'the Streets covered with Tyle-sherds, and Heaps of Rubbish, from the Tops of the Houses, lying almost at every Door', while 'the Distraction and Fury of the Night was visible in the Faces of the People' themselves (p. 33). London looked and felt, as many observers noted at the time, like a city in the aftermath of battle; a scene, as it quickly became apparent, that had been repeated throughout the rest of southern Britain. Defoe realized that this was something to which he, as a leading journalist and pamphleteer, would have to give serious attention, and as he walked through the London streets that morning, inspecting the damage and interviewing his neighbours on their own experiences of the night, he began to take the detailed notes that would lead to the writing of what became his first book: *The Storm*.

As his first full-length work, *The Storm* can be seen as a significant episode in Defoe's literary career. He had, over the previous decade, produced some forty or so political and satirical poems and tracts, some of which, like *The True-Born Englishman* (1701), would prove enduringly popular in his lifetime. But as his first full-length experiment in narrative technique, as well as a move away from the outright polemic of his early works, *The Storm* marked a new departure in his writing career.

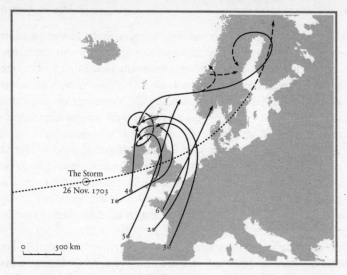

The cyclonic situation over the British Isles in the days leading up to the storm, indicated by the lines numbered in the order in which the cyclones appeared. The storm itself, of 26–7 November 1703, is indicated by the dashed line.

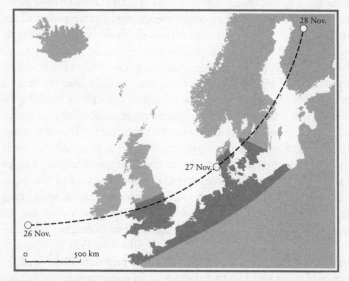

The track of the low pressure centre and the path of the storm from 26 to 28 November 1703 (indicated by the dashed line), and the boundaries of the principal areas of damage caused by the storm (indicated by the shaded area).

Many of the lessons learned during its months of composition would prove invaluable during the writing of his later and better-known novels, such as *Robinson Crusoe* (1719), *Moll Flanders* (1722) and *A Journal of the Plague Year* (1722), not just in his skilled handling of complex structures of space and time, and in his use of varied voices and multiple points of view, but in the unfolding sense of a shared moment of intense historical import. It was as if Defoe had suddenly discovered, amid the trials and losses of his storm-struck neighbours, the two great themes – collective suffering and individual survival – which he would go on to develop as his own.

In fact the storm made such an impression on Defoe that he ended up writing three separate and stylistically distinct pieces in reaction to it, all of which are reproduced in this volume: *The Storm, The Lay-Man's Sermon upon the Late Storm* and *An Essay on the Late Storm* (all 1704). Taken together, the three pieces offer a valuable insight into the apparently contradictory ways in which Defoe reacted to events in both public and private life. It is impossible to know the exact order in which the pieces were started and finished, since Defoe made a habit of working on a number of projects simultaneously, moving between them whenever he alighted upon a suitable idea or phrase, but we know that Defoe began to work on *The Storm* in the days immediately following the event, and we can assume that he composed the other two pieces alongside it. The satirical *Lay-Man's Sermon* was the first of the pieces to be published, appearing in the second week of February 1704, while *The Storm* and the poetic *Essay on the Late Storm* both appeared later on in the summer, by which time most of the physical damage caused by the storm had been repaired. But the memory of the night and its aftermath remained, and, as we will go on to see later in the introduction, Defoe was to make the most of what turned out to be a source of powerful and suggestive imagery.

In every other respect, however, 1703 was a terrible year for Defoe. He had had to spend the first five months of it in hiding, on the move from one safe house to another in and around London and the south of England, and possibly even spending some time in Holland, since a search was conducted for him there. His crime was to have published a satirical pamphlet, *The Shortest-Way with the Dissenters* (1702), which purported to have been written by an apoplectic High-Church Tory minister who proposed that the only sensible recourse for the security of Britain was to do to the Dissenters what Louis XIV had recently done to the Protestant Huguenots of France, that is, get rid of them through massacre and exile. 'They are to be rooted out of this nation, if ever we will live in peace,' wrote Defoe's anonymous High Church minister, a view with which many of his High-flying readers would happily have agreed.[4] The mysterious authorship of *The Shortest-Way* became a public controversy during the last weeks of 1702, but when the sermon was revealed to have been a mischievous hoax, in that it had been written not by an overheated Anglican clergyman but by Daniel Defoe, a well-known Dissenter and political friend of the recently dead King William III, a warrant for his arrest on the charge of 'high crime and misdemeanour' was promptly served by the government. 'The Plot is discovered,' the editor of one London newspaper smirked on 30 December 1702; ''Twas a pretty Sham enough'.[5] But Defoe was now in serious trouble, for it seemed that the sham, whatever its intentions, had grossly insulted the new Queen, Anne, who had read the mock sermon, and was now taking a personal interest in seeing its author punished. Knowing the likely penalties that lay in store for him, Defoe decided to run; not because he imagined that he would never be caught, but to give himself time to negotiate with his enemies in an attempt to defuse their anger.

Defoe was right to be anxious. The sudden death of his patron and employer William III on 8 March 1702 had left Defoe exposed to the resentment of the new administration under Anne. Defoe had devoted much of his time to writing pamphlets and poems in praise of William and his policies of toleration towards the Dissenters, but some of these had included personal attacks on a number of High-Church Tory politicians who now enjoyed influence within the government. They were keen for the slightest excuse to get even with the author of satires such as *The True-Born Englishman* (1701) or *Reformation of Manners*

(1702), the latter of which had poured public scorn on the very judges in front of whom Defoe would soon be standing. He knew that they were unlikely to be lenient, and that the kinds of punishment they might well recommend included whipping, branding, pillorying and imprisonment. Only a few months earlier another Dissenting author, William Fuller, had been found guilty of seditious libel and was pilloried for three days, given thirty-nine lashes and committed to prison with hard labour.

Of all these punishments the pillory was the worst and most feared. The prisoner was made to stand on a platform, usually in a market square or other public place, with his head and hands locked in an upright wooden stocks. There he stood, usually for an hour or two on a series of consecutive days, suffering whatever the assembled crowd of onlookers cared to throw, whether rotten fruit, animal waste, cobblestones or bricks. Pilloried prisoners often died from their injuries, and William Fuller had only barely escaped with his life, having nearly choked to death after he slipped from the stool on which he was standing. As it was, he suffered a broken leg and a fractured skull, as well as the humiliation of his exposure to a crowd that had taken evident pleasure in his downfall. Defoe, who worried that he was 'Unfitt to bear the hardships of a Prison', thought that he might be able to strike some kind of bargain with his pursuers and thus avoid the worst of their hostility.[6] So he ran for cover to give himself time, and the hunt for the satirist was on.

The first arrests to be made in the search for Defoe were of George Croome, the printer of The Shortest-Way, and Edward Bellamy, a known agent of Whig propaganda, who admitted that he had been responsible for supplying Croome with the manuscript, and confirmed that Defoe was its author. A few days later, an advertisement appeared in the London Gazette for 7–11 January 1703, offering a £50 reward for information leading to the arrest of 'Daniel de Fooe'. The following issue of the Gazette carried a revised and expanded version of the ad, which included what has since become a well-known description of Daniel Defoe the fugitive from justice:

St James's, Jan. 10. *Whereas* Daniel de Foe *alias* de Fooe *is charged with writing a Scandalous and Seditious Pamphlet, Entituled,* The Shortest way with the Dissenters, *Whoever shall discover the said* Daniel de Foe, *alias* de Fooe, *to one of Her Majesty's Principal Secretaries of State, or any of Her Majesty's Justices of the Peace, so as he may be apprehended, shall have a Reward of* 50 l. *which Her Majesty has ordered immediately to be paid upon such Discovery*:

He *is a middle Sized Spare Man, about* 40 *years old, of a brown Complexion, and dark brown coloured Hair, but wears a Wig, a hooked Nose, a sharp Chin, grey Eyes, and a large Mould near his Mouth, was born in* London, *and for many years was a Hose Factor in Freeman's-yard, in Cornhill, and now is Owner of the Brick and Pantile Works, near* Tilbury-Fort *in* Essex.[7]

The arrests of Bellamy and Croome had already unsettled Defoe, but the wanted notice, with its detailed description (Cromwellian wart and all) and its reward offered in the name of the Queen herself, nevertheless came as a shock: £50 was a considerable inducement, more than enough for someone to live on for a year, and it was ten times the amount that was offered in the press for the capture of a deserting soldier. Even Jack Sheppard, the famous thief and prison-breaker, whose life story Defoe would later write up for the papers, was only worth a £20 reward. But a seditious author was regarded as a far greater menace than either a prison-breaker or a deserter, for it was as if he had publicly declared himself to be an enemy of the state, which is why the pursuit of Defoe came to occupy the attentions of some of the most powerful men in the land: Robert Harley, Earl of Oxford, the Speaker of the House of Commons; Sidney Godolphin, First Earl of Godolphin, the Lord High Treasurer; and Daniel Finch, Earl of Nottingham, the Secretary of State for the Southern Region and an avowed enemy of the Whigs, to whom the responsibility of actually finding Defoe was given. 'Don Dismal', as Defoe went on to call the Earl of Nottingham, was to find this a difficult and exasperating task, and on 25 February 1703, given Defoe's continuing evasion, he ordered that a copy of *The Shortest-Way* 'be burnt by the hands of the common Hangman, tomorrow in New Palace

Yard'.[8] The sentence was carried out the next day, as instructed.

Defoe, meanwhile, had begun the negotiations which he hoped would soften his enemies. He sent his wife, Mary Tuffley, to face the Earl of Nottingham in person, but Don Dismal merely repeated his demand that Defoe give himself up to the authorities. Defoe then wrote him a pleading letter in which he drew what he hoped was an affecting picture of 'the Cries of a Numerous Ruin'd Family', and offered to answer written questions in return for a sentence 'a Little More Tollerable to me as a Gentleman, Than Prisons, Pillorys, and Such like, which are Worse to me than Death'.[9] He could hardly have expected Dismal Daniel to react to the letter with sympathy, but he ended it with an offer to serve the Queen 'with my hand, my Pen, or my head', which may well have roused the interest of his pursuers. They knew how effective Defoe had been in the service of William III, and there was no denying that his talents as a propagandist and a spy could be put to good use by the new administration. But they remained intent upon catching him first, and were not yet prepared to come to an arrangement with someone they had no reason to trust.

Defoe was finally captured on 21 May 1703, having been betrayed for the reward by an anonymous informer. When he was arrested, at a house in Spitalfields belonging to a French Huguenot weaver named Nathaniel Sammen, he had 'many Libells and papers' on his person, including, it was alleged, an obscene poem that he had written which described the knighting of Dr David Hamilton, physician to the Queen.[10] It took the Earl of Nottingham several days to go through these various papers, but they turned out to contain nothing of any value to the government. Nevertheless, the government remained convinced that Defoe was in the pay of a group of Whig conspirators who were loyal to the ideals of the late King William, and that *The Shortest-Way* was one of their attempts to destabilize the new regime. It is unclear, even now, whether there were reasonable grounds for the Tories' suspicion, but Defoe maintained throughout these events that his sermon had only ever been ironic in intention, not inflammatory. The fault, in other words, lay with the reader, not the writer, a defence which Defoe was soon to use again, in his next mock sermon, *The Lay-Man's Sermon upon the Late Storm*, when he warns the reader that 'he that expected it otherwise than it is tis his Fault, and not Mine' (p. 186). As Defoe had just discovered, although not for the last time in his writing career, the problem with making irony seem real is that the irony is often lost on its audience.

As soon as he was arrested Defoe was committed to Newgate Prison, where he was interrogated for two days by the Earl of Nottingham, who demanded to know who had paid him for his work. Whether or not he had anything to confess, Defoe refused to answer any of Dismal's questions, and on 5 June Nottingham had no choice but to release the prisoner on bail, ordering him to appear in court a month later to face charges. On 5 July he appeared as requested and was charged with seditious libel, the indictment going out of its way to stress that the publication of *The Shortest-Way* had been a 'direct affront to Queen Anne'.[11] Given the wording of the indictment and the obvious animosity of the judges who were appointed to the hearing two days later, Defoe was advised by his defence attorney that the best he could do was to plead guilty and ask for mercy. Defoe reluctantly did what he was told, and the Old Bailey trial, the result of nearly seven months of official investigation, was over in a matter of minutes.

Defoe's sentence, however, was tougher than that which he had been led to expect: a fine of 200 marks (about £133), three days in the pillory, and a return to Newgate Prison for an unspecified period to await Her Majesty's pleasure 'till all be performed'. Given that he was then on the verge of bankruptcy, the payment of the fine was unlikely to be 'performed' for a very long time to come. He was also made to undertake to remain on good behaviour for seven years, which effectively translated into a vow of publishing silence: unthinkable for a writer as compulsive as Defoe. He referred to it, ironically, in his *Essay on the Late Storm* (1704), as his 'sleep of legal Death' (p. 211); ironically, because the period immediately following this sentence of silence was his busiest yet in terms of writing and anonymous publication. By the end of July 1704, only twelve months after the sentence was imposed, Defoe had written and published twenty new works, including the three which are reprinted here.

Defoe had managed to escape hanging or whipping, but he still had to face the prospect of 'Prisons, Pillorys, and Such like, which are Worse to me than Death'. He felt, with some justification, that he had been punished not merely for *The Shortest-Way*, but for all the other satires he had written. The judges and politicians whom he had mocked in the past had taken their opportunity for revenge. So he appealed against his sentence, complaining that he had agreed 'to give the Court No Trouble but to plead Guilty to the Indictment, Even to all the Adverbs, the Seditiously's, the Maliciously's, and a Long Rapsody of the Lawyers et Ceteras; and all this upon promises of being us'd Tenderly'.[12] Defoe thus found himself being interrogated again, this time in the presence of the Queen herself, but his refusal to answer repeated questions about his part in a supposed anti-government conspiracy meant that his appeal was quickly turned down. His dates with the pillory were set for the last three days in July: the first outside the Royal Exchange on Cornhill, near where he used to manage his hosiery warehouse; the second at Cheapside, in sight of the still unfinished St Paul's Cathedral; and the third at Temple Bar on Fleet Street, the future home, appropriately enough, of generations of his fellow libellers.

While awaiting his punishment back in Newgate Prison, Defoe responded in the only way that he had ever responded to a setback: by writing an attack in his defence. *A Hymn to the Pillory*, published on 29 July 1703, the first of his three days of public humiliation, was written specially to be sold to the crowds who came to witness his ordeal. The 450-line poem, an irregular Pindaric ode composed in rhyming couplets addressed directly to the wooden pillory itself, suggests that it is the judges, not Defoe, who rightly belong on its platform, and that his only crime was to have written and published the truth:

> Tell them it was because he was too bold,
> And told those truths, which should not ha' been told.
>   Extol the justice of the land,
> Who punish what they will not understand.[13]

By publicly flouting the no-publications clause of his sentence Defoe was demonstrating a remarkable nerve, and it was partly this that ensured his safety on the stand, for nothing was thrown at him during the entire three days except laughter and the occasional flower. A mid nineteenth-century painting by Eyre Crowe shows Defoe's last day in the pillory at Temple Bar, complete with a basket of roses provided by his admirers. Although it is a later, and highly idealized, artist's impression of the scene, it nevertheless represents the real good humour of the reception given to the by then notorious Defoe, whose courage and convictions had served to win the crowds over to his side. His enemies, of course, were furious, complaining that his printed works were 'Hauk'd and Publickly Sold about the Pillory, while he stood upon it (in Triumph!) for Writing them. And Writes on still',[14] as though Defoe were not a prisoner with his head in the stocks but a tradesman doing business at his stall. Defoe, writing on still, in spite of his sentence, and in the face of open persecution, had survived the most fearful event of his life so far.

Defoe spent the next four months in Newgate Prison, writing and publishing a number of tracts and pamphlets, as well as corresponding with those government ministers with whom he hoped to negotiate his release. Robert Harley, the Speaker of the House of Commons, took over from the Earl of Nottingham as Defoe's main contact, and the two men, despite their obvious political differences, were eventually able to arrive at an understanding. Although he was a Tory, Harley's origins, like Defoe's, were Dissenting, and in many ways he understood and possibly even respected Defoe's outlook and resilience. But he made Defoe wait for his deliverance, knowing that his fear and hatred of prison would make him more receptive to Harley's influence. Defoe's earlier letter, with its offer to help Queen Anne 'with my hand, my Pen, or my head', had been kept on file, and Harley was planning to take him up on the offer, but only when the time was right. As the weeks and months in Newgate went by, Defoe's anxiety and depression increased, while Harley kept a secret watch over his mood. Harley, after all, who was carefully grooming Defoe for his future role as a government propagandist, wanted him suitably softened up for use. 'Foe is much oppressed in his mind,' he noted on 20 September, and since his wish was that Defoe be rendered desperate and compliant rather than broken beyond repair, he began the negotiations that would lead to his release. Defoe, 'friendless and distress'd', as he later described it, 'my Family ruin'd, and my self without Hope of Deliverance', was finally released from prison in the first week of November 1703, and was returned to his long-suffering wife, who, together with their six children, and five months pregnant with their seventh, had moved back in with her mother in Newington Green.[15] 'Whoever Sir Are the Principalls in this Favour,' as Defoe wrote to Robert Harley later that week, 'I Can Not but Profess my Self a Debtor wholly to your Self ... I Take The Freedome to Repeat the Assurance of A Man Ready to Dedicate my Life and all Possible Powers to the Intrest of So Generous and So Bountifull Benefactors, Being Equally Overcome with the Nature as well as the Vallue of the Favour I have Receiv'd.'[16]

The outcome, in other words, was just as Harley had planned. Defoe's release was secured at the price of his convictions, and he was now in the pay of the new regime which he would go on to serve, with energy, devotion and apparent approval of its political aims, for the next ten years of his life.

It was only a few days after his release from prison that Defoe began to notice the increased agitation of the wind. As was described at the beginning of the introduction, these strong November gales continued to blow across the British Isles for ten days or more, rattling windows and shaking trees, until the night of Friday the 26th when the storm itself arrived on the scene, its ferocity undiminished by its long voyage across the Atlantic. It raged until dawn, and nobody that morning who saw the carnage left behind was ever likely to forget it. Defoe, still dazed by his experiences of Newgate, was struck by the impact that the storm had wrought, not just upon the mood of his immediate neighbours but upon the mood of the nation as a whole. It was as if he had stepped out of the half-life of prison into the furious vitality of the wind, and he described the effect of the transformation in his *Essay on the Late Storm*:

> What tho' to Seven Years sleep thou art confin'd,
> Thou well may'st wake with such a Wind,

which is why he decided that the first major task of his post-prison career would be to create what he hoped would prove a lasting memorial to the transient terrors of the storm (p. 211).

So a few days after the storm had passed, Defoe placed an advertisement in both the *Daily Courant* and the *London Gazette* (the same newspaper that had carried the wanted notices for his arrest), in which he requested that first-hand observations of the storm be sent to him, care of one of his regular publishers, near Stationers' Hall on Ludgate Hill:

To preserve the Remembrance of the late Dreadful Tempest, an exact and faithful Collection is preparing of the most remarkable Disasters which happened on that Occasion, with the Places where, and Persons concern'd, whether at Sea or on Shore. For the perfecting so good a Work, 'tis humbly recommended by the Author to all Gentlemen of the Clergy, or others, who have made any Observations of this Calamity, that they would transmit as distinct an Account as possible, of what they have observed, to the Undertakers, directed to John Nutt, near Stationers-hall, London. All Gentlemen that are pleas'd to send any such Accounts, are desired to write no Particulars but that they are well satisfied to be true, and to set their Names to the Observations they send, which the Undertakers of this Work promise shall be faithfully Recorded, and the Favour publickly acknowledged.[17]

What stands out from the wording of this notice, which was copied almost word-for-word from an earlier appeal in the *Athenian Gazette* requesting eyewitness testimonies of providential events, is the strength of its emphasis upon truth. The barrage of terms such as 'exact', 'faithful', 'distinct' and 'true', although part of the everyday currency of the journalist, leaves no doubt that the author intends to compile an account that is

to be read as chronicle rather than legend. As Defoe outlined in
the Preface to *The Storm*, his desire was not '*to forge a Story*'
or to '*sin against Truth*', but to offer an exact narration of the
events of the night, for which he required a stock of reliable
evidence (p. 4).

Defoe's generation of journalists and reporters was the first
to respond to the late-seventeenth-century rise of the empirical
sciences, and they did so by emphasizing the need to gather
first-hand evidence in support of a story; yet there remains
something uniquely defensive about Defoe's protestations in the
Preface to *The Storm*. '*If a Man tells a Lye in Print*,' he declares,
'*he abuses Mankind, and imposes upon the whole World, he
causes our Children to tell Lyes after us, and their Children after
them, to the End of the World*'; he promises, therefore, '*to be
careful of his Words, that nothing pass from him but with an
especial Sanction of Truth*' (p. 3). Ever since his release from
Newgate, Defoe wrote as if he expected to be hauled before the
magistrates at any moment, and his main concern here seems to
be making absolutely sure that the kind of misunderstanding
that saw him pilloried and imprisoned could never happen
again. As both the call for contributions and the Preface to *The
Storm* made clear, this was intended to be a thoroughly unironic
and uninvented production, written not to support the view of
a particular religious or political group, but written, instead, 'to
preserve the Remembrance of the late Dreadful Tempest' on
behalf of the nation as a whole.

Whether or not Defoe managed to stick to this agenda is a
matter for a later paragraph, but in the meantime the first
written responses to the newspaper advertisements had begun
to arrive at his publishers. As Defoe sorted through these letters,
sent from every corner of the storm-battered land, and began
the task of organizing the various sections of the book, he must
have felt that he was finally getting back on course following the
setbacks of the previous twelve months. His financial situation,
however, remained a particular source of worry, both for him
and for his wife Mary, whose £3,700 dowry he had squandered
within a few years of their marriage in 1684. Defoe's first
bankruptcy had come in 1692, when a series of ill-judged invest-

ments collapsed, leaving him £17,000 in debt. Since then he had slowly begun to pay back his creditors, with a successful brick and pantile works at Tilbury, Essex, being his main source of income since he established it, in 1694, with money given to him by his patron William III. The works had done well, supplying the London building boom with high-quality materials, and some of Defoe's bricks were used in the construction of Sir Christopher Wren's great Naval Hospital at Greenwich, while the s-shaped roofing pantiles were used so widely on the hundreds of Nonconformist chapels and meeting houses that were built during the reign of William III that Dissenters became known as 'Pantilers'.[18] Defoe had made an annual profit of around £600 from the Tilbury works, which he put towards paying back some of what he owed, but his flight and imprisonment in 1703 led to the inevitable collapse of his business and to his second experience of bankruptcy. Every day in prison, as Robert Harley was well aware, Defoe's debts and money worries increased, and he was later to describe the moment when a merchant is declared officially bankrupt, which happened to him while he was still in Newgate, as like being 'mortally stabb'd, or, as we may say, shot thro' the head in his trading capacity'.[19]

The timing of the November storm added insult to injury, for had it come just a few months earlier, when his tile business was still a going concern, Defoe would have made a fortune overnight. As he pointed out in *The Storm*, the price of tiles rose 'from 21s. *per* Thousand to 6 *l.* for plain Tiles; and from 50s. *per* Thousand for Pantiles, to 10 *l.* and Bricklayers Labour to 5s. per Day' (p. 57). Although the prices soon came down, tiles remained in high demand, and Defoe knew that had he still been in the roof-tiling business, he would have been in a position to pay off all his debts within a few weeks of the storm. As it was, he had to suffer the success of his old business rivals, and read advertisements such as this one, from the *Daily Courant* for 24 December 1703:

This is to give Notice to all Persons who may have occasion for good new well burnt plain Tyles, that they may be supply'd with what

quantity they want at 3 *l.* 5 *s.* per Thousand, at Mr. *Harvey's* a Timber
Merchant's Yard near *Puddle-Dock*. Likewise good Pan-Tyles to be
sold for 6 *l.* per Thousand.

It reads like a scene from one of his later novels, in which the
fear of debt and failure haunts the narrators, whose economic
fates are meted out with calm Presbyterian irony. ''*Tis an ill
Wind that blows no Body good,*' wrote one of his contemporaries on 29 November, 'but I'm sure both Tilers and Bricklayers
will be much the better for this Storm.'[20] To think what he might
have done with such a windfall! But Defoe always wrote more
compellingly of loss than of gain, and it is here, in *The Storm*,
that he draws closest to its source, where the relationship
between shared disaster and private ruin is evident on almost
every page.

The storm, for Defoe, is the third in the trinity of disasters
which struck the capital city in his lifetime, and he wrote more
than once about each of them in the course of his writing career.
London, 'the monster city' in the words of the historian Jack
Lindsay, is presented by Defoe as a carefully delineated geog-
raphy of suffering, both collective, as in the case of plague, fire
and storm, and personal, as in the case of bankruptcy, prison
and pillory.[21] The London of a *A Journal of the Plague Year*,
for example, like the London of *The Storm*, is filled with scenes
of private suffering played out against a backdrop of public
calamity, with the narrators of both books seen walking through
the disordered streets, collecting evidence and offering reflections on the causes and the consequences of the tragedies. Both
narrators act as implicated observers, giving details of their own
first-hand experiences as well as quoting from material written
and collected by others. The Bills of Mortality, the weekly
printed lists of deaths supplied by every parish, are reproduced
in both books as a kind of recurring motif of loss, as well as an
assessment of the gravity of the unfolding situations. Letters,
diaries and cuttings from newspapers and journals are flourished
throughout the narratives like exhibits at a trial. Even though *A
Journal of the Plague Year* is a work of historical fiction, whereas
The Storm is a work of contemporary reportage, Defoe's

approach to the narrative structure is the same in both cases: a
calm accumulation of facts and circumstances is built up into a
body of evidence, which is then used variously to set the scene,
to explain and interpret the action, and to offer subjects for
conjecture to the reader. It is perhaps the chief characteristic of
Defoe's unmistakable style, regardless of the particular genre in
which any of his works might be cast. His narrative instinct,
both as a journalist and a novelist, lay in his development of a
form of circumstantial realism, the effectiveness of which relied
not so much on his powers of description as on the force of the
submitted evidence.[22]

There is a much-admired passage in an early scene of *Robinson Crusoe*, for example, when Crusoe remembers his shipmates
who were drowned when their vessel was broken on a sandbank
during a storm off the coast of Venezuela: 'as for them,' he
writes, 'I never saw them afterwards, or any sign of them,
except three of their hats, one cap, and two shoes that were not
fellows'.[23] Even in list form such details carry all the emotion
and loss of the moment more effectively, perhaps, than would
a lengthy description of the drownings, and it is in such passages,
with their privileging of evidence over description, that Defoe
demonstrates some of his true greatness as a writer. Similar
touches occur throughout *The Storm*, too, such as the detail of
roof tiles which he saw 'blown from a House above thirty or
forty Yards, and stuck from five to eight Inches into the solid
Earth' (p. 31), or of the lead from church roofs 'roll'd up like a
Roll of Parchment, and blown in some Places clear off from the
Buildings' (p. 60). These images, and others like them, such as
the ship blown from the Thames to the coast of Norway (p. 143),
or the burning windmills, on fire from the friction of their
whirling sails (p. 108), stand out from their surrounding texts
as 'speaking sights', a concept which Defoe first introduced in
The Lay-Man's Sermon upon the Late Storm, when he suggested
that 'in publick Callamities, every Circumstance is a Sermon,
and every thing we see a Preacher' (p. 186). He developed this
idea further in *A Journal of the Plague Year*, when he has a
sexton tell the narrator, who is seeking permission to view a
mass burial pit at Whitechapel: 'depend upon it, 'twill be a

Sermon to you, it may be, the best that ever you heard in your
Life. 'Tis a speaking Sight, says he, and has a Voice with it, and
a loud one, to call us all to Repentance.'[24]

This conviction, that 'every Circumstance is a Sermon, and
every thing we see a Preacher', is what lies behind Defoe's
reliance upon eyewitness descriptions as his guarantee of narrative authenticity. Around sixty of the letters that were submitted
in response to the newspaper advertisements in the *London
Gazette* are included in *The Storm*, and their appearance
undoubtedly heightens the sense of immediacy and crisis which
so characterizes the atmosphere of the book. These individual
stories are so potent and so 'speaking', claims Defoe, that 'their
Testimony is not to be question'd' (p. 64). Yet Defoe worries
throughout *The Storm* that these eyewitness statements are
going to be disbelieved by his readers, and he works hard to
convince us that they are true. '*When I go about a Work in
which I must tell a great many Stories, which may in their own
nature seem incredible, and in which I must expect a great part
of Mankind will question the Sincerity of the Relator,*' he writes
in the Preface, '*I did not do it without a particular sence upon
me of the proper Duty of an Historian*' (pp. 3–4). But the more
that Defoe reiterates the claim, the more cautious we, as readers,
must become. This is Daniel Defoe, after all, the writer famous
for lying like the truth, and there are clues to be found throughout *The Storm* which suggest that not everything that we
encounter there is quite as he insists it is.

In the Preface, for example, he claims to have altered none
of the eyewitnesses' letters, having '*not Arrogance enough to
attempt a Correction either of the Sense or Stile; and if I had
gone about it, should have injur'd both Author and Reader*'
(p. 8). Yet in a later chapter he admits to having done just that,
although he seeks to reassure the reader that he has 'always kept
close to the matter of fact', and that he has only done it in the
interests of greater clarity (p. 65). So how much has he altered
the letters? Some of them, such as the one from Joseph Ralton
in Oxfordshire, the contents of which Defoe describes as 'unaccountably strange', are marked out specifically as having been
reproduced '*verbatim*', which may well have been the case

(p. 66), while others, such as the undated letter from the sailor Miles Norcliffe, the contents of which Defoe describes as 'not litterally True', bear every hallmark of Defoe's characteristic presence: the repetition of the haunting phrase 'all sunk and drowned', the hint of the efficacy of the sailors' prayers, the problem of when the letter was actually written, for it seems to date from several days before Defoe's advertisement, and, most striking of all, the novelistic postscript explaining how the letter came to be dispatched from an apparently sinking ship that was 'expecting every moment to be all drowned', all suggest a high level of fabrication by Defoe (p. 131). We know, as it happens, that Defoe wrote most, if not all, of the 'readers' letters' which appeared in his *Review*, the pro-government newspaper which he produced for his new employers from February 1704 onwards, and we also know that he made good use of the tried-and-tested journalists' trick of inventing insider eye-witnesses to political and courtly events, much in the manner of today's newspapers' 'sources close to the palace' (or 'sources close to the deadline', as many journalists refer to them). This is not to suggest that Defoe wrote every word of the letters which appear in *The Storm*, but we know, from him, that he rewrote them, and we can assume that he did so in order to improve their style: the book was, after all, his own creation, and he would have been understandably reluctant to relinquish too much control over the quality of its contents to a collection of random strangers, no matter how credible their stories might appear.

In fact the problem of assessing the reliability of eyewitness accounts was already a subject for discussion within the newly developing scientific realm. The Royal Society of London, which was founded in 1660 'for the Improving of Natural Knowledge', published its papers and proceedings in a bi-monthly journal, the *Philosophical Transactions*, most of the contents of which took the form of descriptions of natural phenomena which were submitted by correspondents from around the country. But the early editors of the journal faced a recurring problem: there were, as yet, no agreed fieldwork methodologies with which to collect empirical information and no agreed terms in which their contributors could express it on paper, so it remained difficult, if not impossible, to draw meaningful comparisons from the mass of submitted material. One person's remarkable surge of the tide, for example, might be another's everyday ebb and flow, so which of the two accounts should be preserved in the records?

Defoe points to the historical dimensions of this problem in Chapter 2 of *The Storm*, when he writes that 'such Winds as in those Days wou'd have pass'd for Storms, are called only a *Fresh-gale*, or *Blowing hard* . . . when our *Hard Gale* blows, they would have cried a Tempest; and about the *Fret of Wind* they would be all at their Prayers', by which he meant that potentially valuable meteorological comparisons could never be easily drawn, especially from the records of the past (p. 24). He was to remain interested in the problems raised by the use of competing eyewitness testimonies, and later recast this section of *The Storm* into a telling scene in *Robinson Crusoe*, where Crusoe and a shipmate disagree over the weather of the previous night:

I warrant you were frighted, wa'n't you last night, when it blew but a cap full of wind? A cap full d'you call it? said I, *'twas a terrible storm: A storm, you fool you*, replies he, *do you call that a storm why it was nothing at all; give us but a good ship and sea-room, and we think nothing of such a squall of wind as that.*[25]

Defoe was not the first to have realized the implications of these problems, and an article published in the *Philosophical Transactions* for October 1699 offered an attempt to formulate a mathematical model for assessing the value of eyewitness accounts. In an intriguing, if bewildering, piece of applied mathematical logic, the anonymous author (who may well have been Edmond Halley, the astronomer and Clerk to the Royal Society, who loved to get his teeth into just this kind of problem) proceeds to calculate the varying degrees of confidence which ought to be exhibited towards varieties of first-person testimony. To begin with, he writes:

The *Credibility* of any *Reporter* is to be rated (1) by his *Integrity*, or Fidelity; and (2) by his *Ability*: and a double *Ability* is to be considered; both that of *Apprehending*, what is deliver'd; and also of *Retaining* it afterwards, till it be transmitted.

From this basis, the author goes on to factor in the differences in reliability between single and multiple eyewitness accounts, as well as between oral and written testimonies, and after some impressive calculations, he arrives at an average ratio of $\frac{5}{6}$ths believability per person, which is to say, if a single eyewitness passes on six pieces of information, at least one of them can be discounted, although we don't, of course, know which one. Maybe it was this, or something very like it, that Lewis Carroll had in mind when his White Queen explained to Alice that she made a habit of believing six impossible things before breakfast. The mathematical picture soon becomes more complex, however, when multiple accounts of the same events are calculated, and each witness's 'share of Assurance' is factored into the equation:

If Two Concurrent Reporters have, each of them, as $\frac{5}{6}$ths of Certainty; they will both give me an Assurance of $\frac{35}{36}$ths, or of 35 to one: if Three; an Assurance of $\frac{215}{216}$, or of 215 to one,

and so on. Even if each of these eyewitnesses' stories was only 50 per cent reliable, by this calculation, according to the author, two such witnesses would give you $\frac{3}{4}$ths accuracy, three would give you $\frac{7}{8}$ths, while ten would take you up to a level of $\frac{1023}{1024}$ths accuracy, which was just the kind of assurance that Defoe would have liked to have concerning his heterogeneous contributors to *The Storm*.[26]

Apart from the submitted (and his own) eyewitness accounts, Defoe also consulted a wide range of printed sources in the course of compiling *The Storm*, from William Camden's *Britannia*, the celebrated Elizabethan survey of Britain, to the *Philosophical Transactions* of the Royal Society, which produced a kind of storm special for its January–February 1704 edition, with contributions from notable meteorological researchers

such as William Derham, Richard Towneley and the famous
Dutch microscopist Anthony van Leeuwenhoek, all of whom
were cited by Defoe. He also made use of a copy of Ralph
Bohun's *Discourse Concerning the Origine and Properties of
Wind*, a learned volume that had been published in Oxford in
1671. Bohun, who died in 1716, was a fellow of New College,
Oxford, and his *Discourse*, although slightly out of date by
1704, was of particular help to Defoe in compiling the historical
and scientific sections of *The Storm*. Some of his contemporaries,
however, including, presumably, Bohun himself, were quick to
notice a number of unacknowledged borrowings from the book,
and the author of an anonymously published pamphlet, *The
Republican Bullies*, accused Defoe of having stolen 'another
Man's *Philosophical Essay* upon the Winds, in your *Elaborate*
Collection about the late Dreadful Storm, when you made bold
with several Pages from the Learned Dr *Bohun*, without saying
so much to the Dr. for his Assistance as kiss my A—se.'[27]

Plagiarism and piracy were common allegations at the time,
and Defoe could usually refute them with ease, but he was less
able to deal with those same accusers when their laughter was
directed at his pretensions to learning. Like many Dissenters and
Nonconformists, who were barred from attending the English
universities, Defoe was extremely sensitive about his academic
record, even though he had received an excellent all-round
education at the Dissenting Academy in Newington Green. But
Defoe had always thought of himself as a gentleman, complete
with wig and even, on occasions, carrying a sword, and if there
was one kind of laughter that he couldn't bear, it was laughter
at his tradesman's education. In May 1705, for instance, stung
by a reference to his second-rate Latin which appeared in the
pages of the *Observator*, Defoe indulged himself in a long
and uncharacteristically personal response to the newspaper's
editor, John Tutchin:

tell Mr. Tutchin I understand Latin: *non ita Latinus sum ut Latine
loqui.* I easily acknowledge myself blockhead enough to have lost the
fluency of expression in the Latin, and so far trade has been a prejudice
to me; and yet I think I owe this justice to my ancient father, yet living,

and in whose behalf I freely testify that if I am a blockhead it was nobody's fault but my own, he having spared nothing in my education that might qualify me to match the accurate Dr. B or the learned *Observator*.

Defoe then challenged John Tutchin to an extraordinary public contest:

I'll take any Latin author he shall name, and with it one French and one Italian, and I'll translate them into English and after that re-translate them crosswise: the English into French, the French into Italian, and the Italian into Latin. And this I challenge him to perform with him, who does it soonest and best for 20£ each book; and by this he shall have an opportunity to show the world how much Defoe the hosier is inferior in learning to Mr. Tutchin the gentleman.[28]

Defoe was evidently angry and upset, but this moment of self-exposure was just another gift to his enemies, who went on to tease him even more about his lack of classical learning: 'Friend *Daniel*,' laughed the author of *The Republican Bullies*, 'the next time you write any thing in Vindication of your great Skill in the Latin Tongue, let your Quotations come up to your Pretensions, and not make a Jest of your self.'[29]

As was mentioned earlier in the introduction, Defoe intended *The Storm* to be a politically unengaged production, which would lend no overt support to the views of any particular religious or political group. Yet Defoe was by nature a taker of sides, and he could never remain as convincingly neutral as he would have us believe, although he does a much better job of curbing his opinions in the course of *The Storm* than he does in the other two associated pieces. For he felt, overall, that whatever its natural causes may have been, and despite the randomness of the suffering that it caused, as a judgement on his divided nation, the storm had been richly deserved. 'The Storms above reprove the Storms below,' as he wrote in *An Essay on the Late Storm*, the last of the three storm pieces to be published, and it is clear from comments made in the course of all three that he viewed the storm as an act of divine retribution against the antics of the High Church faction (p. 211): ''Tis plain Heaven has suited his Punishment to the Offence, has Punish'd the Stormy Temper of this Party of Men with *Storms of his Vengeance, Storms on their Navies, Storms on their Houses, Storms on their Confederates*, and I question not will at last with *Storms in their Consciences*' (p. 198).

Defoe, newly out of prison and under the protection of Robert Harley, the moderate, if Machiavellian, Tory Speaker of the House of Commons, was keen to point the finger of blame at the enemies who had caused him so much trouble over the previous twelve months, and whose cynicism and treachery were, he felt, at least partly responsible for the terrors unleashed by the storm. His reproaches, however, differed in emphasis across each of the works reprinted here. In *The Lay-Man's Sermon upon the Late Storm*, for example, which was the first to appear, in February 1704, its pretended disguise as a piece of biblical commentary is soon abandoned, and it turns instead into what Defoe happily admits is a 'Discourse ... wholly Civil and Political', in which all the usual suspects, Jacobites, non-jurors and High-Church Tories, are rounded up for vilification by name (p. 186); yet when he exclaims, as he does in the course of *The Storm*, against 'Interest, Parties, Strife, Faction, and particular Malice, with all the scurvy Circumstances attending such things', he is careful to mention no names or labels, although it is obvious who he has in mind (p. 64). And he is also very careful, in the midst of all this political point-scoring, to praise Queen Anne, 'a Mild, Gentle, Just and Protestant Queen', who he wisely exempts from the fanaticism which he holds responsible for the various storms and 'Ecclesiastick Tempests', both political and meteorological, which continued to batter the land (p. 212).

In fact the 1703 storm arrived during an early phase of what was to become known as the War of the Spanish Succession, a twelve-year slog around the fields of western Europe in an attempt to prevent a threatened alliance between the crowns of France and Spain. Its immediate cause was the death, in November 1700, of Charles II of Spain, whose will gifted his throne to the seventeen-year-old Philip, Duke of Anjou, the grandson of the French King, Louis XIV. William III and his Dutch advisors were horrified by this development, and they wanted to see the powerful southern alliance opposed by military force. William signed a treaty, known as the Grand Alliance, with the leaders of the Dutch United Provinces and the Emperor of Austria, all of whom shared the aim of curbing the growing power of the French, who had marched into the Spanish Netherlands in February 1701 and taken control of the fortresses facing the Channel.

The death of William III in 1702, however, had led to the political rise of a group of Tories who disliked the Dutch, were opposed to the idea of the Grand Alliance and intended, while they were at it, to reverse as many of William's other policies as possible, especially his policy of tolerance towards the Dissenters. It was they who had been the target of *The Shortest-Way*, and they who had been instrumental in the harassment of its author. Defoe, who strongly supported the war against France, felt that these Tories cared only about settling domestic scores against their enemies at home, and were doing all they could to undermine the position of the English military commander, the Duke of Marlborough, whom they regarded as William's creation. Defoe's frustration is plain to see in the pages of *The Lay-Man's Sermon upon the Late Storm*, where he openly accuses Marlborough's critics of preferring the defeat of 'the whole *Navy of England*' to the defeat of a single piece of commons legislation (p. 198). Given the storm's recent destruction of so many vessels of the sovereign fleet, as well as the good-behaviour clause that had been added to Defoe's sentence, this was a sensitive area to get into, but Defoe remained unrepentant in his accusations: 'These are the People who Cry out of the Danger from the Dissenters, but are not concerned at our Danger from the *French* . . . God may Thunder from Heaven with Storms upon Storms, Ruin our Fleets, Drown our Sailors and Blow us back from the best contriv'd Expeditions in the World, but they will never believe the case affects them, never look into their own Conduct to see if they have not help'd to bring these heavy Strokes upon the Nation' (p. 198).

The fleet, which had not had a particularly successful campaign during the summer of 1703, had only just returned from
the Mediterranean when the storm came thundering up the
Channel. Defoe, who was already profoundly unimpressed by
the conduct of the admirals at sea, was appalled by their further
failure to have had the main fleet secured in inshore harbours,
rather than leaving it moored and vulnerable on the notorious
Goodwin Sands:

> But O ye Mighty Ships of War!
> What in Winter did you there?
> Wild *November* should our ships restore
> To *Chatham, Portsmouth*, and the *Nore* (p. 207),

and he went further, in the *Lay-Man's Sermon*, suggesting that
the commanders of what remained of the fleet ought to be
removed from their posts, claiming that God 'will never bless
us till they are dismist' (p. 195). Like many others at the time,
he was worried that the uncertain progress of the war so far had
given comfort to the High Church Tories, who wanted to see
an end to the campaigns in Europe as well as an end to moderate
government at home. It was not until the following summer,
with the capture of Gibraltar and the victory at Blenheim, that
any kind of popular support for the war would be heard. Until
then, according to the historian G. M. Trevelyan, the only
significant battle of the war was the one fought (and lost)
against the great November storm, which he described, with
characteristic elegance, as 'no mortal foe'.[30]

In fact the storm inflicted a double defeat upon the battered
English navy, for not only did it destroy a number of valuable
ships but it also felled many of the timber oaks needed to replace
them. Such a serious loss of trees was an emotive subject, and
The Storm has almost as many references to fallen oaks as it
does to flying tiles. Defoe claims to have counted 17,000 of
them during one short trip through Kent, until he got too tired
to carry on counting, 'tho I have great reason to believe I did
not observe one half of the Quantity', and he was also saddened
by the loss of so many apple trees, since 'we shall want Liquor

to make our Hearts merry' (p. 97). He was not alone in his feelings for the battered trees. The diarist John Evelyn, whose country estate in Wotton, Surrey, lost 2,000 oaks during the night of the storm, was grief-struck by the sight which greeted him the following morning: 'Methinks I still hear, and am sure feel the dismal Groans of our *Forests*,' he wrote, 'so many thousand of goodly *Oaks* subverted by that late dreadful *Hurricane*; prostrating the Trees, and crushing all that grew under them, lying in ghastly Postures, like whole *Regiments* fallen in *Battle*.'[31] Evelyn had made a lifetime study of trees and forests, and had published a famous volume in 1664 entitled *Sylva: A Discourse of Forest Trees*. He reissued the book in an updated edition in 1706, using *The Storm* as one of his sources for the new material, and he dedicated it to the cause of replanting oaks on behalf of the Royal Navy, as well as devoting it to the sylvan memory of all those lost trees of England.

Defoe's writing career describes an apparent evolution from his early pamphlets and political tracts into the later novels, travel-books and full-length commentaries upon which his reputation as a writer now stands. Yet throughout this long career Defoe maintained a complex and innovative relationship to the written word, and *The Storm*, in the course of which he describes himself variously as author, editor and the mere 'Collector of these Sheets', as well as 'The Ages Humble Servant', is a particularly good example of this complexity at work. In fact, as a transitional work between the early pamphlets and the later novels it is a valuable indication of his ambitions as a writer as well as of his preoccupations as a social and political observer, for however much we might suspect him of having written most, if not all, of 'these Sheets' himself, he nevertheless sought genuinely to offer equal weight to all manner of eyewitnesses, whether clergyman, farmer, widow or sailor. There is a real attempt, despite his obvious continuing anger at his enemies, to universalize the experience of the storm. He makes the point that its impact was worse than that of the Great Fire of 1666, for 'that Desolation was confin'd to a small Space, the loss fell on the wealthiest part of the People; but this loss is Universal, and its extent general, not a House, not a Family that had anything to lose, but have lost something by this Storm, the Sea, the Land, the Houses, the Churches, the Corn, the Trees, the Rivers, all have felt the fury of the Winds', as if England might at last have found some kind of social unity through its recent exposure to catastrophe (p. 109). And *The Storm*, written as it was for a general audience, and with some of that audience's own words dispensed throughout its pages, was a sincere attempt to represent and commemorate in written form this experience of temporary unity.

Defoe always liked to introduce the sound of multiple voices on the page, just as he liked to introduce the complexity of multiple points of view, and one of the technical distinctions of *The Storm* is the way in which these effects are used to suggest the crowded simultaneity of the events it describes. As Paula R. Backscheider has pointed out, '*The Storm* has sections that show simultaneous events vertically and horizontally; in one moment we may know events in a single house, in adjacent houses, in several parts of town, and in neighboring towns. The book locates events so closely together that the sequence seems to be a single event, each discrete part so integral to the whole that it is indistinguishable from the whole except in memory.'[32] In contrast to *A Journal of the Plague Year*, the main events of which take place over several months, the action of *The Storm* is concentrated instead into a single night of destruction and its aftermath. This is what gives the book such a powerful sense of immediacy and crisis, and, as the picture of a shared catastrophe unfolds before us, Defoe has us listen not only to the sounds of the high wind rising but also to the voices of the eyewitnesses, who clamour for a chance to add their stories and words to the account. Whether these voices were his own creations, or rewritten versions of other people's testimonies, as accounts of loss and survival they exhibit the same kind of narrative power that characterizes the later tales of *Robinson Crusoe* or *Moll Flanders*, whose various sufferings, whether in storms at sea or in Newgate Prison, echo many of the circumstances from which Defoe's first book, *The Storm*, was derived. And the making of this first book, in which many layers of separately narrated but chronologically parallel narratives are presented, required a new creative balance between direct quotation and circumstantial invention, which is something that Defoe pioneered in its pages. By the time he came to write the novels, some fifteen to twenty years later, he had developed this new narrative technique to perfection.

NOTES

1. *London Gazette* 3975 (13–16 December 1703).
2. Richard Chapman, *The Necessity of Repentance Asserted: In Order to Avert those Judgements which the Present War, and Strange Unseasonableness of the Weather at Present, Seem to Threaten this Nation with. In a Sermon Preached on Wednesday the 26th May, 1703* (London: M. Wotton, 1703).
3. Hubert Lamb and Knud Frydendahl, *Historic Storms of the North Sea, British Isles and Northwest Europe* (Cambridge: Cambridge University Press, 1991), p. 62.
4. Daniel Defoe, *The True-Born Englishman and Other Writings*, ed. P. N. Furbank and W. R. Owens (London: Penguin Books, 1997), p. 140.
5. *The Observator* 73 (30 December 1702–2 January 1703).
6. In a letter to the Earl of Nottingham, written on 9 January 1703, in *The Letters of Daniel Defoe*, ed. George Harris Healey (Oxford: Clarendon Press, 1955), p. 1.
7. *London Gazette* 3879 (11–14 January 1703).
8. Cited in Maximillian E. Novak, *Daniel Defoe: Master of Fictions* (Oxford: Oxford University Press, 2001), p. 180.
9. *The Letters of Daniel Defoe*, pp. 1–2.
10. Novak, *Daniel Defoe: Master of Fictions*, p. 183.
11. Novak, *Daniel Defoe: Master of Fictions*, p. 185.
12. Cited in Novak, *Daniel Defoe: Master of Fictions*, p. 189.
13. Defoe, *The True-Born Englishman and Other Writings*, p. 182.
14. Cited in Novak, *Daniel Defoe: Master of Fictions*, p. 191.
15. Novak, *Daniel Defoe: Master of Fictions*, pp. 194–7.
16. *The Letters of Daniel Defoe*, p. 11.
17. *Daily Courant* 409 (2 December 1703); *London Gazette* 3972 (2–6 December 1703).
18. See Paula R. Backscheider, *Daniel Defoe: His Life* (Baltimore: Johns Hopkins University Press, 1989), p. 64.
19. Cited in Novak, *Daniel Defoe: Master of Fictions*, p. 102.

20. *A Letter from a Gentleman in London, to his Friend in the Country; containing an Account of the Dismal Effects of the Terrible Storm of Wind, or, rather, Hurricane, that began in London the 27th November 1703* (London, 29 November 1703). Guildhall Library, London.

21. Jack Lindsay, *The Monster City: Defoe's London, 1688–1730* (London: Granada, 1978).

22. See Mark Schorer, 'A Study in Defoe: Moral Vision and Structural Form', *Thought* 25 (1950), p. 282.

23. Daniel Defoe, *Robinson Crusoe*, ed. John Richetti (London: Penguin Books, 2001), p. 39.

24. Daniel Defoe, *A Journal of the Plague Year*, ed. Cynthia Wall (London: Penguin Books, 2003), p. 60.

25. Defoe, *Robinson Crusoe*, p. 10.

26. 'A Calculation of the Credibility of Human Testimony', *Philosophical Transactions* 21 (1699), pp. 359–65.

27. *The Republican Bullies; Or, a sham Battel between two of a side, in a Dialogue between Mr. Review and the Observator, lately fall'n out about keeping the Queen's Peace* (London: J. Nutt, 1705), p. 2.

28. *The Best of Defoe's Review: An Anthology*, ed. William L. Payne (New York: Columbia University Press, 1951), pp. 14–15.

29. *The Republican Bullies*, p. 7.

30. George Macaulay Trevelyan, *England Under Queen Anne*, 3 vols. (London: Longmans, Green & Co, 1930), I, p. 308.

31. John Evelyn, *Silva: Or a Discourse of Forest-Trees, and the Propagation of Timber in His Majesty's Dominions*, fourth edn (London: Robert Scott, Richard Chiswell, George Sawbridge and Benjamin Tooke, 1706), p. 341.

32. Paula R. Backscheider, *Daniel Defoe: Ambition & Innovation* (Lexington, Kentucky: University Press of Kentucky, 1986), pp. 86–7.

Further Reading

Alkon, Paul K., *Defoe and Fictional Time* (Athens: University of Georgia Press, 1979). Contains a critically acute discussion of the temporal structure of *The Storm*.

Backscheider, Paula R., *Daniel Defoe: Ambition & Innovation* (Lexington, Kentucky: University Press of Kentucky, 1986). Focuses on the technical achievements of Defoe's major narratives.

—, *Daniel Defoe: His Life* (Baltimore: Johns Hopkins University Press, 1989). An excellent and thoroughly researched biography.

Brayne, Martin, *The Greatest Storm* (Stroud: Sutton, 2002). A valuable in-depth study of the 1703 storm and its aftermath.

Defoe, Daniel, *The True-Born Englishman and Other Writings*, ed. P. N. Furbank and W. R. Owens (London: Penguin Books, 1997). Contains the full texts of *The True-Born Englishman, The Shortest-Way with the Dissenters* and *A Hymn to the Pillory*.

Furbank, P. N. and W. R. Owens, *The Canonisation of Daniel Defoe* (New Haven and London: Yale University Press, 1988). A cogent discussion of the changing nature of Defoe's posthumous reputation.

—, *Critical Bibliography of Daniel Defoe* (London: Pickering and Chatto, 1998). The latest and most convincing attempt to solve the ongoing attributions problem, as well as an unparalleled single source of information on everything published by Defoe.

Heller, Keith, *Man's Storm: A Story of London's Parish Watch, 1703* (London: Collins, 1985). Entertaining historical crime novel set during the night of the storm, in which Defoe makes a cameo appearance.

Hill, George, *Hurricane Force: The Story of the Storm of October 1987* (London: Collins, 1988). An illustrated account of the 1987 storm which takes Defoe's earlier study as its template.

Janković, Vladimir, *Reading the Skies: A Cultural History of English Weather, 1650–1820* (Manchester: Manchester University Press, 2001). An excellent background history of early meteorology in Britain.

Lindsay, Jack, *The Monster City: Defoe's London, 1688–1730* (London: Granada, 1978). A guide to the economic and political realities of Defoe's day-to-day existence.

Moore, John Robert, *Defoe in the Pillory, and Other Studies* (Bloomington: Indiana University Press, 1939). Makes the case for viewing 1703 as the turning point in Defoe's life and career.

Novak, Maximillian E., *Daniel Defoe: Master of Fictions* (Oxford: Oxford University Press, 2001). A superb biographical and critical account of Defoe's literary career.

Starr, G. A., *Defoe and Spiritual Autobiography* (Princeton: Princeton University Press, 1965). Relates many of Defoe's works, including *The Storm*, to earlier forms of religious and confessional writing.

Trevelyan, George Macaulay, *England Under Queen Anne*, 3 vols. (London: Longmans, Green & Co, 1930). Trevelyan's remains the best general account of the period, complete with a bravura description of the 1703 storm.

Vickers, Ilsa, *Defoe and the New Sciences* (Cambridge: Cambridge University Press, 1996). Places Defoe in a seventeenth-century scientific context through a study of his education at Newington Green.

West, Richard, *The Life and Strange Surprising Adventures of Daniel Defoe* (London: HarperCollins, 1997). A lively biography which emphasizes Defoe's later career as a journalist and a spy.

A Note on the Texts

This edition of *The Storm* is based on the first edition, which appeared between 14 and 17 July 1704. It was advertised as having appeared 'yesterday' in the *Post-Man* for 15–18 July 1704 and as 'just published' in the *Review* for 29 July 1704. A second edition appeared in January 1713, with a new title-page: *A Collection of the most remarkable Casualties and Disasters, Which happen'd in the late dreadful Tempest, both by Sea and Land, on Friday the Twenty-sixth of November, Seventeen Hundred and Three* (London: George Sawbridge and J. Nutt, 1713). The text itself was unchanged from that of the first edition, and seems likely to have been a reissue of unsold sheets. An expanded version of Defoe's text was published in 1769, with the title *An Historical Narrative of the Great and Tremendous Storm which happened on Nov. 26th, 1703* (London: W. Nicoll, 1769).

The last time *The Storm* was reprinted in full was in 1905, in *The Novels and Miscellaneous Works of Daniel De Foe, with prefaces and notes, including those attributed to Sir Walter Scott*, 6 vols. (London: George Bell, 1904–10), vol. 5. The same volume also included the reprinted text of *An Essay on the Late Storm*.

The Lay-Man's Sermon upon the Late Storm was published in the second week of February 1704, as a 24-page pamphlet. It was advertised as having appeared 'last week' in the *Daily Courant* for 24 February 1704. It was the only edition of the work which, until now, has never been reprinted.

An Essay on the Late Storm was first published in *An Elegy on the Author of the True-Born-English-Man. With an Essay*

on the Late Storm. By the Author of the Hymn to the Pillory
(London, 1704). It was advertised in the *Review* for 15 August
1704. A second edition of the book appeared in 1708.

   I have retained Defoe's original spellings, italicizations, punc-
tuation and capitalizations, with one or two exceptions where
the meaning was obscured, as well as silently correcting a
number of obvious printers' errors. The use of the long 's' and
of continuous quotation marks down the left-hand margin have
also been silently dropped.

THE
STORM:

OR, A

COLLECTION

Of the most Remarkable

CASUALTIES

AND

DISASTERS

Which happen'd in the Late

Dreadful TEMPEST,

BOTH BY

SEA and LAND.

The Lord hath his way in the Whirlwind, and in the Storm, and the Clouds are the dust of his Feet. Nah. I. 3.

LONDON:

Printed for *G. Sawbridge* in *Little Britain,* and Sold by *J. Nutt* near *Stationers-Hall.* M DCC IV.

THE PREFACE

Preaching of Sermons is Speaking to a few of Mankind: Printing of Books is Talking to the whole World. The Parson Prescribes himself, and addresses to the particular Auditory with the Appellation of My Brethren; *but he that Prints a Book, ought to Preface it with a* Noverint Universi, *Know all Men by these Presents.*[1]

The proper Inference drawn from this remarkable Observation, is, That tho' he that Preaches from the Pulpit ought to be careful of his Words, that nothing pass from him but with an especial Sanction of Truth; yet he that Prints and Publishes to all the World, has a tenfold Obligation.

The Sermon is a Sound of Words spoken to the Ear, and prepar'd only for present Meditation, and extends no farther than the strength of Memory can convey it; a Book Printed is a Record; remaining in every Man's Possession, always ready to renew its Acquaintance with his Memory, and always ready to be produc'd as an Authority or Voucher to any Reports he makes out of it, and conveys its Contents for Ages to come, to the Eternity of mortal Time, when the Author is forgotten in his Grave.

If a Sermon be ill grounded, if the Preacher imposes upon us, he trespasses on a few; but if a Book Printed obtrudes a Falshood, if a Man tells a Lye in Print, he abuses Mankind, and imposes upon the whole World, he causes our Children to tell Lyes after us, and their Children after them, to the End of the World.

This Observation I thought good to make by way of Preface, to let the World know, that when I go about a Work in which I must tell a great many Stories, which may in their own nature seem incredible, and in which I must expect a great part of Mankind will question the Sincerity of the Relator; I did not do it without a particular sence upon me of the proper Duty of an Historian, and the abundant Duty laid on him to be very wary what he conveys to Posterity.

I cannot be so ignorant of my own Intentions, as not to know, that in many Cases I shall act the Divine, and draw necessary practical Inferences from the extraordinary Remarkables of this Book, and some Digressions which I hope may not be altogether useless in this Case.

And while I pretend to a thing so solemn, I cannot but premise I should stand convicted of a double Imposture, to forge a Story, and then preach Repentance to the Reader from a Crime greater than that I would have him repent of: endeavouring by a Lye to correct the Reader's Vices, and sin against Truth to bring the Reader off from sinning against Sence.

Upon this score, tho' the Undertaking be very difficult among such an infinite variety of Circumstances, to keep, exactly within the bounds of Truth; yet I have this positive Assurance with me, that in all the subsequent Relation, if the least Mistake happen, it shall not be mine.

If I judge right, 'Tis the Duty of an Historian to set every thing in its own Light, and to convey matter of fact upon its legitimate Authority, and no other: I mean thus, (for I wou'd be as explicit as I can) That where a Story is vouch'd to him with sufficient Authority, he ought to give the World the Special Testimonial of its proper Voucher, or else he is not just to the Story: and where it comes without such sufficient Authority, he ought to say so; otherwise he is not just to himself. In the first Case he injures the History, by leaving it doubtful where it might be confirm'd past all manner of question; in the last he injures his own Reputation, by taking upon himself the Risque, in case it proves a Mistake, of having the World charge him with a Forgery.

And indeed, I cannot but own 'tis just, that if I tell a Story in Print for a Truth which proves otherwise, unless I, at the same time, give proper Caution to the Reader, by owning the Uncer-

tainty of my Knowledge in the matter of fact, 'tis I impose upon the World: my Relater is innocent, and the Lye is my own.

I make all these preliminary Observations, partly to inform the Reader, that I have not undertaken this Work without the serious Consideration of what I owe to Truth, and to Posterity; nor without a Sence of the extraordinary Variety and Novelty of the Relation.

I am sensible, that the want of this Caution is the Foundation of that great Misfortune we have in matters of ancient History; in which the Impudence, the Ribaldry, the empty Flourishes, the little Regard to Truth, and the Fondness of telling a strange Story, has dwindled a great many valuable Pieces of ancient History into meer Romance.

How are the Lives of some of our most famous Men, nay the Actions of whole Ages, drowned in Fable? Not that there wanted Pen-men to write, but that their Writings were continually mixt with such Rhodomontades[2] of the Authors that Posterity rejected them as fabulous.

From hence it comes to pass that Matters of Fact are handed down to Posterity with so little Certainty, that nothing is to be depended upon; from hence the uncertain Account of Things and Actions in the remoter Ages of the World, the confounding the Genealogies as well as Atchievements of Belus, Nimrod, and Nimrus, and their Successors, the Histories and Originals of Saturn, Jupiter,[3] and the rest of the Celestial Rabble, who Mankind would have been asham'd to have call'd Gods, had they had the true Account of their dissolute, exorbitant, and inhumane Lives.

From Men we may descend to Action: and this prodigious Looseness of the Pen has confounded History and Fable from the beginning of both. Thus the great Flood in Deucalion's Time[4] is made to pass for the Universal Deluge: the Ingenuity of Dedalus, who by a Clue of Thread got out of the Egyptian Maze, which was thought impossible, is grown into a Fable of making himself a pair of Wings, and flying through the Air: —[5] the great Drought and violent Heat of Summer, thought to be the Time when the Great Famine was in Samaria, fabl'd by the Poets and Historians into the Story of Phaeton borrowing the

Chariot of the Sun, and giving the Horses their Heads, they run so near the Earth as burnt up all the nearest Parts, and scorch'd the Inhabitants, so that they have been black in those Parts ever since.[6]

These, and such like ridiculous Stuff, have been the Effects of the Pageantry of Historians in former Ages: and I might descend nearer home, to the Legends of Fabulous History which have swallow'd up the Actions of our ancient Predecessors, King Arthur, *the Gyant* Gogmagog, *and the* Britain, *the Stories of* St. George *and the* Dragon, Guy *Earl of* Warwick, Bevis *of* Southampton, *and the like.*[7]

I'll account for better Conduct in the ensuing History: and tho' some Things here related shall have equal Wonder due to them, Posterity shall not have equal Occasion to distrust the Verity of the Relation.

I confess here is room for abundance of Romance, because the Subject may be safer extended than in any other case, no Story being capable to be crowded with such Circumstances, but Infinite Power, which is all along concern'd with us in every Relation, is suppos'd capable of making true.

Yet we shall no where so Trespass upon Fact, as to oblige Infinite Power to the shewing more Miracles than it intended.

It must be allow'd, That when Nature was put into so much Confusion, and the Surface of the Earth and Sea felt such extraordinary a Disorder, innumerable Accidents would fall out that till the like Occasion happen may never more be seen, and unless a like Occasion had happen'd could never before be heard of: wherefore the particular Circumstances being so wonderful, serve but to remember Posterity of the more wonderful Extreme, which was the immediate Cause.

The Uses and Application made from this Terrible Doctrine, I leave to the Men of the Pulpit; only take the freedom to observe, that when Heaven it self lays down the Doctrine, all Men are summon'd to make Applications by themselves.

The main Inference I shall pretend to make or at least venture the exposing to publick View, in this case, is, the strong Evidence God has been pleas'd to give in this terrible manner to his own

Being, which Mankind began more than ever to affront and despise: And I cannot but have so much Charity for the worst of my Fellow-Creatures, that I believe no Man was so hard'ned against the Sence of his Maker, but he felt some Shocks of his wicked Confidence from the Convulsions of Nature at this time.

I cannot believe any Man so rooted in Atheistical Opinions, as not to find some Cause to doubt whether he was not in the Wrong, and a little to apprehend the Possibility of a Supreme Being, when he felt the terrible Blasts of this Tempest. I cannot doubt but the Atheist's hard'ned Soul trembl'd a little as well as his House, and he felt some Nature asking him some little Questions; as these – Am not I mistaken? Certainly there is some such thing as a God – What can all this be? What is the Matter in the World?

Certainly Atheism is one of the most Irrational Principles in the World; there is something incongruous in it with the Test of Humane Policy, because there is a Risque in the Mistake one way, and none another. If the Christian is mistaken, and it should at last appear that there is no Future State, God or Devil, Reward or Punishment, where is the Harm of it? All he has lost is, that he has practis'd a few needless Mortifications, and took the pains to live a little more like a Man than he wou'd have done. But if the Atheist is mistaken, he has brought all the Powers, whose Being he deny'd, upon his Back, has provok'd the Infinite in the highest manner, and must at last sink under the Anger of him whose Nature he has always disown'd.

I would recommend this Thought to any Man to consider of, one Way he can lose nothing, the other he may be undone. Certainly a wise Man would never run such an unequal Risque: a Man cannot answer it to Common Arguments, the Law of Numbers, and the Rules of Proportion are against him. No Gamester will set at such a Main;[8] *no Man will lay such a Wager, where he may lose, but cannot win.*

There is another unhappy Misfortune in the Mistake too, that it can never be discover'd till 'tis too late to remedy. He that resolves to die an Atheist, shuts the Door against being convinc'd in time.

> If it shou'd so fall out, as who can tell,
> But that there is a God, a Heaven, and Hell,
> Mankind had best consider well for Fear,
> 't should be too late when his Mistakes appear.[9]

I should not pretend to set up for an Instructor in this Case, were not the Inference so exceeding just; who can but preach where there is such a Text? when God himself speaks his own Power, he expects we should draw just Inferences from it, both for our Selves and our Friends.

If one Man, in an Hundred Years, shall arrive at a Conviction of the Being of his Maker, 'tis very well worth my While to write it, and to bear the Character of an impertinent Fellow from all the rest.

I thought to make some Apology for the Meanness of Stile, and the Method, which may be a little unusual, of Printing Letters from the Country in their own Stile.

For the last I only leave this short Reason with the Reader, the Desire I had to keep close to the Truth, and hand my Relation with the true Authorities from whence I receiv'd it; together with some Justice to the Gentlemen concern'd, who, especially in Cases of Deliverances, are willing to record the Testimonial of the Mercies they received, and to set their Hands to the humble Acknowledgement. The Plainness and Honesty of the Story will plead for the Meanness of the Stile in many of the Letters, and the Reader cannot want Eyes to see what sort of People some of them come from.

Others speak for themselves, and being writ by Men of Letters, as well as Men of Principles, I have not Arrogance enough to attempt a Correction either of the Sense or Stile; and if I had gone about it, should have injur'd both Author and Reader.

These come dressed in their own Words because I ought not, and those because I could not mend 'em. I am perswaded, they are all dress'd in the desirable, though unfashionable Garb of Truth, and I doubt not but Posterity will read them with Pleasure.

The Gentlemen, who have taken the Pains to collect and transmit the Particular Relations here made publick, I hope will *have their End answered in this Essay, conveying hereby to the Ages to come the Memory of the dreadfulest and most universal Judgment that ever Almighty Power thought fit to bring upon this Part of the World.*

And as this was the true Native and Original Design of the first Undertaking, abstracted from any Part of the Printer's Advantage, the Editor and Undertakers of this Work, having their Ends entirely answer'd, hereby give their humble Thanks to all those Gentlemen who have so far approv'd the Sincerity of their Design as to contribute their Trouble, and help forward by their just Observations, the otherwise very difficult Undertaking.

If Posterity will but make the desired Improvement both of the Collector's Pains, as well as the several Gentlemens Care in furnishing the Particulars, I dare say they will all acknowledge their End fully answer'd, and none more readily than

The Ages Humble Servant.

THE STORM

CHAPTER I

Of the Natural Causes and Original of Winds

Though a System of Exhalation, Dilation, and Extension, things which the Ancients founded the Doctrine of Winds upon, be not my direct Business; yet it cannot but be needful to the present Design to Note, that the Difference in the Opinions of the Ancients, about the Nature and Original of Winds, is a Leading Step to one Assertion which I have advanc'd in all that I have said with Relation to Winds, *viz.* That there seems to be more of God in the whole Appearance, than in any other Part of Operating Nature.

Nor do I think I need explain my self very far in this Notion: I allow the high Original of Nature to be the Great Author of all her Actings, and by the strict Rein of his Providence, is the Continual and Exact Guide of her Executive Power; but still 'tis plain that in Some of the Principal Parts of Nature she is Naked to our Eye, Things appear both in their Causes and Consequences, Demonstration gives its Assistance, and finishes our further Enquiries: for we never enquire after God in those Works of Nature which depending upon the Course of Things are plain and demonstrative; but where we find Nature defective in her Discovery, where we see Effects but cannot reach their Causes; there 'tis most just, and Nature her self seems to direct us to it, to end the rational Enquiry, and resolve it into Speculation: Nature plainly refers us beyond her Self, to the Mighty Hand of Infinite Power, the Author of Nature, and Original of all Causes.

Among these Arcana of the Sovereign Oeconomy, the Winds
are laid as far back as any. Those Ancient Men of Genius who
rifled Nature by the Torch-Light of Reason even to her very
Nudities, have been run a-ground in this unknown Channel; the
Wind has blown out the Candle of Reason, and left them all in
the Dark.

Aristotle, in his Problems, Sect. 23. calls the Wind *Aeris
Impulsum*. *Seneca* says, *Ventus est Aer Fluens*. The *Stoicks* held
it, *Motum aut Fluxionem Aeris*. Mr. *Hobs*, Air mov'd in a
direct or undulating Motion. Fournier, *Le Vent et un Movement
Agitation de l' Air Causi par des Exhalations et Vapours*. The
Moderns, a Hot and Dry Exhalation repuls'd by Antiperistasis;[1]
Des Cartes defines it, *Venti Nihil sunt nisi Moti & Dilati
Vapores*. And various other Opinions are very judiciously
collected by the Learned Mr. *Bohun* in his Treatise of the
Origin and Properties of Wind, P. 7. and concludes, '*That no
one Hypothesis, how Comprehensive soever, has yet been able
to resolve all the Incident Phenomena of Winds*. Bohun *of
Winds*, P. 9.[2]

This is what I quote them for, and this is all my Argument
demands; the deepest Search into the Region of Cause and
Consequence, has found out just enough to leave the wisest
Philosopher in the dark,[3] to bewilder his Head, and drown his
Understanding. You raise a Storm in Nature by the very Inquiry;
and at last, to be rid of you, she confesses the Truth, and tells
you, *It is not in Me, you must go Home and ask my Father*.

Whether then it be the Motion of Air, and what that Air is,
which as yet is undefin'd, whether it is a Dilation, a previous
Contraction, and then violent Extension as in Gun-Powder,
whether the Motion is Direct, Circular, or Oblique, whether
it be an Exhalation repuls'd by the Middle Region, and the
Antiperistasis of that Part of the Heavens which is set as a Wall
of Brass to bind up the Atmosphere, and keep it within its proper
Compass for the Functions of Respiration, Condensing and
Rarifying, without which Nature would be all in Confusion;
whatever are their efficient Causes, 'tis not much to the immediate Design.

'Tis apparent, that God Almighty, whom the Philosophers

care as little as possible to hav~

have reserv'd this, as one of those ~

should more directly guide them to himself. ~ with, seems to

Not but that a Philosopher may be a Christian, a~~ ~~ ~ich

the best of the Latter have been the best of the Former,~

Vossius, Mr. *Boyle*, Sir *Walter Raleigh*, Lord *Verulam*, Dr.

Harvey, and others; and I wish I could say Mr. *Hobbs*, for 'twas

Pity there should lie any just Exceptions to the Piety of a Man,

who had so few to his General Knowledge, and an exalted Spirit

in Philosophy.[4]

When therefore I say the Philosophers do not care to concern

God himself in the Search after Natural Knowledge; I mean, as

it concerns Natural Knowledge, *meerly as such*; for 'tis a Natural

Cause they seek, from a General Maxim, That all Nature has

its Cause within it self: 'tis true, 'tis the Darkest Part of the

Search, to trace the Chain backward; to begin at the Conse-

quence, and from thence *hunt Counter*,[5] as we may call it, to

find out the Cause: 'twould be much easier if we could begin at

the Cause, and trace it to all its Consequences.

I make no Question, the Search would be equally to the

Advantage of Science, and the Improvement of the World; for

without Doubt there are some Consequences of known Causes

which are not yet discover'd, and I am as ready to believe there

are yet in Nature some *Terra Incognita*[6] both as to Cause and

Consequence too.

In this Search after Causes, the Philosopher, tho' he may at

the same Time be a very good Christian, cares not at all to

meddle with his Maker: the Reason is plain; We may at any

time resolve all things into Infinite Power, and we do allow that

the Finger of Infinite is the First Mighty Cause of Nature her

self: but the Treasury of Immediate Cause is generally committed

to Nature; and if at any Time we are driven to look beyond her,

'tis because we are out of the way: 'tis not because it is not in

her, but because we cannot find it.

Two Men met in the Middle of a great Wood; One was

searching for a Plant which grew in the Wood, the Other had

lost himself in the Wood, and wanted to get out: The Latter

rejoyc'd when thro' the Trees he saw the open Country: but the

... not to get out, but to find what he
... Man no more undervalued the Pleasantness
... Champion Country[7] than the other.

Thus in Nature the Philosopher's Business is not to look
through Nature, and come to the vast open Field of Infinite
Power; his Business is in the Wood; there grows the Plant he
looks for; and 'tis there he must find it. Philosophy's a-ground
if it is forc'd to any further Enquiry. The Christian begins just
where the Philosopher ends; and when the Enquirer turns his
Eyes up to Heaven, Farewel Philosopher; 'tis a Sign he can make
nothing of it here.

David was a good Man, the Scripture gives him that Testimony; but I am of the Opinion, he was a better King than a
Scholar, more a Saint than a Philosopher: and it seems very
proper to judge that *David* was upon the Search of Natural
Causes, and found himself puzzled as to the Enquiry, when he
finishes the Enquiry with two pious Ejaculations, *When I view
the Heavens the Works of thy Hands, the Moon and the Stars
which thou hast made; then I say, what is Man!*[8] *David* may
very rationally be suppos'd to be searching the Causes, Motions,
and Influences of Heavenly Bodies; and finding his Philosophy
a-ground, and the Discovery not to answer his Search, he turns
it all to a pious Use, recognizes Infinite Power, and applies it to
the Exstasies and Raptures of his Soul, which were always
employ'd in the Charm of exalted Praise.

Thus in another Place we find him dissecting the Womb of
his Mother, and deep in the Study of Anatomy; but having, as
it may be well supposed, no Help from *Johan Remelini*, or of
the Learned *Riolanus*,[9] and other Anatomists, famous for the
most exquisite Discovery of human Body, and all the Vessels of
Life, with their proper Dimensions and Use, all *David* could say
to the Matter was, *Good Man*, to look up to Heaven, and
admire what he could not understand, *Psal. – I was fearfully
and wonderfully made*, &c.[10]

This is very Good, and well becomes a Pulpit; but what's all
this to a Philosopher? 'Tis not enough for him to know that
God has made the Heavens, the Moon, and the Stars, but must

inform himself where he has plac'd them, and why there; and what their Business, what their Influences, their Functions, and the End of their Being. 'Tis not enough for an Anatomist to know that he is fearfully and wonderfully made in the lowermost Part of the Earth, but he must see those lowermost Parts; search into the Method Nature proceeds upon in the performing the Office appointed, must search the Steps she takes, the Tools she works by; and in short, know all that the God of Nature has permitted to be capable of Demonstration.

And it seems a just Authority for our Search, that some things are so plac'd in Nature by a Chain of Causes and Effects, that upon a diligent Search we may find out what we look for: To search after what God has in his Sovereignty thought fit to conceal, may be criminal, and doubtless is so; and the Fruitlesness of the Enquiry is generally Part of the Punishment to a vain Curiosity: but to search after what our Maker has not hid, only cover'd with a thin Veil of Natural Obscurity, and which upon our Search is plain to be read, seems to be justified by the very Nature of the thing, and the Possibility of the Demonstration is an Argument to prove the Lawfulness of the Enquiry.

The Design of this Digression, is, in short, That as where Nature is plain to be search'd into, and Demonstration easy, the Philosopher is allow'd to seek for it; so where God has, as it were, laid his Hand upon any Place, and Nature presents us with an universal Blank, we are therein led as naturally to recognize the Infinite Wisdom and Power of the God of Nature, as *David* was in the Texts before quoted.

And this is the Case here; the Winds are some of those Inscrutables of Nature, in which humane Search has not yet been able to arrive at any Demonstration.

'The Winds,' *says the Learned Mr.* Bohun, 'are generated in the Intermediate Space between the Earth and the Clouds, either by Rarefaction or Repletion, and sometimes haply by pressure of Clouds, Elastical Virtue of the Air, &c. from the Earth or Seas, as by Submarine or Subterraneal Eruption or Descension or Resilition from the middle Region.'[11]

All this, though no Man is more capable of the Enquiry than

this Gentleman, yet to the Demonstration of the thing, amounts to no more than what we had before, and still leaves it as Abstruse and Cloudy to our Understanding as ever.

Not but that I think my self bound in Duty to Science in General, to pay a just Debt to the Excellency of Philosophical Study, in which I am a meer Junior, and hardly any more than an Admirer; and therefore I cannot but allow that the Demonstrations made of Rarefaction and Dilatation are extraordinary; and that by Fire and Water Wind may be rais'd in a close Room, as the Lord *Verulam* made Experiment in the Case of his Feathers.[12]

But that therefore all the Causes of Wind are from the Influences of the Sun upon vaporous Matter first Exhal'd, which being Dilated are oblig'd to possess themselves of more Space than before, and consequently make the Particles fly before them; this does not seem to be a sufficient Demonstration of Wind: for this, to my weak Apprehension, would rather make a Blow like Gun-Powder than a rushing forward; at best this is indeed a probable Conjecture, but admits not of Demonstration equal to other Phænomena in Nature.

And this is all I am upon, *viz.* That this Case has not equal Proofs of the Natural Causes of it that we meet with in other Cases: The Scripture seems to confirm this, when it says in one Place, *He holds the Wind in his Hand;*[13] as if he should mean, Other things are left to the Common Discoveries of Natural Inquiry, but this is a thing he holds in his own Hand, and has conceal'd it from the Search of the most Diligent and Piercing Understanding: This is further confirm'd by the Words of our Saviour, *The Wind blows where it listeth, and thou hearest the Sound thereof, but knowest not whence it cometh;*[14] 'tis plainly express'd to signify that the Causes of the Wind are not equally discover'd by Natural Enquiry as the rest of Nature is.

If I would carry this Matter on, and travel into the Seas, and Mountains of *America*, where the Mansones,[15] the Trade-Winds, the Sea-Breezes, and such Winds as we have little Knowledge of, are more common; it would yet more plainly appear, *That we hear the Sound, but know not from whence they come.*

Nor is the Cause of their Motion parallel to the Surface of the

Earth, a less Mystery than their real Original, or the Difficulty of their Generation: and though some People have been forward to prove the Gravity of the Particles must cause the Motion to be oblique; 'tis plain it must be very little so, or else Navigation would be impracticable, and in extraordinary Cases where the Pressure above is perpendicular, it has been fatal to Ships, Houses, &c. and would have terrible Effects in the World, if it should more frequently be so.

From this I draw only this Conclusion, That the Winds are a Part of the Works of God by Nature, in which he has been pleased to communicate less of Demonstration to us than in other Cases; that the Particulars more directly lead us to Speculations, and refer us to Infinite Power more than the other Parts of Nature does.

That the Wind is more expressive and adapted to his Immediate Power, as he is pleas'd to exert it in extraordinary Cases in the World.

That 'tis more frequently made use of as the Executioner of his Judgments in the World, and extraordinary Events are brought to pass by it.

From these three Heads we are brought down directly to speak of the Particular Storm before us; *viz*. The Greatest, the Longest in Duration, the widest in Extent, of all the Tempests and Storms that History gives any Account of since the Beginning of Time.

In the further Conduct of the Story, 'twill not be foreign to the Purpose, nor unprofitable to the Reader, to review the Histories of ancient Time and remote Countries, and examine in what Manner God has been pleas'd to execute his Judgments by Storms and Tempests; what kind of things they have been, and what the Consequences of them; and then bring down the Parallel to the Dreadful Instance before us.

We read in the Scripture of Two Great Storms; One past, and the Other to come. Whether the last be not Allegorical rather than Prophetical, I shall not busie my self to determine.

The First was when God caused a strong Wind to blow upon the Face of the Delug'd World; to put a stop to the Flood, and reduce the Waters to their proper Channel.

I wish our Naturalists would explain that Wind to us, and tell us which way it blew, or how it is possible that any direct Wind could cause the Waters to ebb; for to me it seems, that the Deluge being universal, that Wind which blew the Waters from one Part must blow them up in another.

Whether it was not some perpendicular Gusts that might by their Force separate the Water and the Earth, and cause the Water driven from off the Land to *subside* by its own Pressure.

I shall dive no farther into that mysterious Deluge, which has some things in it which recommend the Story rather to our Faith than Demonstration.

The Other Storm I find in the Scripture is in the *God shall rain upon the Wicked, Plagues, Fire, and a horrible Tempest.*[16] What this shall be, we wait to know; and happy are they who shall be secured from its Effects.

Histories are full of Instances of violent Tempests and Storms in sundry particular Places. What that was, which mingled with such violent Lightnings set the Cities of *Sodom* and *Gomorrah* on fire,[17] remains to me yet undecided: nor am I satisfied the Effect it had on the Waters of the Lake, which are to this Day call'd the *Dead Sea*, are such as some fabulous Authors have related, and as Travellers take upon them to say.

CHAPTER II

Of the Opinion of the Ancients, That this Island was more Subject to Storms than other Parts of the World

I am not of Opinion with the early Ages of the World, when these Islands were first known, that they were the most Terrible of any Part of the World for Storms and Tempests.

Cambden tells us,[1] The *Britains* were distinguish'd from all the World by unpassable Seas and terrible Northern Winds, which made the *Albion* Shores dreadful to Sailors; and this part of the World was therefore reckoned the utmost Bounds of the Northern known Land, beyond which none had ever sailed: and

quotes a great variety of ancient Authors to this purpose; some
of which I present as a Specimen.

> *Et Penitus Toto Divisos Orbe Britannos.*
> Britain's disjoyn'd from all the well known World.[2]
> *Quem Littus adusta,*
> *Horrescit Lybiæ, ratibusq; Impervia* *Thule
> *Ignotumq; Fretum.*[3]
>
> Claud.

*Taken frequent-
ly for
Britain.

And if the Notions the World then had were true, it would be
very absurd for us who live here to pretend Miracles in any
Extremes of Tempests; since by what the Poets of those Ages
flourish'd about stormy Weather, was the native and most
proper Epithet of the Place:

> *Belluosus qui remotis*
> *Obstrepit Oceanus* Britannis.[4]
>
> *Hor.*

Nay, some are for placing the Nativity of the Winds hereabouts, as if they had been all generated here, and the Confluence
of Matter had made this Island its General Rendezvouz.

But I shall easily show, that there are several Places in the
World far better adapted to be the General Receptacle or Centre
of Vapours, to supply a Fund of Tempestuous Matter, than
England; as particularly the vast Lakes of *North America*: Of
which afterwards.

And yet I have two Notions, one real, one imaginary, of the
Reasons which gave the Ancients such terrible Apprehensions
of this Part of the World; which of late we find as Habitable and
Navigable as any of the rest.

The real Occasion I suppose thus: That before the Multitude
and Industry of Inhabitants prevail'd to the managing, enclos-
ing, and improving the Country, the vast Tract of Land in this
Island which continually lay open to the Flux of the Sea, and to
the Inundations of Land-Waters, were as so many standing
Lakes; from whence the Sun continually exhaling vast quantities

of moist Vapours, the Air could not but be continually crowded with all those Parts of necessary Matter to which we ascribe the Original of Winds, Rains, Storms, and the like.

He that is acquainted with the situation of *England*, and can reflect on the vast Quantities of flat Grounds, on the Banks of all our navigable Rivers, and the Shores of the Sea, which Lands at Least lying under Water every Spring-Tide, and being thereby continually full of moisture, were like a stagnated standing body of Water brooding Vapours in the Interval of the Tide, must own that at least a fifteenth part of the whole Island may come into this Denomination.

Let him that doubts the Truth of this, examine a little the Particulars; let him stand upon *Shooters-Hill* in *Kent*,[5] and view the Mouth of the River *Thames*, and consider what a River it must be when none of the Marshes on either side were wall'd in from the Sea, and when the Sea without all question flow'd up to the Foot of the Hills on either Shore, and up every Creek, where he must allow is now dry Land on either side the River for two Miles in breadth at least, sometimes three or four, for above forty Miles on both sides the River.

Let him farther reflect, how all these Parts lay when, as our ancient Histories relate, the *Danish* Fleet came up almost to *Hartford*,[6] so that all that Range of fresh Marshes which reach for twenty five Miles in length, from *Ware* to the River *Thames*, must be a Sea.

In short, Let any such considering Person imagine the vast Tract of Marsh-Lands on both sides the River *Thames*, to *Harwich* on the *Essex* side, and to *Whitstable* on the *Kentish* side, the Levels of Marshes up the *Stour* from *Sandwich* to *Canterbury*, the whole Extent of Lowgrounds commonly call'd *Rumney-Marsh*,[7] from *Hythe* to *Winchelsea*, and up the Banks of the *Rother*; all which put together, and being allow'd to be in one place cover'd with Water, what a Lake wou'd it be suppos'd to make? According to the nicest Calculations I can make, it cou'd not amount to less than 500000 Acres of Land.

The Isle of *Ely*, with the *Flats* up the several Rivers from *Yarmouth* to *Norwich*, *Beccles*, &c. the continu'd Levels in the several Counties of *Norfolk*, *Cambridge*, *Suffolk*, *Huntingdon*,

Northampton, and *Lincoln*, I believe do really contain as much Land as the whole County of *Norfolk*; and 'tis not many Ages since these Counties were universally one vast Moras or Lough, and the few solid parts wholly unapproachable: insomuch that the Town of *Ely* it self was a Receptacle for the Malecontents of the Nation, where no reasonable Force cou'd come near to dislodge them.[8]

'Tis needless to reckon up twelve or fourteen like Places in *England*, as the Moores in *Somersetshire*, the Flat-shores in *Lancashire*, *Yorkshire*, and *Durham*, the like in *Hampshire* and *Sussex*; and in short, on the Banks of every Navigable River.

The sum of the matter is this; That while this Nation was thus full of standing Lakes, stagnated Waters, and moist Places, the multitude of Exhalations must furnish the Air with a quantity of Matter for Showers and Storms infinitely more than it can be now supply'd withal, those vast Tracts of Land being now fenc'd off, laid dry, and turn'd into wholsome and profitable Provinces.

This seems demonstrated from *Ireland*, where the multitude of Loughs, Lakes, Bogs, and moist Places, serve the Air with Exhalations, which give themselves back again in Showers, and make it be call'd, *The Piss-pot of the World*.[9]

The imaginary Notion I have to advance on this Head, amounts only to a Reflection upon the Skill of those Ages in the Art of Navigation; which being far short of what it is since arrived to, made these vast Northern Seas too terrible for them to venture in: and accordingly, they rais'd those Apprehensions up to Fable, which began only in their want of Judgment.

The *Phœnicians*,[10] who were our first Navigators, the *Genoese*, and after them the *Portuguese*, who arriv'd to extra-ordinary Proficiency in Sea Affairs, were yet all of them, *as we say*, Fair-weather Sea-men: The chief of their Navigation was Coasting; and if they were driven out of their Knowledge, had work enough to find their way home, and sometimes never found it at all; but one Sea convey'd them directly into the last Ocean, from whence no Navigation cou'd return them.

When these, by Adventures, or Misadventures rather, had at any time extended their Voyaging as far as this Island, which,

by the way, they always perform'd round the Coast of *Spain,
Portugal*, and *France*; if ever such a Vessel return'd, if ever the
bold Navigator arriv'd at home, he had done enough to talk
on all his Days, and needed no other Diversion among his
Neighbours, than to give an Account of the vast Seas, mighty
Rocks, deep Gulfs, and prodigious Storms he met with in these
remote Parts of the known World: and this, magnified by the
Poetical Arts of the Learned Men of those times, grew into a
receiv'd Maxim of Navigation, That these Parts were so full of
constant Tempests, Storms, and dangerous Seas, that 'twas
present Death to come near them, and none but Madmen and
Desperadoes could have any Business there, since they were
Places where Ships never came, and Navigation was not proper
in the Place.

> And *Thule*, where no Passage was
> For Ships their Sails to bear.[11]

Horace has reference to this horrid Part of the World, as a
Place full of terrible Monsters, and fit only for their Habitation,
in the Words before quoted.

> *Belluosus qui remotis
> Obstrepit Oceanus Britannis.*

Juvenal follows his Steps;

> *Quanto Delphino Balæna Britannica major.*[12]
> Juv.

Such horrid Apprehensions those Ages had of these Parts,
which by our Experience, and the Prodigy to which Navigation
in particular, and Sciential Knowledge in general, is since grown,
appear very ridiculous.

For we find no Danger in our Shores, no uncertain wavering
in our Tides, no frightful Gulfs, no horrid Monsters, but what
the bold Mariner has made familiar to him. The Gulfs which
frighted those early Sons of *Neptune* are search'd out by our

Seamen, and made useful Bays, Roads, and Harbours of Safety. The Promontories which running out into the Sea gave them terrible Apprehensions of Danger, are our Safety, and make the Sailors Hearts glad, as they are the first Lands they make when they are coming Home from a long Voyage, or as they are a good shelter when in a Storm our Ships get *under their Lee*.

Our Shores are sounded, the Sands and Flats are discovered, which they knew little or nothing of, and in which more real Danger lies, than in all the frightful Stories they told us; useful Sea-marks and Land-figures are plac'd on the Shore, Buoys on the Water, Light-houses on the highest Rocks; and all these dreadful Parts of the World are become the Seat of Trade, and the Centre of Navigation: Art has reconcil'd all the Difficulties, and Use made all the *Horribles* and *Terribles* of those Ages become as natural and familiar as Day-light.

The Hidden Sands, almost the only real Dread of a Sailor, and by which till the Channels between them were found out, our Eastern Coast must be really unpassable, now serve to make Harbours: and *Yarmouth* Road was made a safe Place for Shipping by them.[13] Nay, when *Portsmouth, Plymouth*, and other good Harbours would not defend our Ships in the Violent Tempest we are treating of, here was the least Damage done of any Place in *England*, considering the Number of Ships which lay at Anchor, and the Openness of the Place.

So that upon the whole it seems plain to me, that all the dismal things the Ancients told us of *Britain*, and her terrible Shores, arose from the Infancy of Marine Knowledge, and the Weakness of the Sailor's Courage.

Not but that I readily allow we are more subject to bad Weather and hard Gales of Wind than the Coasts of *Spain, Italy*, and *Barbary*.[14] But if this be allow'd, our Improvement in the Art of Building Ships is so considerable, our Vessels are so prepar'd to ride out the most violent Storms, that the Fury of the Sea is the least thing our Sailors fear: Keep them but from *a Lee Shore*,[15] or touching upon a Sand, they'll venture all the rest: and nothing is a greater satisfaction to them, if they have a Storm in view, than a sound Bottom and good *Sea-room*.[16]

From hence it comes to pass, that such Winds as in those Days wou'd have pass'd for Storms, are called only a *Fresh-gale*, or *Blowing hard*. If it blows enough to fright a South Country Sailor, we laugh at it: and if our Sailors bald Terms were set down in a Table of Degrees, it will explain what we mean.

Stark Calm.	*A Top-sail Gale.*
Calm Weather.	*Blows fresh.*
Little Wind.	*A hard Gale of Wind.*
A fine Breeze.	*A Fret of Wind.*
A small Gale.	*A Storm.*
A fresh Gale.	*A Tempest.*

Just half these Tarpawlin Articles, I presume, would have pass'd in those Days for a Storm; and that our Sailors call a Top-sail Gale would have drove the Navigators of those Ages into Harbours: when our Sailors reef a Top-sail, they would have handed all their Sails; and when we go under a main Course,[17] they would have run *afore it* for Life to the next Port they could make: when our *Hard Gale* blows, they would have cried a Tempest; and about the *Fret of Wind* they would be all at their Prayers.

And if we should reckon by this Account we are a stormy Country indeed, our Seas are no more Navigable now for such Sailors than they were then: If the *Japoneses*, the *East Indians*, and such like Navigators, were to come with their thin Cockle-shell Barks and Calico Sails; if *Cleopatra*'s Fleet, or *Cæsar*'s great Ships with which he fought the Battle of *Actium*,[18] were to come upon our Seas, there hardly comes a *March* or a *September* in twenty Years but would blow them to Pieces, and then the poor Remnant that got Home, would go and talk of a terrible Country where there's nothing but Storms and Tempests; when all the Matter is, the Weakness of their Shipping, and the Ignorance of their Sea-men: and I make no question but our Ships ride out many a worse Storm than that terrible Tempest which scatter'd *Julius Cæsar*'s Fleet, or the same that drove *Æneas* on the Coast of *Carthage*.[19]

And in more modern times we have a famous Instance in the *Spanish Armada*; which, after it was rather frighted than damag'd by Sir *Francis Drake*'s Machines, not then known by the Name of Fireships, were scatter'd by a terrible Storm, and lost upon every Shore.[20]

The Case is plain, 'Twas all owing to the Accident of Navigation: They had, no doubt, a hard Gale of Wind, and perhaps a Storm; but they were also on an Enemy's Coast, their Pilots out of their Knowledge, no Harbour to run into, and an Enemy a-stern, that when once they separated, Fear drove them from one Danger to another, and away they went to the Northward, where they had nothing but God's Mercy, and the Winds and Seas to help them. In all those Storms and Distresses which ruin'd that Fleet, we do not find an Account of the Loss of one Ship, either of the *English* or *Dutch*; the Queen's Fleet rode it out in the *Downs*,[21] which all Men know is none of the best Roads in the World; and the *Dutch* rode among the Flats of the *Flemish* Coast, while the vast Galleons, not so well fitted for the Weather, were forc'd to keep the Sea, and were driven to and fro till they had got out of their Knowledge; and like Men desperate, embrac'd every Danger they came near.

This long Digression I could not but think needful, in order to clear up the Case, having never met with any thing on this Head before: At the same time 'tis allow'd, and Histories are full of the Particulars, that we have often very high Winds, and sometimes violent Tempests in these Northen Parts of the World; but I am still of opinion, such a Tempest never happen'd before as that which is the Subject of these Sheets: and I refer the Reader to the Particulars.

CHAPTER III

Of the Storm in General

Before we come to examine the Damage suffer'd by this terrible
Night, and give a particular Relation of its dismal Effects; 'tis
necessary to give a summary Account of the thing it self, with
all its affrightning Circumstances.

It had blown exceeding hard, as I have already observ'd, for
about fourteen Days past; and that so hard, that we thought it
terrible Weather: Several Stacks of Chimnies were blown down,
and several Ships were lost, and the Tiles in many Places were
blown off from the Houses; and the nearer it came to the
fatal 26*th* of *November*, the Tempestuousness of the Weather
encreas'd.

On the *Wednesday* Morning before, being the 24*th* of *November*, it was fair Weather, and blew hard; but not so as to give
any Apprehensions, till about 4 a Clock in the Afternoon the
Wind encreased, and with Squauls of Rain and terrible Gusts
blew very furiously.

The Collector of these Sheets narrowly escap'd the Mischief
of a Part of a House, which fell on the Evening of that Day by
the Violence of the Wind; and abundance of Tiles were blown
off the Houses that Night: the Wind continued with unusual
Violence all the next Day and Night; and had not the Great
Storm follow'd so soon, this had pass'd for a great Wind.

On *Friday* Morning it continued to blow exceeding hard, but
not so as that it gave any Apprehensions of Danger within
Doors; towards Night it encreased: and about 10 a Clock,
our Barometers[1] inform'd us that the Night would be very
tempestuous; the *Mercury* sunk lower than ever I had observ'd
it on any Occasion whatsoever, which made me suppose the
Tube had been handled and disturb'd by the Children.

But as my Observations of this Nature are not regular enough
to supply the Reader with a full Information, the Disorders
of that dreadful Night having found me other Imployment,
expecting every Moment when the House I was in would bury

us all in its own Ruins; I have therefore subjoin'd a Letter from
an Ingenious Gentleman on this very Head, directed to the *Royal
Society*, and printed in the *Philosophical Transactions*, No. 289.
P. 1530. as follows.[2]

A Letter from the Reverend Mr. William Derham, F.R.S.[3] Containing his Observations concerning the late Storm.

SIR,

According to my Promise at the general Meeting of the *R. S.* on
St. *Andrews* Day,[4] I here send you inclos'd the Account of my
Ingenious and Inquisitive Friend *Richard Townely*, Esq;[5] concerning the State of the Atmosphere in that Part of *Lancashire* where
he liveth, in the late dismal Storm. And I hope it will not be
unaccepable, to accompany his with my own Observations at
Upminster; especially since I shall not weary you with a long
History of the Devastations, *&c.* but rather some Particulars of a
more Philosophical Consideration.

And first, I do not think it improper to look back to the
preceding Seasons of the Year. I scarce believe I shall go out of
the way, to reflect as far back as *April, May, June* and *July*;
because all these were wet Months in our Southern Parts. In *April*
there fell 12,49 *l.*[6] of Rain through my Tunnel:[7] And about 6, 7,
8, or 9, *l.* I esteem a moderate quantity for *Upminster*. *In* May
there fell more than in any Month of any Year since the Year
1696, viz. 20,77 *l.* June likewise was a dripping Month, in which
fell 14,55 *l.* And *July*, although it had considerable Intermissions,
yet had 14,19 *l.* above 11 *l.* of which fell on *July* 28*th* and 29*th*
in violent Showers. And I remember the News Papers gave
Accounts of great Rains that Month from divers Places of *Europe*;
but the *North of England* (which also escaped the Violence of the
late Storm) was not so remarkably wet in any of those Months;
at least not in that great proportion more than we, as usually they
are; as I guess from the Tables of Rain, with which Mr. *Towneley*
hath favoured me. Particularly *July* was a dry Month with them,
there being no more than 3,65 *l.* of Rain fell through Mr. *Towneley*'s Tunnel of the same Diameter with mine.

From these Months let us pass to *September*, and that we shall find to have been a wet Month, especially the latter part of it; there fell of Rain in that Month, 14,86 *l*.

October and *November* last, although not remarkably wet, yet have been open warm Months for the most part. My Thermometer (whose freezing Point is about 84) hath been very seldom below 100 all this Winter, and especially in *November*.

Thus I have laid before you as short Account as I could of the preceding Disposition of the Year, particularly as to wet and warmth, because I am of opinion that these had a great Influence in the late Storm; not only in causing a Repletion of Vapours in the Atmosphere, but also in raising such Nitro-sulphureous or other heterogeneous matter, which when mix'd together might make a sort of Explosion (like fired Gun-powder) in the Atmosphere.[8] And from this Explosion I judge those Corruscations or Flashes in the Storm to have proceeded, which most People as well as my self observed, and which some took for Lightning. But these things I leave to better Judgments, such as that very ingenious Member of our Society, who hath undertaken the Province of the late Tempest; to whom, if you please, you may impart these Papers; Mr. *Halley*[9] you know I mean.

From Preliminaries it is time to proceed nearer to the Tempest it self. And the foregoing Day, *viz. Thursday, Nov.* 25. I think deserveth regard. In the Morning of that day was a little Rain, the Winds high in the Afternoon: S.b.E. and S. In the Evening there was Lightning; and between 9 and 10 of the Clock at Night, a violent, but short Storm of Wind, and much Rain at *Upminster*; and of Hail in some other Places, which did some Damage: There fell in that Storm 1,65 *l*. of Rain. The next Morning, which was *Friday, Novem.* 26. the Wind was S. S. W. and high all Day, and so continued till I was in Bed and asleep. About 12 that Night, the Storm awaken'd me, which gradually encreas'd till near 3 that Morning; and from thence till near 7 it continued in the greatest excess: and then began slowly to abate, and the *Mercury* to rise swiftly. The Barometer I found at 12 h.$\frac{1}{2}$ P. M. at 28,72, where it continued till about 6 the next Morning, or $6\frac{1}{4}$, and then hastily rose; so that it was gotten to 82 about 8 of the Clock, as in the Table.

How the Wind sat during the late Storm I cannot positively

say, it being excessively dark all the while, and my Vane blown down also, when I could have seen: But by Information from Millers, and others that were forc'd to venture abroad; and by my own guess, I imagin it to have blown about S. W. by S. or nearer to the S. in the beginning, and to veer about towards the West towards the End of the Storm, as far as W. S. W.

The degrees of the Wind's Strength being not measurable (that I know of, though talk'd of) but by guess, I thus determine, with respect to other Storms. On *Feb. 7. 169*$\frac{8}{9}$. was a terrible Storm that did much damage. This I number 10 degrees; the Wind then W. N. W. *vid. Ph. Tr. No.* 262.[10] Another remarkable Storm was *Feb. 3. 170*$\frac{1}{2}$. at which time was the greatest descent of the ☿[11] ever known: This I number 9 degrees. But this last of *November*, I number at least 15 degrees.

As to the *Stations* of the *Barometer*, you have Mr. *Towneley*'s and mine in the following Table to be seen at one View.

A Table shewing the Height of the *Mercury* in the Barometer, at *Townely* and *Upminster*, before, in, and after the Storm

Townely.			*Upminster.*		
Day	Hour	Height of ☿	Day	Hour	Height of ☿
Novr.	7	28 98	Novr.	8	29 50
25	3	64	25	12	39
	9$\frac{1}{2}$	61		9	14
	7	80		8	33
26	3	70	26	12	28
				9	10
	9$\frac{1}{8}$	47		12$\frac{1}{2}$	28 72
	7	50		7$\frac{1}{2}$	82
27	3	81	27	12	29 31
	9$\frac{1}{2}$	95		9	42
	7	29 34		8	65
28	3	62	28	12	83
	9	84		9	30 07
29	7	88	29	8	25

As to *November* 17*th* (whereon Mr. *Towneley* mentions a violent Storm in *Oxfordshire*) it was a Stormy Afternoon here at *Upminster*, accompanied with Rain, but not violent, nor ☿ very low. *November* 11*th* and 12*th* had both higher Winds and more Rain; and the ☿ was those Days lower than even in the last Storm of *November* 26*th*.

Thus, Sir, I have given you the truest Account I can, of what I thought most to deserve Observation, both before, and in the late Storm. I could have added some other particulars, but that I fear I have already made my Letter long, and am tedious. I shall therefore only add, that I have Accounts of the Violence of the Storm at *Norwich, Beccles, Sudbury, Colchester, Rochford*, and several other intermediate places; but I need not tell Particulars, because I question not but you have better Informations.

Thus far Mr. Derham's *Letter.*

It did not blow so hard till Twelve a Clock at Night, but that most Families went to Bed; though many of them not without some Concern at the terrible Wind, which then blew: But about One, or at least by Two a Clock, 'tis suppos'd, few People, that were capable of any Sense of Danger, were so hardy as to lie in Bed. And the Fury of the Tempest encreased to such a Degree, that as the Editor of this Account being in *London*, and conversing with the People the next Days, understood, most People expected the Fall of their Houses.

And yet in this general Apprehension, no body durst quit their tottering Habitations; for whatever the Danger was within doors, 'twas worse without; the Bricks, Tiles, and Stones, from the Tops of the Houses, flew with such force, and so thick in the Streets, that no one thought fit to venture out, tho' their Houses were near demolish'd within.

The Author of this Relation was in a well-built brick House in the skirts of the City; and a Stack of Chimneys falling in upon the next Houses, gave the House such a Shock, that they thought it was just coming down upon their Heads: but opening the Door to attempt an Escape into a Garden, the Danger was so apparent, that they all thought fit to surrender to the Disposal

of Almighty Providence, and expect their Graves in the Ruins
of the House, rather than to meet most certain Destruction in
the open Garden: for unless they cou'd have gone above two
hundred Yards from any Building, there had been no Security,
for the Force of the Wind blew the Tiles point-blank, tho' their
weight inclines them downward: and in several very broad
Streets, we saw the Windows broken by the flying of Tile-sherds
from the other side: and where there was room for them to fly,
the Author of this has seen Tiles blown from a House above
thirty or forty Yards, and stuck from five to eight Inches into
the solid Earth. Pieces of Timber, Iron, and Sheets of Lead,
have from higher Buildings been blown much farther; as in the
Particulars hereafter will appear.

It is the receiv'd Opinion of abundance of People, that they
felt, during the impetuous fury of the Wind, several Movements
of the Earth; and we have several Letters which affirm it: But as
an Earthquake must have been so general, that every body must
have discern'd it; and as the People were in their Houses when
they imagin'd they felt it, the Shaking and Terror of which might
deceive their Imagination, and impose upon their Judgment; I
shall not venture to affirm it was so: And being resolv'd to use
so much Caution in this Relation as to transmit nothing to
Posterity without authentick Vouchers, and such Testimony as
no reasonable Man will dispute; so if any Relation come in our
way, which may afford us a Probability, tho' it may be related
for the sake of its Strangeness or Novelty, it shall nevertheless
come in the Company of all its Uncertainties, and the Reader
left to judge of its Truth: for this Account had not been undertaken, but with design to undeceive the World in false Relations,
and to give an Account back'd with such Authorities, as that
the Credit of it shou'd admit of no Disputes.

For this reason I cannot venture to affirm that there was any
such thing as an Earthquake; but the Concern and Consternation of all People was so great, that I cannot wonder at their
imagining several things which were not, any more than their
enlarging on things that were, since nothing is more frequent,
than for Fear to double every Object, and impose upon the
Understanding, strong Apprehensions being apt very often to

perswade us of the Reality of such things which we have no other reasons to shew for the probability of, than what are grounded in those Fears which prevail at that juncture.

Others thought they heard it thunder. 'Tis confess'd, the Wind by its unusual Violence made such a noise in the Air as had a resemblance to Thunder; and 'twas observ'd, the roaring had a Voice as much louder than usual, as the Fury of the Wind was greater than was ever known: the Noise had also something in it more formidable; it sounded aloft, and roar'd not very much unlike remote Thunder.

And yet tho' I cannot remember to have heard it thunder, or that I saw any Lightning, or heard of any that did in or near *London*; yet in the Counties the Air was seen full of Meteors and vaporous Fires: and in some places both Thundrings and unusual Flashes of Lightning, to the great terror of the Inhabitants.

And yet I cannot but observe here, how fearless such People as are addicted to Wickedness, are both of God's Judgments and uncommon Prodigies; which is visible in this Particular, That a Gang of hardned Rogues assaulted a Family at *Poplar*, in the very Height of the Storm, broke into the House, and robb'd them: it is observable, that the People cryed Thieves, and after that cryed Fire, in hopes to raise the Neighbourhood, and to get some Assistance; but such is the Power of Self-Preservation, and such was the Fear, the Minds of the People were possess'd with, that no Body would venture out to the Assistance of the distressed Family, who were rifled and plundered in the middle of all the Extremity of the Tempest.

It would admit of a large Comment here, and perhaps not very unprofitable, to examine from what sad Defect in Principle it must be that Men can be so destitute of all manner of Regard to invisible and superiour Power, to be acting one of the vilest Parts of a Villain, while infinite Power was threatning the whole World with Disolation, and Multitudes of People expected the Last Day was at Hand.

Several Women in the City of *London* who were in Travail,[12] or who fell into Travail by the Fright of the Storm, were oblig'd to run the risque of being delivered with such Help as they had;

and Midwives found their own Lives in such Danger, that few of them thought themselves oblig'd to shew any Concern for the Lives of others.

Fire was the only Mischief that did not happen to make the Night compleatly dreadful; and yet that was not so every where, for in *Norfolk* the Town of — was almost ruin'd by a furious Fire, which burnt with such Vehemence, and was so fann'd by the Tempest, that the Inhabitants had no Power to concern themselves in the extinguishing it; the Wind blew the Flames, together with the Ruines, so about, that there was no standing near it; for if the People came to Windward they were in Danger to be blown into the Flames; and if to Leeward the Flames were so blown up in their Faces, they could not bear to come near it.

If this Disaster had happen'd in *London*, it must have been very fatal; for as no regular Application could have been made for the extinguishing it, so the very People in Danger would have had no Opportunity to have sav'd their Goods, and hardly their Lives: for though a Man will run any Risque to avoid being burnt, yet it must have been next to a Miracle, if any Person so oblig'd to escape from the Flames had escap'd being knock'd on the Head in the Streets; for the Bricks and Tiles flew about like small Shot; and 'twas a miserable Sight, in the Morning after the Storm, to see the Streets covered with Tyle-sherds, and Heaps of Rubbish, from the Tops of the Houses, lying almost at every Door.

From Two of the Clock the Storm continued, and encreased till Five in the Morning; and from Five, to half an Hour after Six, it blew with the greatest Violence: the Fury of it was so exceeding great for that particular Hour and half, that if it had not abated as it did, nothing could have stood its Violence much longer.

In this last Part of the Time the greatest Part of the Damage was done: Several Ships that rode it out till now, gave up all; for no Anchor could hold. Even the Ships in the River of *Thames* were all blown away from their Moorings, and from *Execution-Dock* to *Lime-House Hole* there was but four Ships that rid it out, the rest were driven down into the *Bite*, as the Sailors call it, from *Bell-Wharf* to *Lime-House*; where they were huddeld together and drove on Shore, Heads and Sterns, one upon another, in such a manner, as any one would have thought it had been impossible: and the Damage done on that Account was incredible.

Together with the Violence of the Wind, the Darkness of the Night added to the Terror of it; and as it was just New Moon, the Spring Tides being then up at about Four a Clock, made the Vessels, which were a-float in the River, drive the farther up upon the Shore: of all which, in the Process of this Story, we shall find very strange Instances.

The Points from whence the Wind blew, are variously reported from various Hands: 'Tis certain, it blew all the Day before at S. W. and I thought it continued so till about Two a Clock; when, as near as I could judge by the Impressions it made on the House, for we durst not look out, it veer'd to the S. S. W. then to the W. and about Six a Clock to W. by N. and still the more Northward it shifted, the harder it blew, till it shifted again Southerly about Seven a Clock; and as it did so, it gradually abated.

About Eight a Clock in the Morning it ceased so much, that our Fears were also abated, and People began to peep out of Doors; but 'tis impossible to express the Concern that appear'd in every Place: the Distraction and Fury of the Night was visible in the Faces of the People, and every Body's first Work was to visit and enquire after Friends and Relations. The next Day or Two was almost entirely spent in the Curiosity of the People, in viewing the Havock the Storm had made, which was so universal in *London*, and especially in the Out-Parts,[13] that nothing can be said sufficient to describe it.

Another unhappy Circumstance with which this Disaster was join'd, was a prodigious Tide, which happen'd the next Day but one, and was occasion'd by the Fury of the Winds: which is also a Demonstration, that the Winds veer'd for Part of the Time to the Northward: and as it is observable, and known by all that understand our Sea Affairs, that a North West Wind makes the Highest Tide, so this blowing to the Northward, and that with such unusual Violence, brought up the Sea raging in such a manner, that in some Parts of *England* 'twas incredible, the Water rising Six or Eight Foot higher than it was ever known to do in the Memory of Man; by which Ships were fleeted up upon the firm Land several Rods[14] off from the Banks, and an incredible Number of Cattle and People drown'd; as in the Pursuit of this Story will appear.

It was a special Providence that so directed the Waters, that in the River of *Thames*, the Tide, though it rise higher than usual, yet it did not so prodigiously exceed; but the Height of them as it was, prov'd very prejudicial to abundance of People whose Cellars and Ware-houses were near the River; and had the Water risen a Foot higher, all the Marshes and Levels on both sides the River had been over-flowed, and a great part of the Cattle drowned.

Though the Storm abated with the rising of the Sun, it still blew exceeding hard; so hard, that no Boats durst stir out on the River, but on extraordinary Occasions: and about Three a Clock in the Afternoon, the next Day being *Saturday*, it increas'd again, and we were in a fresh Consternation, lest it should return with the same Violence. At Four it blew an extreme Storm, with Sudden Gusts as violent as any time of the Night; but as it came with a great black Cloud, and some Thunder, it brought a hasty Shower of Rain which allay'd the Storm: so that in a quarter of an Hour it went off, and only continued blowing as before.

This sort of Weather held all *Sabbath-Day* and *Monday*, till on *Tuesday* Afternoon it encreased again; and all *Tuesday* Night it blew with such Fury, that many Families were afraid to go to Bed: And had not the former terrible Night harden'd the People to all things less than it self, this Night would have pass'd for a Storm fit to have been noted in our Almanacks.[15] Several Stacks of Chimneys that stood out the great Storm, were blown down in this; several Ships which escap'd in the great Storm, perish'd this Night; and several People who had repair'd their Houses, had them untiled again. Not but that I may allow those Chimneys that fell now might have been disabled before.

At this Rate it held blowing till *Wednesday* about One a Clock in the Afternoon, which was that Day Seven-night on which it began; so that it might be called one continued Storm from *Wednesday* Noon to *Wednesday* Noon: in all which time, there was not one Interval of Time in which a Sailor would not have acknowledged it blew a Storm; and in that time two such terrible Nights as I have describ'd.

And this I particularly noted as to Time, *Wednesday*, *Nov.* the 24*th* was a calm fine Day as at that time of Year shall be seen; till above Four a Clock, when it began to be Cloudy, and the Wind rose of a sudden, and in half an Hours Time it blew a Storm. *Wednesday*, *Dec.* the 2*d.* it was very tempestuous all the Morning; at One a Clock the Wind abated, the Sky clear'd, and by Four a Clock there was not a Breath of Wind.

Thus ended the Greatest and the Longest Storm that ever the World saw. The Effects of this terrible Providence are the Subject of the ensuing Chapter; and I close this with a Pastoral Poem sent us among the Accounts of the Storm from a very ingenious Author, and desir'd to be publish'd in this Account.

A PASTORAL, Occasion'd by the Late Violent Storm

Damon, Melibæus.[16]

DAM.

Walking alone by pleasant Isis[17] *side*
Where the two Streams their wanton course divide,
And gently forward in soft Murmurs glide;
Pensive and sad I Melibæus *meet,*
And thus the melancholy Shepherd greet.
    Kind Swain, what Cloud dares overcast your brow,
Bright as the Skies o're happy Nile *till now!*
Does Chloe *prove unkind, or some new Fair?*

MEL.

No Damon, *mine's a publick, nobler, Care;*
Such in which you and all the World must share.
One Friend may mollifie another's Grief,
But publick Loss admits of no relief.   *10*

DAM.

I guess your Cause: O you that use to sing

Of Beauty's Charms and the Delights of Spring;
Now change your Note, and let your Lute rehearse
The dismal Tale in melancholy Verse.

MEL.

Prepare then, lovely Swain; prepare to hear,
The worst Report that ever reach'd your Ear.
  My Bower you know, hard by yon shady Grove,
A fit Recess for Damon's pensive Love: 20
As there dissolv'd I in sweet Slumbers lay,
Tir'd with the Toils of the precedent Day,
The blust'ring Winds disturb my kind Repose,
Till frightned with the threatning Blasts, I rose.
But O, what havock did the Day disclose!
Those charming Willows which on Cherwel's banks[18]
Flourish'd, and thriv'd, and grew in evener ranks
Than those which follow'd the Divine Command
Of Orpheus Lyre, or sweet Amphion's Hand,[19]
By hundreds fall, while hardly twenty stand.   30
The stately Oaks which reach'd the azure Sky,
And kiss'd the very Clouds, now prostrate lie.
Long a huge Pine did with the Winds contend;
This way, and that, his reeling Trunk they bend,
Till forc'd at last to yield, with hideous Sound
He falls, and all the Country feels the Wound.
  Nor was the God of Winds content with these;
Such humble Victims can't his Wrath appease:
The Rivers swell, not like the happy Nile,
To fatten, dew, and fructifie our Isle: 40
But like the Deluge, by great Jove design'd
To drown the Universe, and scourge Mankind.
In vain the frighted Cattel climb so high,
In vain for Refuge to the Hills they fly;
The Waters know no Limits but the Sky.
So now the bleating Flock exchange in vain,
For barren Clifts, their dewy fertil Plain:
In vain, their fatal Destiny to shun,
From Severn's Banks to higher Grounds they run.
  Nor has the Navy better Quarter found;   50

There we've receiv'd our worst, our deepest Wound.
The Billows swell, and haughty Neptune[20] raves,
The Winds insulting o're th' impetuous Waves.
Thetis[21] incens'd, rises with angry Frown,
And once more threatens all the World to drown,
And owns no Power, but England's and her own.
Yet the Æolian God[22] dares vent his Rage;
And ev'n the Sovereign of the Seas engage.
What tho' the mighty Charles of Spain's[23] on board,
The Winds obey none but their blust'ring Lord.   60
Some Ships were stranded, some by Surges rent,
Down with their Cargo to the bottom went.
Th' absorbent Ocean could desire no more;
So well regal'd he never was before.
The hungry Fish could hardly wait the day,
When the Sun's beams should chase the Storm away,
But quickly seize with greedy Jaws their Prey.

DAM.

So the great Trojan, by the Hand of Fate,
And haughty Power of angry Juno's Hate,[24]
While with like aim he cross'd the Seas, was tost,   70
From Shore to Shore, from foreign Coast to Coast:
Yet safe at last his mighty Point he gain'd;
In charming promis'd Peace and Splendor reign'd.

MEL.

So may Great Charles, whom equal Glories move,
Like the great Dardan Prince[25] successful prove:
Like him, with Honour may he mount the Throne,
And long enjoy a brighter destin'd Crown.

CHAPTER IV

Of the Extent of this Storm, and from what Parts it was suppos'd to come; with some Circumstances as to the Time of it

As all our Histories are full of the Relations of Tempests and Storms which have happened in various Parts of the World, I hope it may not be improper that some of them have been thus observ'd with their remarkable Effects.

But as I have all along insisted, that no Storm since the Universal Deluge was like this, either in its Violence or its Duration, so I must also confirm it as to the particular of its prodigious Extent.

All the Storms and Tempests we have heard of in the World, have been Gusts or Squauls of Wind that have been carried on in their proper Channels, and have spent their Force in a shorter space.

We feel nothing here of the Hurricanes of *Barbadoes*, the North-Wests of *New England* and *Virginia*, the terrible Gusts of the *Levant*, or the frequent Tempests of the *North Cape*. When Sir *Francis Wheeler*'s Squadron perish'd at *Gibralter*, when the City of *Straelsond*[1] was almost ruin'd by a Storm, *England* felt it not, nor was the Air here disturb'd with the Motion. Even at home we have had Storms of violent Wind in one part of *England* which have not been felt in another. And if what I have been told has any truth in it, in St. *George*'s Channel there has frequently blown a Storm at Sea right up and down the Channel, which has been felt on neither Coast, tho it is not above 20 Leagues from the *English* to the *Irish* Shore.

Sir *William Temple*[2] gives us the Particulars of two terrible Storms in *Holland* while he was there; in one of which the great Cathedral Church at *Utrecht* was utterly destroy'd: and after that there was a Storm so violent in *Holland*, that 46 Vessels were cast away at the *Texel*,[3] and almost all the Men drowned: and yet we felt none of these Storms here.

And for this very reason I have reserv'd an Abridgment of

these former Cases to this place; which as they are recited by Sir
William Temple, I shall put them down in his own Words, being
not capable to mend them, and not vain enough to pretend
to it.

'I stay'd only a Night at *Antwerp*, which pass'd with so great
Thunders and Lightnings, that I promis'd my self a very fair
Day after it, to go back to *Rotterdam* in the *States* Yacht, that
still attended me. The Morning prov'd so; but towards Evening
the Sky grew foul, and the Sea men presag'd ill Weather, and so
resolved to lie at Anchor before *Bergen ap Zoom*, the Wind
being cross and little. When the Night was fallen as black as
ever I saw, it soon began to clear up, with the most violent
Flashes of Lightning as well as Cracks of Thunder, that I believe
have ever been heard in our Age and Climate. This continued
all Night; and we felt such a fierce Heat from every great Flash
of Lightning, that the Captain apprehended it would fire his
Ship. But about 8 the next Morning the Wind changed, and
came up with so strong a Gale, that we came to *Rotterdam* in
about 4 Hours, and there found all Mouths full of the Mischiefs
and Accidents that the last Night's Tempest had occasioned
both among the Boats and the Houses, by the Thunder, Lightning, Hail, or Whirlwinds. But the Day after came Stories to the
Hague from all Parts, of such violent Effects as were almost
incredible: At *Amsterdam* they were deplorable, many Trees
torn up by the Roots, Ships sunk in the Harbour, and Boats in
the Channels; Houses beaten down, and several People were
snatch'd from the Ground as they walk'd the Streets, and thrown
into the Canals. But all was silenc'd by the Relations from
Utrecht, where the Great and Ancient Cathedral was torn in
pieces by the Violences of this Storm; and the vast Pillars of
Stone that supported it, were wreathed like a twisted Club,
having been so strongly compos'd and cimented, as rather to
suffer such a Change of Figure than break in pieces, as other
Parts of the Fabrick did; hardly any Church in the Town escap'd
the Violence of this Storm; and very few Houses without the
Marks of it; Nor were the Effects of it less astonishing by
the Relations from *France* and *Brussels*, where the Damages
were infinite, as well from Whirlwinds, Thunder, Lightning, as

from Hail-stones of prodigious Bigness. This was in the Year 1674.

'In *November*, 1675, happen'd a Storm at *North-West*, with a Spring-tide, so violent, as gave apprehensions of some loss irrecoverable to the Province of *Holland*, and by several breaches in the great Diques near *Enchusen*, and others between *Amsterdam* and *Harlem*, made way for such Inundations as had not been seen before by any man then alive, and fill'd the Country with many relations of most deplorable Events. But the incredible Diligence and unanimous Endeavours of the People upon such occasions, gave a stop to the Fury of that Element, and made way for recovering next Year all the Lands, though not the People, Cattel, and Houses that had been lost.'[4]

Thus far Sir William Temple.

I am also credibly inform'd that the greatest Storm that ever we had in *England* before, and which was as universal here as this, did no Damage in *Holland* or *France*, comparable to this Tempest: I mean the great Wind in 1661. An Abstract of which, as it was printed in *Mirabilis Annis*,[5] an unknown, but unquestion'd Author, take as follows, in his own Words.

A dreadful Storm of Wind, accompanied with Thunder, Lightning, Hail and Rain; together with the sad Effects of it in many Parts of the Nation.

Upon the 18*th* of *February*, 1661, being *Tuesday*, very early in the Morning, there began a very great and dreadful Storm of Wind (accompanied with Thunder, Lightning, Hail, and Rain, which in many Places were as salt as Brine) which continued with a strange and unusual Violence till almost Night: the sad Effects whereof throughout the Nation are so many, that a very great Volume is not sufficient to contain the Narrative of them. And indeed some of them are so stupendious and amazing, that the Report of them, though from never so authentick Hands, will scarce gain Credit among any but those that have an affectionate Sense of the unlimited Power of the Almighty, knowing and believing that there is nothing too hard for Him to do.

Some few of which wonderful Effects we shall give a brief Account of, as we have received them from Persons of most unquestionable Credit in the several Parts of the Nation.

In the City of *London*, and in *Covent Garden* and other Parts about *London* and *Westminster*, five or six Persons were killed outright by the Fall of Houses and Chimneys; especially one Mr. *Luke Blith* an Attorney, that lived at or near *Stamford* in the County of *Lincoln*, was killed that Day by the fall of a Riding-House not far from *Pickadilla*: and there are some very remarkable Circumstances in this Man's Case, which do make his Death to appear at least like a most eminent Judgment and severe Stroak of the Lord's Hand upon him.

From other Parts likewise we have received certain Information, that divers Persons were killed by the Effects of this great Wind.

At *Chiltenham* in *Gloucestershire*, a Maid was killed by the Fall of a Tree, in or near the Church-Yard.

An honest Yeoman likewise of *Scaldwel* in *Northamptonshire*, being upon a Ladder to save his Hovel, was blown off, and fell upon a Plough, died outright, and never spoke Word more.

Also at *Tewksbury* in *Gloucestershire*, a Man was blown from an House, and broken to Pieces.

At *Elsbury* likewise in the same County, a Woman was killed by the Fall of Tiles or Bricks from an House.

And not far from the same Place, a Girl was killed by the Fall of a Tree.

Near *Northampton*, a Man was killed by the Fall of a great Barn.

Near *Colchester*, a Young-man was killed by the Fall of a Wind-mill.

Not far from *Ipswich* in *Suffolk*, a Man was killed by the Fall of a Barn.

And about two Miles from the said Town of *Ipswich*, a Man was killed by the Fall of a Tree.

At *Langton*, or near to it, in the County of *Leicester*, one Mr. *Roberts* had a Wind-mill blown down, in which were three Men; and by the Fall of it, one of them was killed outright, a second had his Back broken, and the other had his Arm or Leg struck off; and both of them (according to our best Information) are since dead.

Several other Instances there are of the like Nature; but it would be too tedious to mention them: Let these therefore suffice to stir us up to Repentance, *lest we likewise perish*.[6]

There are also many Effects of this Storm which are of another Nature, whereof we shall give this following brief Account.

The Wind hath very much prejudiced many Churches in several Parts of the Nation.

At *Tewksbury* in *Gloucestershire*, it blew down a very fair Window belonging to the Church there, both the Glass, and the Stone-work also; the Doors likewise of that Church were blown open, much of the Lead torn up, and some Part of a fair Pinnacle thrown down.

Also at *Red-Marly* and *Newin*, not far from *Tewksbury*, their Churches are extreamly broken and shatter'd, if not a considerable part of them blown down. The like was done to most, if not all the Publick Meeting-places at *Gloucester* City. And it is reported, that some Hundreds of Pounds will not suffice to repair the Damage done to the Cathedral at *Worcester*, especially in that Part that is over the Quire.

The like Fate happen'd to many more of them, as *Hereford*, and *Leighton Beau-desart* in *Bedfordshire*, and *Eaton-Soken* in the same County; where they had newly erected a very fair Cross of Stone, which the Wind blew down: and, as some of the Inhabitants did observe, that was the first Damage which that Town sustained by the Storm, though afterwards in other respects also they were in the same Condition with their Neighbours. The Steeples also, and other Parts of the Churches of *Shenley, Waddon*, and *Woolston* in the County of *Bucks*, have been very much rent and torn by the Wind. The Spire of *Finchinfield* Steeple in the County of *Essex*, was blown down, and it brake through the Body of the Church, and spoil'd many of the Pews; some Hundreds of Pounds will not repair that Loss. But that which is most remarkable of this kind, is, the Fall of that most famous Spire, or Pinnacle of the Tower-Church in *Ipswich*: it was blown down upon the Body of the Church, and fell reversed, the sharp End of the Shaft striking through the Leads on the South-side of the Church, carried much of the Timber-work down before it into the Alley just behind the Pulpit, and took off one Side of the Sounding-board over the Pulpit: it shattered many Pews: The Weather-Cock, and the Iron upon which it stood, broke off as it fell; but the narrowest Part of the Wood-work, upon which the Fane[7] stood, fell into the Alley, broke quite through a Grave-stone, and ran shoring under two Coffins that had been placed there one on another; that Part of the Spire which was pluck'd up was about three Yards deep in the Earth, and it is believed some Part of it is yet behind in the Ground: some Hundreds of Pounds will not make good the Detriment done to the Church by the Fall of this Pinnacle.

Very great Prejudice has been done to private Houses; many of them blown down, and others extreamly shattered and torn. It is thought that five thousand Pounds will not make good the Repairs at *Audley-End House*, which belongs to the Earl of *Suffolk*.[8] A good Part also of the Crown-Office in the *Temple* is blown down. The Instances of this kind are so many and so obvious, that it would needlesly take up too much time to give the Reader an Account of the Collection of them; only there has been such a wonderful Destruction of Barns, that (looking so much like a Judgment from the Lord, who the last Year took away our Corn, and this our Barns) we cannot but give a short Account of some Part of that Intelligence which hath come to our Hands of that Nature.

A Gentleman, of good Account, in *Ipswich*, affirms, that in a few Miles riding that Day, there was eleven Barns and Out-houses blown down in the Road within his View; and within a very few Miles of *Ipswich* round about, above thirty Barns, and many of them with Corn in them, were blown down. At *Southold* not far from the Place before mentioned, many new Houses and Barns (built since a late Fire that happened there) are blown down; as also a Salt-house is destroyed there: and a thousand Pounds, as it is believed, will not make up that particular Loss.

From *Tewksbury* it is certified, that an incredible Number of Barns have been blown down in the small Towns and Villages thereabouts. At *Twyning*, at least eleven Barns are blown down.

In *Ashchurch* Parish seven or eight. At *Lee*, five. At *Norton*, a very great Number, three whereof belonging to one Man. The great Abby-Barn also at *Tewksbury* is blown down.

It is credibly reported, that within a very few Miles Circumference in *Worcestershire*, about an hundred and forty Barns are blown down. At *Finchinfield* in *Essex*, which is but an ordinary Village, about sixteen Barns were blown down. Also at a Town called *Wilchamsted* in the County of *Bedford* (a very small Village) fifteen Barns at least are blown down. But especially the Parsonage Barns went to wrack in many Places throughout the Land: In a few Miles Compass in *Bedfordshire*, and so in *Northamptonshire*, and other Places, eight, ten, and twelve are blown down; and at *Yielding Parsonage* in the County of *Bedford* (out of which was thrust by Oppression and Violence the late Incumbent) all the Barns belonging to it are down. The Instances also of this kind are innumerable, which we shall therefore forbear to make further mention of.

We have also a large Account of the blowing down of a very great and considerable Number of Fruit-Trees, and other Trees in several Parts; we shall only pick out two or three Passages which are the most remarkable. In the Counties of *Gloucester, Hereford*, and *Worcester*, several Persons have lost whole Orchards of Fruit-Trees; and many particular Mens Loss hath amounted to the Value of forty or fifty Pounds at the least, meerly by Destruction of their Fruit-Trees: and so in other Parts of *England* proportionably the like Damage hath been sustained in this Respect. And as for other Trees, there has been a great Destruction made of them in many Places, by this Storm. Several were blown down at *Hampton-Court*.[9] And three thousand brave Oaks at least, but in one principal Part of the Forest of *Dean*, belonging to his Majesty. In a little Grove at *Ipswich*, belonging to the Lord of *Hereford* (which together with the Spire of the Steeple before-mentioned, were the most considerable Ornaments of that Town) are blown down at least two hundred goodly Trees, one of which was an Ash, which had ten Load of Wood upon it: there are now few Trees left there.

In *Bramton Bryan Park* in the County of *Hereford*, belonging to Sir *Edward Harly*,[10] one of the late Knights of the *Bath*, above thirteen hundred Trees are blown down; and above six hundred in *Hopton Park* not far from it: and thus it is proportionably in most Places where this Storm was felt. And the Truth is, the Damage which the People of this Nation have sustained upon all Accounts by this Storm, is not easily to be valued: some sober and discreet People, who have endeavoured to compute the Loss of the several Counties one with another, by the Destruction of Houses and Barns, the blowing away of Hovels and Ricks of Corn, the falling of Trees, *&c.* do believe it can come to little less than two Millions of Money.

There are yet behind many Particulars of a distinct Nature from those that have been spoken of; some whereof are very wonderful, and call for a very serious Observation of them.

In the Cities of *London* and *Westminster*, especially on the Bridge and near *Wallingford-house*, several Persons were blown down one on the Top of another.

In *Hertfordshire*, a Man was taken up, carried a Pole in Length,[11] and blown over a very high Hedge; and the like in other Places.

The Water in the River of *Thames*, and other Places, was in a very strange manner blown up into the Air: Yea, in the new Pond in *James's Park*, the Fish, to the Number of at least two Hundred, where blown out and lay by the Bank-side, whereof many were Eye-witnesses.

At *Moreclack* in *Surry*, the *Birds*, as they attempted to fly, were beaten down to the Ground by the Violence of the Wind.

At *Epping* in the County of *Essex*, a very great Oak was blown down, which of it self was raised again, and doth grow firmly at this Day.

At *Taunton*, a great Tree was blown down, the upper Part whereof rested upon a Brick or Stone-wall, and after a little time, by the force of the Wind, the lower part of the Tree was blown quite over the Wall.

In the City of *Hereford*, several persons were, by the Violence of the Wind, borne up from the Ground; one Man (as it is credibly reported) at least six Yards.

The great Fane at *Whitehall* was blown down; and one of the four which were upon the *white Tower*,[12] and two more of them strangely bent; which are to be seen at this Day, to the Admiration of all that behold them.

The several *Triumphant Arches*[13] in the City of *London* were much shattered and torn; That in *Leaden-hall-Street* lost the King's Arms, and many other rare Pieces that were affixed to it; That in *Cheapside*, which represented the Church, suffered very much by the Fury of the Storm; and a great Part of that in *Fleet Street* (which represented Plenty) was blown down: but, blessed be God, none as we hear of were either killed or hurt by the Fall of it.

The Wind was so strong, that it blew down several Carts loaded with Hay in the Road between *Barnet* and *London*; and in other Roads leading to the City of *London*.

Norwich Coach, with four or six Horses, was not able to come towards *London*, but stayed by the way till the Storm was somewhat abated.

It is also credibly reported, That all, or some of the Heads which were set up upon *Westminster-Hall*,[14] were that Day blown down.

There was a very dreadful Lightning which did at first accompany the Storm, and by it some of his Majesty's Houshold conceive that the Fire which happened at *Whitehall* that Morning, was kindled; as also that at *Greenwich*, by which (as we are informed) seven or eight Houses were burnt down.

Thus far the Author of Mirabilis Annis.

'Tis very observable, that this Storm blew from the same Quarter as the last, and that they had less of it Northward than here; in which they were much alike.

Now as these Storms were perhaps very furious in some Places, yet they neither came up to the Violence of this, nor any way to be compar'd for the Extent, and when ruinous in one County, were hardly heard of in the next.

But this terrible Night shook all *Europe*; and how much farther it extended, he only knows who *has his way in the Whirlwind, and in the Storm, and the Clouds are the Dust of his Feet.*[15]

As this Storm was first felt from the West, some have conjectur'd that the first Generation or rather Collection of Materials, was from the Continent of *America*, possibly from that part of *Florida* and *Virginia* where, if we respect natural Causes, the Confluence of Vapours rais'd by the Sun from the vast and unknown Lakes and Inland Seas of Water, which as some relate are incredibly large as well as numerous, might afford sufficient Matter for the Exhalation; and where time adding to the Preparation, God, who has generally confin'd his Providence to the Chain of natural Causes, might muster together those Troops of Combustion till they made a sufficient Army duly proportion'd to the Expedition design'd.

I am the rather inclin'd to this Opinion, because we are told, they felt upon that Coast an unusual Tempest a few Days before the fatal 27th of *November*.

I confess, I have never studied the Motion of the Clouds so nicely, as to calculate how long time this Army of Terror might take up in its furious March; possibly the Velocity of its Motion might not be so great at its first setting out as it was afterward, as a Horse that is to run a Race does not immediately put himself into the height of his Speed: and tho' it may be true, that by the length of the way the force of the Wind spends it self, and so by degrees ceases as the Vapour finds more room for Dilation; besides, yet we may suppose a Conjunction of some confederate Matter which might fall in with it by the way, or which meeting it at its Arrival here, might join Forces in executing the Commission receiv'd from above, all natural Causes being allow'd a Subserviency to the Direction of the great supream Cause; yet where the vast Collection of Matter had its first Motion, as it did not all take Motion in one and the same moment, so when all the Parts had felt the Influence, as they advanc'd and press'd those before them, the Violence must increase in proportion: and thus we may conceive that the Motion might not have arriv'd at its Meridian[16] Violence till it reach'd our Island; and even then it blew some Days with more than common fury, yet much less than that last Night of its force; and even that Night the Violence was not at its extremity till about an hour before Sun-rise, and then it continued declining, tho' it blew a full Storm for four Days after it.

Thus Providence, by whose special Direction the Quantity and Conduct of this Judgment was manag'd, seem'd to proportion things so, as that by the course of things the proportion of Matter being suited to Distance of Place, the Motion shou'd arrive at its full Force just at the Place where its Execution was to begin.

As then our Island was the first, this way, to receive the Impressions of the violent Motion, it had the terriblest Effects here; and continuing its steady Course, we find it carried a true Line clear over the Continent of *Europe*, travers'd *England*, *France*, *Germany*, the *Baltick* Sea, and passing the Northern Continent of *Sweedland, Finland, Muscovy*, and part of *Tartary*, must at last lose it self in the vast Northern Ocean, where Man never came, and Ship never sail'd; and its Violence cou'd have no effect, but upon the vast Mountains of Ice and the huge Drifts of Snow, in which Abyss of Moisture and Cold it is very probable the Force of it was check'd, and the World restor'd to Calmness and Quiet: and in this Circle of Fury it might find its End not far off from where it had its Beginning, the Fierceness of the Motion perhaps not arriving to a Period, till having pass'd the Pole, it reached again the Northern Parts of *America*.

The Effects of this impetuous Course, are the proper Subjects of this Book; and what they might be before our Island felt its Fury, who can tell? Those unhappy Wretches who had the misfortune to meet it in its first Approach, can tell us little, having been hurried by its irresistible Force directly into Eternity: how many they are, we cannot pretend to give an Account; we are told of about seventeen Ships, which having been out at Sea are never heard of: which is the common way of Discourse of Ships founder'd in the Ocean: and indeed all we can say of them is, the fearful *Exit* they have made among the Mountains of Waters, can only be duly reflected on by those who have seen those Wonders of God in the Deep.

Yet I cannot omit here to observe, That this Loss was in all probability much less than it would otherwise have been; because the Winds having blown with very great Fury, at the same Point, for near fourteen Days before the Violence grew to its more uncommon height, all those Ships which were newly gone to Sea were forc'd back, of which some were driven into *Plymouth* and *Falmouth* who had been above a hundred and fifty Leagues[17] at Sea; others, which had been farther, took Sanctuary in *Ireland*.

On the other hand, All those Ships which were homeward bound, and were within 500 Leagues of the *English* Shore, had been hurried so furiously on *afore it (as the Seamen say)* that they had reach'd their Port before the Extremity of the Storm came on; so that the Sea was as it were swept clean of all Shipping, those which were coming home were blown home before their time; those that had attempted to put to Sea, were driven back again in spight of all their Skill and Courage: for the Wind had blown so very hard, directly into the Channel, that there was no possibility of their keeping the Sea whose Course was not right afore the Wind.

On the other hand, these two Circumstances had fill'd all our Ports with unusual Fleets of Ships, either just come home or outward-bound, and consequently the Loss among them was very terrible; and the Havock it made among them, tho' it was not so much as every body expected, was such as no Age or Circumstance can ever parallel, and we hope will never feel again.

Nay, so high the Winds blew even before *that we call the Storm*, that had not that intolerable Tempest follow'd so soon after, we should have counted those Winds extraordinary high: and any one may judge of the Truth of this from these few Particulars; That the *Russia* Fleet, compos'd of near a hundred Sail, which happen'd to be then upon the Coast, was absolutely dispers'd and scatter'd, some got into *Newcastle*, some into *Hull*, and some into *Yarmouth* Roads; two founder'd in the Sea; one or two more run a-shore, and were lost; and the *Reserve* Frigat, their Convoy, founder'd in *Yarmouth* Roads, all her Men being lost, and no Boat from the Shore durst go off to relieve her, tho' it was in the Day-time, but all her Men perished.

In the same previous Storms the — Man of War was lost off of *Harwich*; but by the help of smaller Vessels most of her Men were sav'd.

And so high the Winds blew for near a Fortnight, that no Ship stirr'd out of Harbour; and all the Vessels, great or small, that were out at Sea, made for some Port or other for shelter.

In this juncture of time it happen'd, that together with the *Russia* Fleet, a great Fleet of Laden Colliers, near 400 Sail, were just put out of the River *Tine*: and these being generally deep and unweildy Ships, met with hard measure, tho' not so fatal to them as was expected: such of them as could run in for *Humber*, where a great many were lost afterwards, as I shall relate in its course; some got shelter under the high Lands of *Cromer* and the Northern Shores of the County of *Norfolk*, and the greater number reach'd into *Yarmouth* Roads.

So that when the Great Storm came, our Ports round the Sea-Coast of *England* were exceeding full of Ships of all sorts: a brief account whereof take as follows.

At *Grimsby*, *Hull*, and the other Roads of the *Humber*, lay about 80 Sail, great and small, of which about 50 were Colliers, and part of the *Russia* Fleet as aforesaid.

In *Yarmouth* Roads there rode at least 400 Sail, being most of them Laden Colliers, *Russia* Men, and Coasters from *Lynn* and *Hull*.

In the River of *Thames*, at the *Nore*,[18] lay about 12 Sail of the Queen's hir'd Ships and Store-ships, and only two Men of War.

Sir *Cloudsly Shovel*[19] was just arriv'd from the *Mediterranean* with the Royal Navy: Part of them lay at *St. Hellens*, part in the *Downs*, and with 12 of the biggest Ships he was coming round the *Foreland* to bring them into *Chatham*; and when the Great Storm began was at an Anchor at the *Gunfleet*,[20] from whence the *Association* was driven off from Sea as far as the Coast of *Norway*: What became of the rest, I refer to a Chapter by it self.

At *Gravesend* there rode five *East India* Men, and about 30 Sail of other Merchant-men, all outward bound.

In the *Downs* 160 Sail of Merchant Ships outward bound, besides that part of the Fleet which came in with Sir *Cloudsly Shovel*, which consisted of about 18 Men of War, with Tenders and Victuallers.[21]

At *Portsmouth* and *Cowes* there lay three Fleets; first, a Fleet of Transports and Tenders, who with Admiral *Dilks* brought the Forces from *Ireland* that were to accompany the King of

Spain to *Lisbon*;[22] secondly, a great Fleet of Victuallers, Tenders, Store-ships, and Transports, which lay ready for the same Voyage, together with about 40 Merchant-ships, who lay for the benefit of their Convoy; and the third Article was, the Remainder of the Grand Fleet which came in with Sir *Cloudsly Shovel*; in all almost 300 Sail, great and small.

In *Plymouth* Sound, *Falmouth* and *Milford* Havens, were particularly several small Fleets of Merchant-ships, driven in for Shelter and Harbour from the Storm, most homeward bound from the Islands and Colonies of *America*.

The *Virginia* Fleet, *Barbadoes* Fleet, and some *East India* Men, lay scatter'd in all our Ports, and in *Kinsale* in *Ireland* there lay near 80 Sail, homeward bound and richly laden.

At *Bristol* about 20 Sail of home-bound *West India* Men, not yet unladen.

In *Holland*, the Fleet of Transports for *Lisbon* waited for the King of *Spain*, and several *English* Men of War lay at *Helvoet Sluice*; the *Dutch* Fleet from the *Texel* lay off of *Cadsandt*, with their Forces on Board, under the Admiral *Callenberge*.[23] Both these Fleets made 180 Sail.

I think I may very safely affirm, That hardly in the Memory of the oldest Man living, was a juncture of Time when an Accident of this nature could have happen'd, that so much Shipping, laden out and home, ever was in Port at one time.

No Man will wonder that the Damages to this Nation were so great, if they consider these unhappy Circumstances: it shou'd rather be wonder'd at, that we have no more Disasters to account to Posterity, but that the Navigation of this Country came off so well.

And therefore some People have excus'd the Extravagancies of the *Paris Gazetteer*,[24] who affirm'd in Print, that there was 30000 Sea-men lost in the several Ports of *England*, and 300 Sail of Ships; which they say was a probable Conjecture; and that considering the multitude of Shipping, the Openness of the Roads in the *Downs*, *Yarmouth*, and the *Nore*, and the prodigious Fury of the Wind, any Man would have guess'd the same as he.

'Tis certain, It is a thing wonderful to consider, that especially

in the *Downs* and *Yarmouth* Roads any thing shou'd be safe:
all Men that know how wild a Road the first is, and what
Crowds of Ships there lay in the last; how almost every thing
quitted the Road, and neither Anchor nor Cable would hold;
must wonder what Shift or what Course the Mariners could
direct themselves to for Safety.

Some which had not a Mast standing, nor an Anchor or Cable
left them, went out to Sea wherever the Winds drove them; and
lying like a Trough in the Water, wallow'd about till the Winds
abated; and after were driven, some into one Port, some into
another, as Providence guided them.

In short, Horror and Confusion seiz'd upon all, whether on
Shore or at Sea: No Pen can describe it, no Tongue can express
it, no Thought conceive it, unless some of those who were in the
Extremity of it; and who, being touch'd with a due sense of the
sparing Mercy of their Maker, retain the deep Impressions of
his Goodness upon their Minds, tho' the Danger be past: and
of those I doubt the Number is but few.

OF THE EFFECTS OF
THE STORM

The particular dreadful Effects of this Tempest, are the Subject of the ensuing Part of this History: And tho' the Reader is not to expect that all the Particulars can be put into this Account, and perhaps many very remarkable Passages may never come to our Knowledge; yet as we have endeavour'd to furnish our selves with the most authentick Accounts we could from all Parts of the Nation, and a great many worthy Gentlemen have contributed their Assistance in various, and some very exact Relations and curious Remarks; so we pretend, not to be meanly furnish'd for this Work.

Some Gentlemen, whose Accounts are but of common and trivial Damages, we hope will not take it ill from the Author, if they are not inserted at large; for that we are willing to put in nothing here common with other Accidents of like nature; or which may not be worthy of a History and a Historian to record them; nothing but, what may serve to assist in convincing Posterity that this was the most violent Tempest the World ever saw.

From hence 'twill follow, that those Towns who only had their Houses until'd, their Barns and Hovels levell'd with the Ground, and the like, will find very little notice taken of them in this Account; because if these were to be the Subject of a History, I presume it must be equally voluminous with *Fox*, *Grimston*, *Holinshead* or *Stow*.[1]

Nor shall I often trouble the Reader with the Multitude or Magnitude of Trees blown down, whole Parks ruin'd, fine Walks defac'd, and Orchards laid flat, and the like: and tho' I had, my self, the Curiosity to count the Number of Trees, in a Circuit I rode, over most part of *Kent*, in which being tired with the Number, I left off reckoning after I had gone on to 17000; and tho' I have great reason to believe I did not observe one half of the Quantity; yet in some Parts of *England*, as in *Devonshire* especially, and the Counties of *Worcester, Gloucester,* and *Hereford*, which are full of very large Orchards of Fruit-Trees, they had much more mischief.

In the Pursuit of this Work, I shall divide it into the following Chapters or Sections, that I may put it into as good Order as possible.

1. Of the Damage in the City of *London*, &c.
2.   in the Counties.
3. } *On the Water* { in the Royal Navy.
4. }   to Shipping in general.
5.   by Earthquake.
6.   by High Tides.
7. Remarkable Providences and Deliverances.
8. Hardned and blasphemous Contemners both of the Storm and its Effects.
9. Some Calculations of Damage sustain'd.
10. The Conclusion.

We had design'd a Chapter for the Damages abroad, and have been at no small Charge to procure the Particulars from foreign Parts; which are now doing in a very authentick manner: but as the World has been long expecting this Work, and several Gentlemen who were not a little contributing to the Information of the Author, being unwilling to stay any longer for the Account, it was resolved to put it into the Press without any farther Delay: and if the foreign Accounts can be obtain'd in time, they shall be a Supplement to the Work; if not, some other Method shall be found out to make them publick.

I. Of the Damages in the City of London, and Parts adjacent

Indeed the City was a strange Spectacle, the Morning after the Storm, as soon as the People could put their Heads out of Doors: though I believe, every Body expected the Destruction was bad enough; yet I question very much, if any Body believed the Hundredth Part of what they saw.

The Streets lay so covered with Tiles and Slates, from the Tops of the Houses, especially in the Out-parts, that the Quantity is incredible: and the Houses were so universally stript, that all the Tiles in Fifty Miles round would be able to repair but a small Part of it.

Something may be guest at on this Head, from the sudden Rise of the Price of Tiles; which rise from 21 s. per Thousand to 6 l. for plain Tiles; and from 50s. per Thousand for Pantiles, to 10 l. and Bricklayers Labour to 5s. per Day: And tho' after the first Hurry the Prices fell again, it was not that the Quantity was supply'd; but because,

1st, The Charge was so extravagant, that an universal Neglect of themselves, appear'd both in Landlord and Tenant; an incredible Number of Houses remain'd all the Winter uncovered, and expos'd to all the Inconveniences of Wet and Cold; and are so even at the Writing of this Chapter.

2. Those People who found it absolutely necessary to cover their Houses, but were unwilling to go to the extravagant Price of Tiles; chang'd their Covering to that of Wood, as a present Expedient, till the Season for making of Tiles should come on; and the first Hurry being over, the Prices abate: and 'tis on this Score, that we see, to this Day, whole Ranks of Buildings, as in *Christ Church Hospital*, the *Temple*, *Asks-Hospital*, *Old-street*, *Hogsden-Squares*, and infinite other Places, covered entirely with Deal Boards; and are like to continue so, perhaps a Year or two longer, for Want of Tiles.

These two Reasons reduc'd the Tile-Merchants to sell at a more moderate Price: But 'tis not an irrational Suggestion, that all the Tiles which shall be made this whole Summer, will not repair the Damage in the covering of Houses within the Circumference of the City, and Ten Miles round.

The next Article in our Street Damage was, the Fall of Chimneys; and as the Chimneys in the City Buildings are built in large Stacks, the Houses being so high, the Fall of them had the more Power, by their own Weight, to demolish the Houses they fell upon.

'Tis not possible to give a distinct Account of the Number, or particular Stacks of Chimneys, which fell in this fatal Night; but the Reader may guess by this Particular, that in *Cambray-House*, commonly so called, a great House near *Islington*, belonging to the Family of the *Comptons*, Earls of *Northampton*,[1] but now let out into Tenements; the Collector of these Remarks counted Eleven or Thirteen Stacks of Chimneys, either wholly thrown in, or the greatest Parts of them at least, what was expos'd to the Wind, blown off. I have heard Persons, who pretended to observe the Desolation of that terrible Night very nicely; and who, by what they had seen and enquired into, thought themselves capable of making some Calculations, affirm, They could give an Account of above Two Thousand Stacks of Chimneys blown down in and about *London*; besides Gable Ends of Houses, some whole Roofs, and Sixteen or Twenty whole Houses in the Out-Parts.

Under the Disaster of this Article, it seems most proper to place the Loss of the Peoples Lives, who fell in this Calamity; since most of those, who had the Misfortune to be killed, were buried, or beaten to Pieces with the Rubbish of the several Stacks of Chimneys that fell.

Of these, our Weekly Bills of Mortality[2] gave us an Account of Twenty One; besides such as were drown'd in the River, and never found: and besides above Two Hundred People very much wounded and maim'd.

One Woman was kill'd by the Fall of a Chimney in or near the Palace of St. *James*'s, and a Stack of Chimneys falling in the new unfinish'd Building there, and carried away a Piece of the Coin of the House.[3]

Nine Souldiers were hurt, with the Fall of the Roof of the Guard-house at *Whitehall*, but none of them died.

A Distiller in *Duke-Street*, with his Wife, and Maid-servant, were all buried in the Rubbish of a Stack of Chimneys, which forced all the Floors, and broke down to the Bottom of the House; the Wife was taken out alive, though very much bruised, but her Husband and the Maid lost their Lives.

One Mr. *Dyer*, a Plaisterer in *Fetter-Lane*, finding the Danger he was in by the shaking of the House, jumpt out of Bed to save himself; and had, in all Probability, Time enough to have got out of the House, but staying to strike a Light, a Stack of Chimneys fell in upon him, kill'd him, and wounded his Wife.

Two Boys at one Mr. *Purefoy's*, in *Cross-Street Hatton-Garden*, were both kill'd, and buried in the Rubbish of a Stack of Chimneys; and a third very much wounded.

A Woman in *Jewin-Street*, and Two Persons more near *Aldersgate-Street*, were kill'd; the first, as it is reported, by venturing to run out of the House into the Street; and the other Two by the Fall of a House.

In *Threadneedle-Street*, one Mr. *Simpson*, a Scrivener being in Bed and fast a-sleep, heard nothing of the Storm; but the rest of the Family being more sensible of Danger, some of them went up, and wak'd him; and telling him their own Apprehensions, press'd him to rise; but he too fatally sleepy, and consequently unconcern'd at the Danger, told them, he did not apprehend any Thing; and so, notwithstanding all their Persuasions, could not be prevailed with to rise: they had not been gone many Minutes out of his Chamber, before the Chimneys fell in, broke through the Roof over him, and kill'd him in his Bed.

A Carpenter in *White-Cross-Street* was kill'd almost in the same Manner, by a Stack of Chimneys of the *Swan* Tavern, which fell into his House; it was reported, That his Wife earnestly desir'd him not to go to Bed; and had prevail'd upon him to sit up till near two a Clock, but then finding himself very heavy, he would go to Bed against all his Wife's Intreaties; after which she wak'd him, and desir'd him to rise, which he refus'd, being something angry for being disturb'd; and going to sleep again, was kill'd in his Bed: and his Wife, who would not go to Bed, escap'd.

In this Manner, our Weekly Bills gave us an Account of Twenty One Persons kill'd in the City of *London*, and Parts adjacent.

Some of our printed Accounts give us larger and plainer Accounts of the Loss of Lives, than I will venture to affirm for Truth; as of several Houses near *Moor-Fields* levell'd with the Ground: Fourteen People drowned in a Wherry[4] going to *Gravesend*, and Five in a Wherry from *Chelsey*. Not that it is not very probable to be true; but as I resolve not to hand any thing to Posterity, but what comes very well attested, I omit such Relations as I have not extraordinary Assurance as to the Fact.

The Fall of Brick-Walls, by the Fury of this Tempest, in and about *London*, would make a little Book of it self; and as this affects the Out-Parts chiefly, where the Gardens and Yards are wall'd in, so few such have escap'd; at St. *James*'s a considerable part of the Garden Wall; at *Greenwich Park* there are several pieces of the Wall down for an Hundred Rods in a Place; and some much more, at *Battersey*, *Chelsey*, *Putney*, at *Clapham*, at *Deptford*, at *Hackney*, *Islington*, *Hogsden*, *Wood's Close* by St. *John's Street*, and on every side the City, the Walls of the Gardens have generally felt the Shock, and lie flat on the Ground twenty, thirty Rod of walling in a Place.

The publick Edifices of the City come next under our Consideration; and these have had their Share in the Fury of this terrible Night.

A part of her Majesty's Palace, as is before observ'd, with a Stack of Chimneys in the Centre of the new Buildings, then not quite finished, fell with such a terrible Noise as very much alarm'd the whole Houshold.

The Roof of the Guard-house at *Whitehall*, as is also observ'd before, was quite blown off; and the great Vane, or Weather-Cock at *Whitehall* blown down.

The Lead, on the Tops of the Churches and other Buildings, was in many Places roll'd up like a Roll of Parchment, and blown in some Places clear off from the Buildings; as at *Westminster Abby*, St. *Andrews Holbourn*, *Christ-Church Hospital*, and abundance of other Places.

Two of the new built Turrets, on the Top of St. *Mary Alder-mary Church*, were blown off, whereof One fell upon the Roof of the Church; of Eight Pinnacles on the Top of St. *Albans Woodstreet*, Five of them were blown down; Part of One of the Spires of St. *Mary Overies* blown off; Four Pinnacles on the Steeple of St. *Michael Crooked Lane* blown quite off: The Vanes and Spindles of the Weather-Cocks, in many places, bent quite down; as on St. *Michael Cornhil*, St. *Sepulchres*, the *Tower*, and divers other Places.

It was very remarkable, that the Bridge over the *Thames* received but little Damage, and not in Proportion to what in common Reason might be expected; since the Buildings there stand high, and are not sheltered, as they are in the Streets, one by another.

If I may be allow'd to give this Philosophical Account of it, I hope it may not be absurd; that the Indraft[5] of the Arches underneath the Houses giving Vent to the Air, it past there with a more than common Current; and consequently relieved the Buildings, by diverting the Force of the Storm: I ask Pardon of the ingenious Reader for this Opinion, if it be not regular, and only present it to the World for Want of a better; if those better furnished *that Way* will supply us with a truer Account, I shall withdraw mine, and submit to theirs. The Fact however is certain, that the Houses on the *Bridge* did not suffer in Proportion to the other Places; though all must allow, they do not seem to be stronger built, than other Streets of the same sort.

Another Observation I cannot but make; to which, as I have Hundreds of Instances, so I have many more Witnesses to the Truth of Fact, and the uncommon Experiment has made it the more observ'd.

The Wind blew, during the whole Storm, between the Points of S. W. and N. W., not that I mean it blew at all these Points, but I take a Latitude of Eight Points to avoid Exceptions, and to confirm my Argument; since what I am insisting upon, could not be a natural Cause from the Winds blowing in any of those particular Points.

If a Building stood North and South, it must be a Consequence that the East-side Slope of the Roof must be the Lee-side, lie out of the Wind, be weather'd by the Ridge, and consequently receive no Damage in a direct Line.

But against this rational way of arguing, we are convinced by Demonstration and Experiment, after which Argument must be silent. It was not in one Place or Two, but in many Places; that where a Building stood ranging North and South, the Sides or Slopes of the Roof to the East and the West, the East-side of the Roof would be stript and untiled by the Violence of the Wind; and the West Side, which lay open to the Wind, be sound and untouch'd.

This, I conceive, must happen either where the Building had some open Part, as Windows or Doors to receive the Wind in the Inside, which being pusht forward by the succeeding Particles of the Air, must force its Way forward, and so lift off the Tiling on the Leeward side of the Building; or it must happen from the Position of such Building near some other higher Place or Build-ing, where the Wind being repuls'd, must be forc'd back again in Eddies; and consequently taking the Tiles from the lower Side of the Roof, rip them up with the more Ease.

However it was, it appear'd in many Places, the Windward Side of the Roof would be whole, and the Leeward Side, or the Side from the Wind, be untiled; in other Places, a high Building next the Wind has been not much hurt, and a lower Building on the Leeward Side of the high One clean ript, and hardly a Tile left upon it: this is plain in the Building of *Christ Church Hospital* in *London*, where the Building on the West and South Side of the Cloyster was at least Twenty Five Foot higher than the East Side, and yet the Roof of the lower Side on the East was quite untiled by the Storm; and remains at the Writing of This covered with Deal Boards above an Hundred Foot in Length.

The blowing down of Trees may come in for another Article in this Part; of which, in Proportion to the Quantity, here was as much as in any Part of *England*: Some printed Accounts tell us of Seventy Trees in *Moorfields* blown down, which may be true; but that some of them were Three Yards about, as is affirmed by the Authors, I cannot allow: above a Hundred Elms in St. *James's Park*, some whereof were of such Growth, as they tell us they were planted by Cardinal *Woolsey*;[6] whether that Part of it be true or not, is little to the Matter, but only to imply that they were very great Trees: about *Baums*, commonly call'd *Whitmore house*, there were above Two Hundred Trees blown down, and some of them of extraordinary Size broken off in the middle.

And 'twas observ'd, that in the Morning after the Storm was abated, it blew so hard, the Women, who usually go for Milk to the Cow-keepers in the Villages round the City, were not able to go along with their Pails on their Heads; and One, that was more hardy than the rest, was blown away by the Fury of the Storm, and forced into a Pond, but by strugling hard got out, and avoided being drowned; and some that ventured out with Milk the Evening after, had their Pails and Milk blown off from their Heads.

'Tis impossible to enumerate the Particulars of the Damage suffered, and of the Accidents which happened under these several Heads, in and about the City of *London*: The Houses looked like Skeletons, and an universal Air of Horror seem'd to sit on the Countenances of the People; all Business seem'd to be laid aside for the Time, and People were generally intent upon getting Help to repair their Habitations.

It pleased God so to direct things, that there fell no Rain in any considerable Quantity, except what fell the same Night or the ensuing Day, for near Three Weeks after the Storm, though it was a Time of the Year that is generally dripping. Had a wet Rainy Season followed the Storm, the Damage which would have been suffered in and about this City to Houshold Goods, Furniture and Merchandise, would have been incredible, and might have equall'd all the the rest of the Calamity: but the Weather prov'd fair and temperate for near a Month after the Storm, which gave People a great deal of Leisure in providing themselves Shelter, and fortifying their Houses against the Accidents of Weather by Deal Boards, old Tiles, Pieces of Sail-Cloth, Tarpaulin, and the like.

II. Of the Damages in the Country

As the Author of this was an Eye-witness and Sharer of the Particulars in the former Chapter; so, to furnish the Reader with Accounts as authentick, and which he has as much cause to depend upon as if he had seen them, he has the several Particulars following from like Eye-witnesses; and that in such a manner, as I think their Testimony is not to be question'd, most of the Gentlemen being of Piety and Reputation.

And as a Publication was made to desire all Persons who were willing to contribute to the forwarding this Work, and to transmit the Memory of so signal a Judgment to Posterity, that they would be pleas'd to send up such authentick Accounts of the Mischiefs, Damages, and Disasters in their respective Counties that the World might rely on; it cannot, without a great breach of Charity, be suppos'd that Men mov'd by such Principles, without any private Interest or Advantage, would forge any thing to impose upon the World, and abuse Mankind in Ages to come.

Interest, Parties, Strife, Faction, and particular Malice, with all the scurvy Circumstances attending such things, may prompt Men to strain a Tale beyond its real Extent; but, that Men shou'd invent a Story to amuse Posterity, in a case where they have no manner of Motive, where the only Design is to preserve the Remembrance of Divine Vengeance, and put our Children in mind of God's Judgments upon their sinful Fathers, this would be telling a Lye for God's sake, and doing Evil for the sake of it self, which is a step beyond the Devil.

Besides, as most of our Relators have not only given us their Names, and sign'd the Accounts they have sent, but have also given us Leave to hand their Names down to Posterity with the Record of the Relation they give, we would hope no Man will be so uncharitable to believe that Men would be forward to set their Names to a voluntary Untruth, and have themselves recorded to Posterity for having, without Motion, Hope, Reward, or any other reason, impos'd a Falsity upon the World, and dishonour'd our Relation with the useless Banter of an Untruth.

We cannot therefore but think, that as the Author believes himself sufficiently back'd by the Authority of the Vouchers he presents, so after what has been here premis'd, no Man will have any room to suspect us of Forgery.

The ensuing Relation therefore, as to Damages in the Country, shall consist chiefly of Letters from the respective Places where such things have happen'd; only that as all our Letters are not concise enough to be printed as they are, where it is otherwise the Letter is digested into a Relation only; in which the Reader is assur'd we have always kept close to the matter of fact.

And first, I shall present such Accounts as are entire, and related by Men of Letters, principally by the Clergy; which shall be given you in their own Words.

The first is from *Stowmarket* in *Suffolk*, where, by the Violence of the Storm, the finest Spire in that County, and but new built, *viz.* within thirty Years, was overthrown, and fell upon the Church. The Letter is sign'd by the reverend Minister of the Place, and vouched by two of the principal Inhabitants, as follows.

SIR,

Having seen an Advertisement of a Design to perpetuate the Remembrance of the late dreadful Storm, by publishing a Collection of all the remarkable Accidents occasion'd by it, and supposing the Damage done to our Church to be none of the least, we were willing to contribute something to your Design, by sending you an Account thereof as follows.

We had formerly a Spire of Timber covered with Lead, of the height of 77 Foot; which being in danger of falling, was taken down: and in the Year 1674, with the Addition of 10 Loads of new Timber, 21 thousand and 8 hundred weight of Lead, a new one was erected, 100 Foot high from the Steeple, with a Gallery at the height of 40 Foot all open, wherein hung a Clock-Bell of between 2 and 3 hundred Weight. The Spire stood but 8 Yards above the Roof of the Church; and yet by the extreme Violence of the Storm, a little before 6 in the Morning the Spire was thrown down; and carrying with it all the Battlements on the East side, it fell upon the Church at the distance of 28 Foot; for so much is the distance between the Steeple and the first Breach, which is on the North-side of the middle Roof, of the length of 17 Foot, where it brake down 9 Spars clean, each 23 Foot long, and severally supported with very strong Braces. The Spire inclining to the North, fell cross the middle Wall, and broke off at the Gallery, the lower part falling in at the aforesaid Breach, and the upper upon the North Isle, which is 24 Foot wide, with a flat Roof lately built, all new and very strong: It carried all before it from side to side, making a Breach 37 Foot long, breaking in sunder two large Beams that went a-cross, which were 12 Inches broad and 15 deep, besides several other smaller. Besides these two Breaches, there is a great deal of Damage done by the Fall of great Stones upon other parts of the Roof, as well as by the Wind's riving[1] up the Lead, and a third part of the Pews broken all in pieces, every thing falling into the Church, except the Weather-cock, which was found in the Church-yard, at a considerable distance, in the great Path that goes cross by the East End of the Church. It will cost above 400*l.* to make all good as it was before. There were 3 single Chimneys blown down, and a Stack of 4 more together, all about the same time; and some others so shaken, that they were forc'd to be pull'd down; but, we thank God, no body hurt, tho' one Bed was broken in pieces that was very oft lain in: no body lay in it that Night. Most Houses suffered something in their Tiling, and generally all round the Country, there is incredible Damage done to Churches, Houses, and Barns.

> *Samuel Farr*, Vicar.
> *John Gaudy.*
> *William Garrard.*

From *Oxfordshire* we have an Account very authentick, and yet unaccountably strange: but the reverend Author of the Story being a Gentleman whose Credit we cannot dispute, in acknowledgment to his Civility, and for the Advantage of our true Design, we give his Letter also *verbatim*.

SIR,

Meeting with an Advertisement of yours in the *Gazette* of *Monday* last, I very much approved of the Design, thinking it might be a great Motive towards making People, when they hear the Fate of others, return Thanks to Almighty God for his Providence in preserving them. I accordingly was resolved to send you all I knew. The Place where I have for some time lived is *Besselsleigh*, in *Barkshire*, about four Miles S. W. of *Oxon*. The Wind began with us much about One of the Clock in the Morning, and did not do much harm, only in untiling Houses, blowing down a Chimney or two, without any Person hurt, and a few Trees: but what was the only thing that was strange, and to be observed, was a very tall Elm, which was found the next Morning standing, but perfectly twisted round; the Root a little loosen'd, but not torn up. But what happened the Afternoon preceding, is abundantly more surprizing, and is indeed the Intent of this Letter.

On *Friday* the 26th of *November*, in the Afternoon, about Four of the Clock, a Country Fellow came running to me in a great Fright, and very earnestly entreated me to go and see a Pillar, as he call'd it, in the Air, in a Field hard by. I went with the Fellow; and when I came, found it to be a Spout marching directly with the Wind: and I can think of nothing I can compare it to better than the Trunk of an Elephant, which it resembled, only much bigger. It was extended to a great Length, and swept the Ground as it went, leaving a Mark behind. It crossed a Field; and what was very strange (and which I should scarce have been induced to believe had I not my self seen it, besides several Country-men who were astonish'd at it) meeting with an Oak that stood towards the middle of the Field snapped the Body of it asunder. Afterwards crossing a Road, it sucked up the Water that was in the Cart-ruts: then coming to an old Barn, it tumbled it down, and the Thatch that was on the Top was carried about by the Wind, which was then very high, in great confusion. After this I followed it no farther, and therefore saw no more of it. But a Parishoner of mine going from hence to *Hinksey*, in a Field about a quarter of a Mile off of this Place, was on the sudden knock'd down, and lay upon the Place till some People came by and brought him home; and he is not yet quite recovered. Having examined him, by all I can collect both from the Time, and Place, and Manner of his being knock'd down, I must conclude it was done by the Spout, which, if its Force had not been much abated, had certainly kill'd him: and indeed I attribute his Illness more to the Fright, than the sudden Force with which he was struck down.

I will not now enter into a Dissertation on the Cause of Spouts, but by what I can understand they are caused by nothing but the Circumgyration[2] of the Clouds, made by two contrary Winds meeting in a Point, and condensing the Cloud till it falls in the Shape we see it; which by the twisting Motion sucks up Water, and doth much Mischief to Ships at Sea, where they happen oftner than at Land. Whichever of the two Winds prevails, as in the above-mentioned was the S. W. at last dissolves and dissipates the Cloud, and then the Spout disappears.

This is all I have to communicate to you, wishing you all imaginable Success in your Collection. Whether you insert this Account, I leave wholly to your own Discretion; but can assure you, that to most of these things, tho' very surprizing, I was my self an Eye-witness. I am,

SIR,

Your humble Servant,

Dec. 12. 1703.   Joseph Ralton.

The judicious Reader will observe here, that this strange Spout, or Cloud, or what else it may be call'd, was seen the Evening before the great Storm: from whence is confirm'd what I have said before of the violent Agitation of the Air for some time before the Tempest.

A short, but very regular Account, from *Northampton*, the Reader may take in the following Letter; the Person being of undoubted Credit and Reputation in the Town, and the Particulars very well worth remark.

SIR,

Having seen in the *Gazette* an Intimation, that there would be a Memorial drawn up of the late terrible Wind, and the Effects of it, and that the Composer desired Informations from credible

Persons, the better to enable him to do the same, I thought good
to intimate what happen'd in this Town, and its Neighbourhood.
1. The Weather-cock of *All-Saints* Church being placed on a
mighty Spindle of Iron, was bowed together, and made useless.
Many Sheets of Lead on that Church, as also on St. *Giles*'s and
St. *Sepulchres*, rowled up like a Scroll. Three Windmills belonging
to the Town blown down, to the Amazement of all Beholders; the
mighty upright Post below the Floor of the Mills being snapt in
two like a Reed. Two entire Stacks of Chimneys in a House
uninhabited fell on two several Roofs, and made a most amazing
Ruin in the Chambers, Floors, and even to the lower Windows
and Wainscot, splitting and tearing it as if a Blow by Gun-powder
had happen'd. The Floods at this instant about the South Bridge,
from a violent S. W. Wind, rose to a great and amazing height;
the Wind coming over or a-thwart large open Meadows, did
exceeding damage in that part of the Town, by blowing down
some whole Houses, carrying whole Roofs at once into the Streets,
and very many lesser Buildings of Tanners, Fell-mongers,[3] Dyers,
Glue-makers, *&c.* yet, through the Goodness of God, no Person
killed or maimed: the mighty Doors of the Sessions-house, barr'd
and lock'd, forced open, whereby the Wind entring, made a
miserable Havock of the large and lofty Windows: a Pinnacle on
the *Guild-hall*, with the Fane, was also blown down. To speak
of Houses shatter'd, Corn-ricks and Hovels blown from their
Standings, would be endless. In Sir *Thomas Samwell*'s Park a very
great headed Elm was blown over the Park-Wall into the Road,
and yet never touched the Wall, being carried some Yards. I have
confined my self to this Town. If the Composer finds any thing
agreeable to his Design, he may use it or dismiss it at his Discretion. Such Works of Providence are worth recording. I am

                                        Your loving Friend,

Northampton,
Dec. 12. 1703.   Ben. Bullivant.

The following Account from *Berkly* and other Places in *Glouces-*
tershire and *Somersetshire*, &c. are the sad Effects of the
prodigious Tide in the *Severn*. The Wind blowing directly into

the Mouth of that Channel we call the *Severn* Sea, forced the Waters up in such quantity, that 'tis allow'd the Flood was eight Foot higher than ever was known in the Memory of Man; and at one Place, near *Huntspill*, it drove several Vessels a long way upon the Land; from whence, no succeeding Tide rising to near that height, they can never be gotten off: as will appear in the two following Letters.

SIR,

This Parish is a very large one in the County of *Gloucester*, on one Side whereof runneth the River *Severn*, which by Reason of the Violence of the late Storm beat down and tore to pieces the Sea Wall (which is made of great Stones, and Sticks which they call Rouses;[4] a Yard and half long, about the Bigness of ones Thigh rammed into the Ground as firm as possible) in many Places, and levell'd it almost with the Ground, forcing vast Quantities of Earth a great Distance from the Shore, and Stones, many of which were above a Hundred Weight: and hereby the *Severn* was let in above a Mile over one part of the Parish, and did great Damage to the Land; it carried away one House which was by the Sea-side, and a Gentleman's Stable, wherein was a Horse, into the next Ground; and then the Stable fell to pieces, and so the Horse came out. There is one thing more remarkable in this Parish, and 'tis this: Twenty Six Sheets of Lead, hanging all together, were blown off from the middle Isle of our Church, and were carried over the North Isle, which is a very large one, without touching it; and into the Church-yard ten Yards distant from the Church; and they were took up all joyned together as they were on the Roof; the Plummer[5] told me that the Sheets weighed each Three Hundred and a half one with another. This is what is most observable in our Parish; but I shall give you an Account of one thing (which perhaps you may have from other Hands) that happen'd in another, call'd *Kingscote*, a little Village about Three Miles from *Tedbury*, and Seven from us; where *William Kingscote* Esq; has many Woods; among which was one Grove of very tall Trees, being each near Eighty Foot high; the which he greatly valued for the Tallness and Prospect of them, and therefore resolv'd never to cut them down: But it so happen'd, that Six

Hundred of them, within the Compass of Five Acres were wholly blown down; (and suppos'd to be much at the same time) each Tree tearing up the Ground with its Root; so that the Roots of most of the Trees, with the Turf and Earth about them, stood up at least Fifteen or Sixteen Foot high; the lying down of which Trees is an amazing Sight to all Beholders. This Account was given by the Gentleman himself, whom I know very well. I have no more to add, but that I am, *Your humble Servant*, wishing you good Success in your Undertaking,

Henry Head, Vicar of *Berkly*.

Jan. 24.

The Damage of the Sea-wall may amount to about five Hundred Pounds.

SIR,

I Received a printed Paper sometime since, wherein I was desired to send you an Account of what happen'd in the late Storm: and I should have answered it sooner, but was willing to make some Enquiry first about this County; and by what I can hear or learn, the dismal Accident of our late Bishop and Lady was most remarkable;[6] who was killed by the Fall of two Chimney Stacks, which fell on the Roof, and drove it in upon my Lord's Bed, forced it quite through the next Flower down into the Hall, and buried them both in the Rubbish; and 'tis suppos'd my Lord was getting up, for he was found some Distance from my Lady, who was found in her Bed; but my Lord had his Morning Gown on, so that 'tis suppos'd he was coming from the Bed just as it fell. We had likewise two small Houses blown flat down just as the People were gone out to a Neighbour's House; and several other Chimney Stacks fell down, and some through the Roof, but no other Accident as to Death in this Town or near it: abundance of Tiles are blown off, and likewise Thatch in and about this Town, and several Houses uncover'd, in the Country all about us, abundance of Apple and Elm Trees are rooted up by the Ground; and also abundance of Wheat and Hay-mows blown down: at *Huntspil*, about twelve Miles from this Town, there was Four or

Five small Vessels drove a-shoar which remain there still, and 'tis suppos'd cannot be got off; and in the same Parish, the Tide broke in Breast high; but all the People escap'd only one Woman, who was drowned. These are all the remarkable Things that happen'd near us, as I can hear of; and is all, but my humble Service; and beg Leave to subscribe my self,

   SIR,

        Your most humble Servant,

Wells in *Somersetshire*,
Feb. 9. 1703.   Edith. Conyers.

SIR,
The Dreadful Storm did this Church but little Damage, but our Houses were terribly shaken hereabouts, and the Tide drowned the greatest part of the Sheep on our Common; as it likewise did, besides many Cows, between this Place and *Bristol*; on the opposite Shore of *Glamorganshire*, as (I suppose you may also know) it brake down part of *Chepstow* Bridge, o'er the *Wye*. In the midst of this Church-yard grew a vast Tree, thought to be the most large and flourishing Elm in the Land which was torn up by the Roots, some of which are really bigger than ones Middle, and several than a Man's Thigh; the Compass of them curiously interwoven with the Earth, being from the Surface (or Turf) to the Basis, full an Ell[7] in Depth, and Eighteen Foot and half in the Diameter, and yet thrown up near Perpendicular; the Trunk, together with the loaden Roots, is well judg'd to be Thirteen Tun at least, and the Limbs to make Six Load of Billets with Faggots; and, about Two Years since, our Minister observ'd, that the circumambient Boughs dropt round above Two Hundred Yards: He hath given it for a SINGERS SEAT in our said Church, with this Inscription thereon; *Nov.* 27. *A.D.* 1703. *Miserere*, &c.[8]

Slimbrige near Severn
Dec. 28. 1703.   *William Frith* Church-Warden.

SIR,

By the late Dreadful Storm a considerable Breach was made in our Town Wall, and Part of the Church Steeple blown down; besides most of the Inhabitants suffered very much by untiling their Houses, *&c.* and abundance of Trees unrooted: at the same time our River overflowed, and drowned the low Grounds of both Sides the Town, whereby several Hundreds of Sheep were lost, and some Cattle; and one of our Market Boats lifted upon our Key. This is a true Account of most of our Damages. I am,

Your humble Servant,

Cardiff,
Jan. 10. 1703.   William Jones.

Honour'd Sir,

In Obedience to your Request I have here sent you a particular Account of the damages sustain'd in our Parish by the late Violent Storm; and because that of our Church is the most material which I have to impart to you, I shall therefore begin with it. It is the fineness of our Church which magnifies our present loss, for in the whole it is a large and noble structure, compos'd within and without of Ashler[9] curiously wrought, and consisting of a stately Roof in the middle, and two Isles runing a considerable length from one end of it to the other, makes a very beautiful Figure. It is also adorn'd with 28 admired and Celebrated Windows, which, for the variety and fineness of the Painted Glass that was in them, do justly attract the Eyes of all curious Travellers to inspect and behold them; nor is it more famous for its Glass, than newly renown'd for the Beauty of its Seats and Paving, both being chiefly the noble Gift of that pious and worthy Gentleman *Andrew Barker*, Esq; the late Deceas'd Lord of the Mannor. So that all things consider'd, it does equal, at least, if not exceed, any Parochial Church in *England*. Now that part of it which most of all felt the fury of the Winds, was, a large middle West Window, in Dimension about 15 Foot wide, and 25 Foot high: it represents the general Judgment, and is so fine a piece of Art, that 1500 *l.* has formerly been bidden for it, a price, though very tempting, yet were the Parishoners so just and honest as to refuse it. The upper part of this Window, just above the place where our Saviour's Picture is drawn sitting on a Rainbow, and the Earth his Foot-stool, is entirely ruin'd, and both sides are so shatter'd and torn, especially the left, that upon a general Computation, a fourth part, at least, is blown down and destroy'd. The like Fate has another West Window on the left side of the former, in Dimension about 10 Foot broad, and 15 Foot high, sustain'd; the upper half of which is totally broke, excepting one Stone Munnel.[10] Now if this were but ordinary Glass, we might quickly compute what our repairs would Cost, but we the more lament our misfortune herein, because the Paint of these two, as of all the other Windows in our Church, is stain'd thro' the Body of the Glass; so that if that be true which is generally said, that this Art is lost, then have we an irretrievable loss. There are other damages about our Church, which, tho' not so great as the former, do yet as much testify how strong and boisterous the Winds were, for they unbedded 3 Sheets of Lead upon the uppermost Roof, and roll'd them up like so much Paper. Over the Church-porch, a large Pinnacle and two Battlements were blown down upon the leads of it, but resting there, and their fall being short, these will be repair'd with little Cost. This is all I have to say concerning our Church: Our Houses come next to be considered, and here I may tell you, that (thanks be to God) the effects of the Storm were not so great as they have been in many other places; several Chimneys, and Tiles, and Slats, were thrown down, but no body kill'd or wounded. Some of the Poor, because their Houses were Thatch'd, were the greatest sufferers; but to be particular herein, would be very frivolous, as well as vexatious. One Instance of Note ought not to omitted; on *Saturday* the 26th, being the day after the Storm, about 2-a-Clock in the Afternoon, without any previous warning, a sudden flash of Lightning, with a short, but violent clap of Thunder, immediately following it like the Discharge of Ordnance, fell upon a new and strong built House in the middle of our Town, and at the same time disjointed two Chimneys, melted some of the Lead of an upper Window, and struck the Mistress of the House into a Swoon, but this, as appear'd afterwards, prov'd the effect more of fear, than of any real considerable hurt to be found about her. I have nothing more to add, unless it be the fall of several Trees and Ricks of Hay amongst us, but these being so common every where, and not very many in number here, I shall Conclude this tedious Scrible, and Subscribe my self,

> SIR,

> > *Your most Obedient and Humble Servant,*

Fairford, Gloucest.

January 170¾. Edw. Shipton, *Vic.*

The following Letters, tho' in a homely stile, are written by very honest, plain and observing Persons, to whom entire Credit may be given.

BREWTON.

SIR,

Some time since I received a Letter from you, to give you an Account of the most particular Things that hapned in the late dreadful Tempest of Wind, and in the first Place is the Copy of a Letter from a Brother of mine, that was an Exciseman of *Axbridge*, in the West of our County of *Somerset*; these are his Words,

What I know of the Winds in these Parts, are, that it broke down many Trees, and that the House of one *Richard Henden*; of *Charter-House* on *Mendip*, call'd *Piney*, was almost blown down, and in saving their House, they, and the Servants, and others, heard grievous Cries and Scrieches in the Air. The Tower of *Compton Bishop* was much shatter'd, and the Leads that cover'd it were taken clean away, and laid flat in the Church-Yard: The House of *John Cray* of that place, received much and strange Damages, which together with his part in the Sea-wall, amounted to 500 *l*. Near the Salt-works in the Parish of *Burnham*, was driven five trading Vessels, as Colliers and Corn-dealers, betwixt *Wales* and *Bridgwater*, at least 100 Yards on Pasture Ground. In the North Marsh, on the sides of *Bristol* River, near *Ken* at *Walton Woodspring*, the Waters broke with such Violence, that it came six Miles into the Country drowning much Cattel, carrying away several Hay-ricks and Stacks of Corn: And at a Farm at

Churchill near *Wrington*, it blew down 150 Elms that grew most in Rows, and were laid as Uniform as Soldiers lodge their Arms.

At *Cheddar* near *Axbridge*, was much harm done in Apple-trees, Houses, and such like; but what's worth remark, tho' not the very Night of the Tempest, a Company of wicked People being at a Wedding of one *Thomas Marshall, John*, the Father of the said *Thomas*, being as most of the Company was very Drunk, after much filthy Discourse while he was eating, a strange Cat pulling something from his Trenchard,[11] he Cursing her, stoopt to take it up, and died immediately.

At *Brewton* what was most Remarkable, was this, that one *John Dicer* of that Town, lay the Night as the Tempest was, in the Barn of one *John Seller*, the Violence of the Wind broke down the Roof of the Barn, but fortunately for him there was a Ladder which staid up a Rafter, which would have fell upon the said *John Dicer*; but he narrowly escaping being killed, did slide himself thro' the broken Roof, and so got over the Wall without any great hurt. What hurt was done more about that Town is not so considerable as in other Places; Such as blowing off the Thatch from a great many back Houses of the Town; for the Town is most tiled with a sort of heavy Tile, that the Wind had no power to move; there was some hurt done to the Church, which was not above 40s. besides the Windows, where was a considerable damage, the Lady *Fitzharding*'s House standing by the Church, the Battlement with part of the Wall of the House was blown down, which 'tis said, above 20 Men with all their strength could not have thrown down; besides, a great many Trees in the Park torn up by the Roots, and laid in very good Order one after another; it was taken notice that the Wind did not come in a full Body at once, but it came in several Gusts, as my self have taken Notice as I rid the Country, that in half a Miles riding I could not see a Tree down, nor much hurt to Houses, then again I might for some space see the Trees down, and all the Houses shattred: and I have taken Notice that it run so all up the Country in such a Line as the Wind sat; about One of the Clock it turn'd to the North West, but at the beginning was at South West; I my self was up until One and then I went to Bed, but the highest of the Wind was after that, so that my Bed did shake with me.

What was about *Wincanton*, was, that one Mrs. *Gapper* had 36 Elm-trees growing together in a Row, 35 of them was blown down; and one *Edgehill* of the same Town, and his Family being a Bed did arise, hearing the House begin to Crak, and got out of the Doors with his whole Family, and as soon as they were out the Roof of the House fell in, and the Violence of the Wind took of the Children's Head-cloaths, that they never saw them afterwards.

At *Evercreech*, three Miles from *Brewton*, there were a poor Woman beg'd for Lodging in the Barn of one *Edmond Peny* that same Night that the Storm was, she was wet the Day before in Travelling, so she hung up her Cloaths in the Barn, and lay in the Straw; but when the Storm came it blew down the Roof of the Barn where she lay, and she narrowly escaped with her Life, being much bruised, and got out almost naked through the Roof where it was broken most, and went to the dwelling House of the said *Edmond Peny*, and they did arise, and did help her to something to cover her, till they could get out her Cloaths; that place of *Evercreech* received a great deal of hurt in their Houses, which is too large to put here.

At *Batcomb* Easterly of *Evercreech*, they had a great deal of Damage done as I said before, it lay exactly with the Wind from *Evercreech*, and both places received a great deal of Damage; there was one Widow *Walter* lived in a House by it self, the Wind carried away the Roof, and the Woman's pair of Bodice, that was never heard of again, and the whole Family escaped narrowly with their Lives; all the Battlements of the Church on that side of the Tower next to the Wind was blown in, and a great deal of Damage done to the Church.

At *Shipton Mallet* was great Damages done, as I was told by the Post that comes to *Brewton*, that the Tiles of the Meeting House was blown off, and being a sort of light Tiles they flew against the Neighbouring Windows, and broke them to pieces:

And at *Chalton* near *Shepton Mallet* at one *Abbot*'s, the Roof was carried from the Walls of the House and the House mightily shaken, and seemingly the Foundation removed, and in the Morning they found a Foundation Stone of the House upon the top of the Wall, where was a shew in the Ground of its being driven out. At *Dinder* within two Miles of *Shepton*, there was one *John Allen*, and his Son, being out of Doors in the midst of the Tempest, they saw a great Body of Fire flying on the side of a Hill, call'd *Dinder-hill*, about half a Mile from them, with a Shew of black in the midst of it, and another Body of Fire following it, something smaller than the former.

There has been a strange thing at *Butly*, eight Miles from *Brewton*, which was thought to be Witchcraft, where a great many unusual Things happened to one *Pope*, and his Family, especially to a Boy, that was his Son, that having lain several Hours Dead, when he came to himself, he told his Father, and several of his Neighbours, Strange Stories of his being carried away by some of his Neighbours that have been counted wicked Persons; the Things have been so strangely related that Thousands of People have gone to see and hear it; it lasted about a Year or more: But since the Storm I have inquired of the Neighbours how it was, and they tell me, that since the late Tempest of Wind the House and People have been quiet; for its generally said, that there was some Conjuration in quieting of that House. If you have a desire to hear any farther Account of it, I will make it my Business to inquire farther of it, for there were such. Things happened in that time which is seldom heard of,

Your humble Servant

Hu. Ash.

Our Town of Butly *lyes in such a place, that no Post-House is in a great many Miles of it, or you should hear oftner.*

SIR,

I received yours, desiring an Account of the Damage done by the late great Wind about us. At *Wilsnorton*, three Miles from *Wittney*, the Lead of the Church was rouled, and great Damage done to the Church, many great Elms were tore up by the Roots: At *Helford*, two Miles from us, a Rookery of Elms, was most of it tore up by the Roots: At *Cockeup*, two Miles from us, was a Barn blown down, and several Elms blown down a Cross the High-way, so that there was no passage; a great Oak of about nine or ten Loads[12] was blown down, having a Raven sitting in it, his Wing-feathers got between two Bows, and held him fast; but the Raven received no hurt: At *Duckelton*, a little thatch't House was taken off the Ground-pening, and removed a distance from the place, the covering not damaged. Hay-recks abundance are torn to pieces: At *Wittney*, six Stacks of Chimneys blown down, one House had a sheet of Lead taken from one side and blown over to the other, and many Houses were quite torn to pieces; several Hundred Trees blown down, some broke in the middle, and some torn up by the Roots. Blessed be God, I hear neither Man, Woman nor Child that received any harm about us.

Your Servant,

Wittney, Oxfordsh. Richard Abenell.

ILMISTER, *Somerset*

Brief but exact Remarks on the late Dreadful Storms of Wind, as it affected the Town, and the Parts adjacent.

Imprimus.[13] At *Ashil*-Parish 3 Miles West from this Town, the Stable belonging to the Hare and Hounds Inn was blown down, in which were three Horses, one kill'd, another very much bruised.

2. At *Jurdans*, a Gentleman's Seat in the same Parish, there was a Brick Stable, whose Roof, one Back, and one End Wall, were all thrown down, and four foot in depth of the Fore Wall; in this Stable were 4 Horses, which by reason of the Hay-loft that bore up the Roof, were all preserv'd.

3. At *Sevington* Parish, three Miles East from this Town, *John* Hutkens had the Roof of a new built House heaved clean off the Walls. *Note*, the House was not glazed, and the Roof was thatch'd.

4. In *White Larkington* Park, a Mile East from this Town,

besides four or five hundred tall Trees broken and blown down, (admirable to behold, what great Roots was turned up) there were three very large Beaches, two of them that were near five Foot thick in the Stem were broken off, one of them near the Root, the other was broken off twelve Foot above, and from that place down home to the Root was shattered and flown; the other that was not broken, cannot have less than forty Waggon Loads in it; a very fine Walk of Trees before the House all blown down, and broke down the Roof of a Pidgeon House, the Rookery carried away in Lanes, the Lodg-House damaged in the Roof, and one End by the fall of Trees. In the Garden belonging to the House, was a very fine Walk of tall Firrs, twenty of which were broken down.

5. The damage in the Thatch of Houses, (which is the usual Covering in these Parts) is so great and general, that the price of Reed arose from twenty Shillings to fifty or three Pounds a Hundred; insomuch that to shelter themselves from the open Air, many poor People were glad to use Bean, Helm and Furse, to thatch their Houses with, Things never known to be put to such Use before.

6. At *Kingston*, a Mile distance from this Town, the Church was very much shattered in its Roof, and Walls too, and all our Country Churches much shattered, so that Churches and Gentlemen's Houses which were tiled, were so shatter'd in their Roofs, that at present, they are generally patch'd with Reed, not in Compliance with the Mode, but the Necessity of the Times.

7. At *Broadway*, two Miles West of this Town, *Hugh Betty*, his Wife, and four Children being in his House, it was by the violence of the Storm blown down, one of his Children killed, his Wife wounded, but recovered, the rest escaped with their Lives. A large Alms-house had most of the Tile blown off, and other Houses much shattered; a very large Brick Barn blown down, Walls and Roof to the Ground.

8. Many large Stacks of Wheat were broken, some of the Sheaves carried two or three Hundred Yards from the Place, many Stacks of Hay turned over, some Stacks of Corn heaved off the Stadle,[14] and set down on the Ground, and not broken.

9. *Dowlish Walk*, two Miles South East, the Church was very

much shattered, several Load of Stones fell down, not as yet repair'd, therefore can't express the damage. A very large Barn broken down that stood near the Church, much damage was done to Orchards, not only in this Place, but in all places round, some very fine Orchards quite destroyed: some to their great Cost had the Trees set up right again, but a Storm of Wind came after, which threw down many of the Trees again; as to Timber Trees, almost all our high Trees were broken down in that violent Storm.

10. In this Town *Henry Dunster*, his Wife and 2 Children, was in their House when it was blown down, but they all escaped with their Lives, only one of them had a small Bruise with a piece of Timber, as she was going out of the Chamber when the Roof broke in.

The Church, in this Place, scap'd very well, as to its Roof, being cover'd with Lead only on the Chancel; the Lead was at the top of the Roof heaved up, and roll'd together, more than ten Men could turn back again, without cutting the Sheets of Lead, which was done to put it in its place again: But in general the Houses much broken and shatter'd, besides the fall of some.

This is a short, but true Account. I have heard of several other things which I have not mentioned, because I could not be positive in the truth of them, unless I had seen it. This is what I have been to see the truth of. You may enlarge on these short Heads, and methodize 'em as you see good.

At *Henton St. George*, at the Lord *Pawlet*'s, a new Brick Wall was broken down by the Wind for above 100 foot, the Wall being built not above 2 years since, as also above 60 Trees near 100 foot high.

At *Barrington*, about 2 miles North of this Town, there was blown down above eight-score Trees, being of an extraordinary height, at the Lady *Strouds*.

As we shall not crow'd our Relation with many Letters from the same places, so it cannot be amiss to let the World have, at least, one Authentick Account from most of those Places where any Capital Damages have been sustain'd and to summ up the rest in a general Head at the end of this Chapter.

From Wiltshire *we have the following Account from the Reverend the Minister of Upper* Donhead *near* Shaftsbury; *to which the Reader is referr'd as follows.*

SIR,

As the Undertaking you are engag'd in, to preserve the Remembrance of the late dreadful Tempest, is very commendable in it self, and may in several respects be serviceable not only to the present Age, but also to Posterity; so it merits a suitable Encouragement, and, 'tis hop'd, it will meet with such, from all that have either a true sense of Religion, or have had any sensible share of the care of Providence over them, or of the goodness of God unto them in the Land of the Living, upon that occasion. There are doubtless vast numbers of People in all Parts (where the Tempest raged) that have the greatest reason (as the Author of this Paper for one hath) to bless God for their wonderful preservation, and to tell it to the Generation following. But to detain you no longer with Preliminaries, I shall give you a faithful Account of what occurr'd in my Neighbourhood (according to the Conditions mention'd in the Advertisement in the *Gazette*) worthy, at least, of my notice, if not of the Undertakers; and I can assure you, that the several Particulars were either such as I can vouch-for on my own certain Knowledge and Observation, or else such as I am satisfy'd of the truth of by the Testimony of others, whose Integrity I have no reason to suspect. I will say no more than this in general, concerning the Storm, that, at its height, it seem'd, for some hours, to be a perfect Hurrican, the Wind raging from every Quarter, especially from all the Points of the Compass, from *N. E.* to the *N. W.* as the dismal Effects of it in these Parts do evidently demonstrate, in the demolishing of Buildings (or impairing 'em at best) and in the throwing up vast numbers of Trees by the Roots, or snapping them off in their Bodies, or larger Limbs. But as to some remarkable Particulars, you may take these following, *viz.*

1. The Parish-Church receiv'd little damage, tho' it stands high, the chief was in some of the Windows on the N. side, and in the fall of the Top-stone of one of the Pinnacles, which fell on a House adjoining to the Tower with little hurt to the Roof, from

which glancing it rested on the Leads of the South-Isle of the Church. At the fall of it an aged Woman living in the said House on which the Stone fell, heard horrible Scrieches (as she constantly averrs) in the Air, but none before nor afterwards.

2. Two stone Chimney-tops were thrown down, and 2 broad Stones of each of them lay at even poize on the respective ridges of both the Houses, and tho' the Wind sat full against one of them to have thrown it off, (and then it had fallen over a Door, in and out at which several People were passing during the Storm) and tho' the other fell against the Wind, yet neither of the said Stones stirr'd.

3. A Stone of near 400 Weight, having lain about 7 Years under a Bank, defended from the Wind as it then sat, tho' it lay so long as to be fix'd in the ground, and was as much out of the Wind, as could be, being fenced by the Bank, and a low Stone-wall upon the Bank, none of which was demolish'd, tho' 2 small Holms[15] standing in the Bank between the Wall, and the Stone, at the foot of the Bank were blown up by the roots; I say, this Stone, tho' thus fenced from the Storm, was carried from the place where it lay, into an hollow-way beneath, at least seven Yards from the place, where it was known to have lain for 7 Years before.

4. A Widdow-woman living in one part of an House by her self, kept her Bed till the House over her was uncover'd, and she expected the fall of the Timber and Walls; but getting below Stairs in the dark, and opening the Door to fly for shelter, the Wind was so strong in the Door, that she could neither get out at it, tho' she attempted to go out on her knees and hands, nor could she shut the Door again with all her strength, but was forced to sit alone for several hours ('till the Storm slacken'd), fearing every Gust would have buried her in the Ruins; and yet it pleas'd God to preserve her, for the House (tho' a feeble one) stood over the Storm.

5. Another, who made Malt in his Barn, had been turning his Malt sometime before the Storm was at its height, and another of the Family being desirous to go again into the said Barn sometime after, was disswaded from it, and immediately thereupon the said Barn was thrown down by the Storm.

6. But a much narrower Escape had one, for whose safety the

Collector of these Passages has the greatest reason to bless and
praise the great Preserver of Men, who was twice in his Bed that
dismal Night (tho' he had warning sufficient to deter him the first
time by the falling of some of the Seiling on his Back and Shoul-
ders, as he was preparing to go to Bed) and was altogether
insensible of the great danger he was in, 'till the next morning
after the Day-light appear'd, when he found the Tiles, on the side
of the House opposite to the main Stress of the Weather, blown
up in two places, one of which was over his Beds-head (about
9 foot above it) in which 2 or 3 Laths being broken, let down a
Square of 8 or 10 Stone Tiles upon one single Lath, where they
hung dropping inward a little, and bended the Lath like a Bow,
but fell not: What the consequence of their Fall had been, was
obvious to as many as saw it, and none has more reason to
magnify God's great Goodness, in this rescue of his Providence,
than the Relater.

7. A young Man of the same Parish, who was sent abroad to
look after some black Cattle and Sheep that fed in an Inclosure,
in, or near to which there were some Stacks of Corn blown down,
reports, That tho' he had much difficulty to find the Inclosure in
the dark, and to get thither by reason of the Tempest then raging
in the height of its fury; yet being there, he saw a mighty Body of
Fire on an high ridge of Hills, about 3 parts of a Mile from the
said Inclosure, which gave so clear a Light into the Valley below,
as that by it the said young Man could distinctly descry all the
Sheep and Cattle in the said Pasture, so as to perceive there was
not one wanting.

8. At *Ashegrove*, in the same Parish (where many tall Trees
were standing on the steep side of an Hill) there were two Trees
of considerable bigness blown up against the side of the Hill,
which seems somewhat strange, to such as have seen how many
are blown, at the same place, a quite contrary way, *i.e.* down the
Hill; and to fall downwards was to fall with the Wind, as upward,
was to fall against it.

9. One in this Neighbourhood had a Poplar in his Back-side of
near 16 Yards high blown down, which standing near a small
Current of Water, the Roots brought up near a Tun of Earth with

them, and there the Tree lay for some days after the Storm; but when the Top or Head of the Tree was saw'd off from the Body (tho' the Boughs were nothing to the weight of the But End, yet) the Tree mounted, and fell back into its place, and stood as upright without its Head, as ever it had done with it. And the same happen'd at the Lady *Banks* her House near *Shaftsbury*, where a Wall-nut-Tree was thrown down in a place that declin'd somewhat, and after the greater Limbs had been cut off in the day time, went back in the Night following, of it self, and now stands in the same place and posture it stood in before it was blown down. I saw it standing the 14th of this Instant, and could hardly perceive any Token of its having been Down, so very exactly it fell back into it's place. This is somewhat the more remarkable, because the Ground (as I said) was declining, and consequently the Tree raised against the Hill. To this I shall only add, at present, that

10. This Relator lately riding thro' a neighbouring Parish, saw two Trees near two Houses thrown besides the said Houses, and very near each House, which yet did little or no harm, when if they had fallen with the Wind, they must needs have fallen directly upon the said Houses. And

11. That this Relator had two very tall Elms thrown up by the Roots, which fell in among five young Walnut Trees, without injuring a Twig or Bud of either of them, as rais'd the admiration of such as saw it.

12. In the same place, the Top of another Elm yet standing, was carry'd of from the Body of the Tree, a good part of 20 Yards.

SIR; I shall trouble you no further at present, you may perhaps think this enough, and too much; but however that may be, you, or your ingenious Undertakers are left at liberty to publish so much, or so little of this Narrative, as shall be thought fit for the Service of the Publick. I must confess the particular Deliverances were what chiefly induced me to set Pen to Paper, tho' the other Matters are Considerable, but whatever regard you shew to the latter, in Justice you should publish the former to the World, as the Glory of God is therein concern'd more immediately, to promote which, is the only aim of this Paper. And the more effectually to induce you to do me Right, (for contributing a slender Mite towards your very laudable Undertaking) I make no manner of Scruple to subscribe my self,

Upper Donhead,   *Sir, Yours,* &c.
Decemb. 18*th* 1703.   Rice Adams.
           Rector of Upper Donhead Wilts near *Shaftsbury.*

From Littleton *in* Worcestershire, *and* Middleton *in* Oxfordshire, *the following Letters may be a Specimen of what those whole Counties felt, and of which we have several other particular Accounts.*

SIR,

Publick notice being given of a designed Collection of the most Prodigious, as well as lamentable Effects of the last dreadful Tempest of Wind. There are many Persons hereabouts, and I suppose in many other places, wish all speedy furtherance and good Success to that so useful and pious Undertaking, for it may very well be thought to have a good Influence both upon the present Age, and succeeding Generation, to beget in them a holy admiration and fear of that tremendous Power and Majesty, which as one Prophet tells us, *Causeth the Vapours to ascend from the Ends of the Earth, and bringeth the Wind out of his Treasures, and as the Priest Saith, hath so done his marvellous Works, that they ought to be had in remembrance.*[16] As to these Villages of *Littleton* in *Worcestershire*, I can only give this Information, that this violent Hurricane visited us also in its passage to the great Terror of the Inhabitants, who although by the gracious Providence of God all escaped with their Lives and Limbs, and the main Fabrick of their Houses stood; tho' with much shaking, and some damage in the Roofs of many of them: Yet when the Morning Light appeared after that dismal Night, they were surpris'd with fresh apprehensions of the Dangers escaped, when they discover'd the sad Havock that was made among the Trees of their Orchards and Closes,[17] very many Fruit Trees, and many mighty Elms being torn up, and one Elm above the rest, of very great Bulk and ancient Growth I observed, which might have defied the Strength of all the Men and Teams in the Parish, (tho' assaulted in every Branch with Roaps and Chains) was found torn up by the Roots, all sound, and of vast Strength and Thickness, and with its fall (as was thought) by the help of the same impetuous Gusts, broke off in the middle of the Timber another great Elm its Fellow, and next Neighbour. And that which may exercise the Thoughts of the Curious, some little Houses and Out-houses that seemed to stand in the same Current, and without any visible Burrough or Shelter, escaped in their Roofs, without any, or very little Damage: What Accidents of Note hapned in our Neighbouring Parishes, I suppose you may receive from other Hands. This, (I thank God) is all that I have to transmit unto you from this place, but that I am a Well-wisher to your Work in Hand, *And your Humble Servant,*

Littleton, Decem. 20.   *Ralph Norris.*

Middleton-Stony in *Oxfordshire*, Nov. 26. 1703

The Wind being South West and by West, it began to blow very hard at 12 of the Clock at Night, and about four or five in the Morning *Nov.* 27, the Hurricane was very terrible; many large Trees were torn up by the Roots in this Place; the Leads of the Church were Roll'd up, the Stone Battlements of the Tower were blown upon the Leads, several Houses and Barns were uncover'd, part of a new built Wall of Brick, belonging to a Stable was blown down, and very much damage, of the like Nature, was done by the Wind in the Towns and Villages adjacent.

                    William Offley, Rector of *Middleton-Stony*.

From Leamington Hasting, *near* Dun-*Church in* Warwickshire, *we have the following Account.*

SIR,
I find in the Advertisments a Desire to have an Account of what happen'd remarkable in the late terrible Storm in the Country; the Stories every where are very many, and several of them such

as will scarce gain Credit; one of them I send here an Account of being an Eye Witness, and living upon the place: The Storm here began on the 26th of *Novem.* 1703. about 12-a-clock, but the severest Blasts were between 5 and six in the Morning, and between Eight and Nine the 27th I went up to the Church, where I found all the middle Isle clearly stript of the Lead from one End to the other, and a great many of the Sheets lying on the East End upon the Church, roll'd up like a piece of Cloth: I found on the Ground six Sheets of Lead, at least 50 Hundred weight, all joyn'd together, not the least parted, but as they lay upon the Isle, which six Sheets of Lead were so carried in the Air by the Wind fifty Yards and a Foot, measured by a Workman exactly as cou'd be, from the place of the Isle where they lay, to the place they fell; and they might have been carried a great way further, had they not happen'd in their way upon a Tree, struck off an Arm of it near 17 Yards high; the End of one Sheet was twisted round the Body of the Tree, and the rest all joyn'd together lay at length, having broke down the Pales first where the Tree stood, and lay upon the Pales on the Ground, with one End of them, as I said before, round the Body of the Tree.

At the same time at *Marson*, in the County of *Warwick*, about 4 Miles from this place, a great Rick of Wheat was blown off from its Staddles, and set down without one Sheaf remov'd, or disturb'd, or without standing away 20 Yards from the place.

If you have a mind to be farther satisfied in this Matter, let me hear from you, and I will endeavour it: But I am in great hast at this time, which forces me to be confus'd.

I am your Friend,

E. Kingsburgh.

The following Account we have from Fareham *and* Christ Church *in* Hampshire, *which are also well attested.*

SIR,

I received yours, and in Answer these are to acquaint you; That we about us came no ways behind the rest of our Neighbours in

that mighty Storm or Hurricane. As for our own Parish, very few
Houses or Outhouses escaped. There was in the Parish of *Fareham*
six Barns blown down, with divers other Outhouses, and many
Trees blown up by the Roots, and other broken off in the middle;
by the fall of a large Elm, a very large Stone Window at the West
End of our Church was broken down; there was but two Stacks
of Chimneys thrown down in all our Parish that I know of, and
those without hurting any Person. There was in a *Coppice* called
Pupal Coppice, an Oak Tree, of about a Load of Timber, that
was twisted off with the Wind, and the Body that was left standing
down to the very Roots so shivered, that if it were cut into
Lengths, it would fall all in pieces. Notwithstanding so many
Trees, and so much Out-Housing was blown down, I do not hear
of one Beast that was killed or hurt. There was on the *Down*
called *Portsdown*, in the Parish of *Southwick*, within three Miles
of us, a Wind-Mill was blown down, that had not been up very
many Years, with great damage in the said Parish to Mr. *Norton*,
by the fall of many Chimneys and Trees. The damage sustained
by us in the *Healing* is such, that we are obliged to make use of
Slit Deals[18] to supply the want of Slats and Tyles until Summer
come to make some. And so much Thatching wanting, that it
cannot be all repaired till after another Harvest. As for Sea Affairs
about us, we had but one Vessel abroad at that time, which was
one *John Watson*, the Master of which was never heard of yet,
and I am afraid never will; I have just reason to lament her Loss,
having a great deal of Goods aboard of her. If at any time any
particular Relation that is true, come to my knowledge in any
convenient time, I will not fail to give you an Account, and at all
times remain

Fareham,   *Your Servant,*
January the 23d. 170¾.   Hen. Stanton.

SIR,

In Answer to yours, relating to the Damages done by the late
Storm in, and about out Town, is, that we had great part of the
Roof of our Church uncover'd, which was cover'd with very large
Purbick-stone, and the Battlements of the Tower, and part of the

Leads blown down, some Stones of a vast weight blown from the Tower, several of them between two or three hundred weight, were blown some Rods or Perches[19] distance from the Church; and 12 Sheets of Lead rouled up together, that 20 Men could not have done the like, to the great Amasement of those that saw 'em: And several Houses and Barns blown down, with many hundreds of Trees of all sorts; several Stacks of Chimneys being blown down, and particularly of one *Thomas Spencer*'s of this Town, who had his Top of a Brick Chimney taken off by the House, and blown a cross a Cart Road, and lighting upon a Barn of *Richard Holloway*'s, broke down the end of the said Barn, and fell upright upon one End, on a Mow of Corn in the Barn; but the said *Spencer* and his Wife, al-tho' they were then sitting by the Fire, knew nothing thereof until the Morning: And a Stack of Chimneys of one Mr. *Imber*'s fell down upon a young Gentlewoman's Bed, she having but just before got out of the same, and several Outhouses and Stables were blown down, some Cattel killed; and some Wheat-ricks entirely blown off their Stafolds; and lighted on their bottom without any other damage; this is all the Relation I can give you that is Remarkable about us,

> *I remain your Friend and Servant,*
> William Mitchel.

At *Ringwood* and *Fording-Bridge*, several Houses and Trees are blown down, and many more Houses uncovered.

From Oxford *the following Account was sent, enclosed in the other, and are confirm'd by Letters from other Hands.*

SIR,

The inclos'd is a very exact, and I am sure, faithful Account of the Damages done by the late Violent Tempest in *Oxford*. The particulars of my Lord Bishop of *Bath* and *Wells*, and his Ladies Misfortune are as follows, The Palace is the Relicks of a very old decay'd Castle, only one Corner is new built; and had the Bishop had the good Fortune to have lain in those Apartments that Night, he had sav'd his Life. He perceiv'd the fall before it came, and accordingly jump't out of Bed, and made towards the Door, where he was found with his Brains dash'd out; his Lady perceiving it, wrapt all the Bed-cloaths about her, and in that manner was found smother'd in Bed. This account is Authentick,

I am, Sir, yours,

Dec. 9. 1703.   J. Bagshot.

SIR,

I give you many thanks for your account from *London*: We were no less terrified in *Oxon* with the Violence of the Storm, tho' we suffer'd in comparison but little Damage. The most considerable was, a Child kill'd in St. *Giles*'s by the fall of an House; two Pinnacles taken off from the Top of *Magdalen* Tower, one from *Merton*; about 12 Trees blown down in *Christ* Church long walk, some of the Battlements from the Body of the Cathedral, and two or three Ranges of Rails on the Top of the great Quadrangle: Part of the great Elm in University Garden was blown off, and a Branch of the Oak in *Magdalen* walks; the rest of the Colleges scaped tolerably well, and the Schools and Theatre intirely. A very remarkable passage happened at Queen's College, several Sheets of Lead judged near 6000 *l.* weight, were taken off from the Top of Sir *J. Williamson*'s Buildings, and blown against the West-end of St. Peter's Church with such Violence, that they broke an Iron-bar in the Window, making such a prodigious Noise with the fall, that some who heard it, thought the Tower had been falling. The rest of our Losses consisted for the most part in Pinnacles, Chimneys, Trees, Slates, Tiles, Windows, *&c.* amounting in all, according to Computation, to not above 1000 *l.*

Ox. Dec. 7. 1703.

From Kingstone-upon-Thames, *the following Letter is very particular, and the truth of it may be depended upon.*

SIR,

I have inform'd my self of the following Matters; here was blown down a Stack of Chimneys of Mrs. *Copper*, Widow, which fell on the Bed, on which she lay; but she being just got up, and gone down, she received no harm on her Body: Likewise, here was a Stack of Chimnies of one Mr. *Robert Banford*'s blown down, which fell on a Bed, on which his Son and Daughter lay, he was about 14 years and the Daughter 16; but they likewise were just got down Stairs, and received no harm: A Stack of Chimnies at the *Bull-Inn* was blown down, and broke way down into the Kitchen, but hurt no Body: Here was a new Brick Malt-House of one Mr. *Francis Best* blown down, had not been built above two Years, blown off at the second Floor: besides many Barns, and out Houses; and very few Houses in the Town but lost Tiling, some more, some less, and Multitudes of Trees, in particular. 11 Elms of one Mr. *John Bowles*, Shooe-maker: About 30 Apple-trees of one *Mr. Peirce*'s: And of one *John Andrew*, a Gardiner, 100 Apple-trees blown to the Ground: One *Walter Kent*, Esq; had about 20 Rod of new Brick-wall of his Garden blown down: One Mr. *Tiringam*, Gentleman, likewise about 10 Rod of new Brick-wall blown down: Mr. *George Cole*, Merchant, had also some Rods of new Brickwall blown down: Also Mr. *Blitha*, Merchant, had all his Walling blown down, and other extraordinary Losses. These are the most considerable Damages done here,

Your humble Servant,

C. Castleman.

From Teuxbury *in* Gloucestershire, *and from* Hatfield *in* Hertfordshire, *the following Letters are sent us from the Ministers of the respective Places.*

SIR,

Our Church, tho' a very large one, suffered no great discernable Damage. The Lead Roof, by the force of the Wind was strangely ruffled, but was laid down without any great cost or trouble. Two well-grown Elms, that stood before a sort of Alms-house in the Church-yard had a different Treatment; the one was broken short in the Trunck, and the head turn'd Southward, the other tore up by the Roots, and cast Northward: Divers Chimnies were blown down, to the great Damage and Consternation of the Inhabitants: And one rising in the middle of two Chambers fell so violently, that it broke thro' the Roof and Cieling of the Chamber, and fell by the Bed of Mr. *W. M.* and bruised some part of the Bed-teaster[20] and Furniture; but himself, Wife and Child were signally preserved: An Out-house of Mr. *F. M.* (containing a Stable, Millhouse, and a sort of Barn, judged about 40 Foot in length) standing at the end of our Town, and much expos'd to the Wind, intirely fell, which was the most considerable Damage: Not one of our Town was kill'd, or notably hurt; tho' scarce any but were terribly alarm'd by the dreadful Violence of it, which remitted about five in the Morning: The beautiful Cathedral Church of *Glocester* suffer'd much; but of that I suppose you will have an account from some proper Hand: This I was willing to signifie to you, in answer to your Letter, not that I think them worthy of a publick Memorial; but the Preservation of *W. M.* his Wife and Child was remarkable,

> *Your unknown Friend*
> *and Servant,*

Teuxbury Jan. 12. 170¾.   John Matthews.

Bishop's Hatfield, Decem. 9. 1703.

SIR,

I perceive by an Advertisement in the *Gazette* of last *Monday*, that a Relation of some considerable Things which happened in the late Tempest is intended to be printed, which design I believe will be well approved of, that the Memory of it may be perpetuated. I will give you an Account of some of the observable Damages done in this Parish: The Church which was Til'd is so shattered, that the Body of it is entirely to be ripp'd. Two Barns, and a Stable have been blown down; in the latter were 13 Horses, and none of them hurt, tho' there was but one to be seen when the Men first came. I have number'd about 20 large Trees blown down, which stood in the regular Walks in the Park here. It is said, that all the Trees blown down in both the Parks will make above an hundred Stacks of Wood. A Summer-house which stood on the East-side of the Bowling-green at *Hatfield*-House, was blown against the Wall, and broken, and a large part of it carried over the Wall, beyond a Cartway into the plowed Grounds. A great part of the South-wall belonging to one of the Gardens was levelled with the Ground; tho' it was so strong, that great part of it continues cemented, tho' it fell upon a Gravel-walk. Several Things which happened, incline me to think that there was something of an *Hurricane*. Part of the fine painted Glass-window in my Lord *Salisbury*'s Chapel was broken, tho' it looked towards the East. The North-side of an House was untiled several Yards square. In some places the Lead has been raised up, and over one Portal quite blown off. In *Brocket-hall* Park belonging to Sir *John Reade*, so many Trees are blown down, that lying as they do, they can scarce be numbred, but by a moderate Computation, they are said to amount to above a Thousand. The Damages which this Parish hath sustained, undoubtedly amount to many hundred Pounds, some of the most considerable I have mentioned to you, of which I have been in great Measure an Eye-witness, and have had the rest from Credible Persons, especially the matter of *Brocket-hall* Park, it being two Miles out of Town, tho' in this Parish. I am,

Sir, Your humble Servant,
George Hemsworth, *M. A.*
Curate of Bishop's Hatfield, *in Hartfordshire.*

The shorter Accounts which have been sent up from almost all parts of England, *especially to the South of the* Trent; *tho' we do not transmit them at large as the abovesaid Letters are, shall be faithfully abridg'd for the readier comprising them within the due compass of our Volume.*

From Kent *we have many strange Accounts of the Violence of the Storm, besides what relate to the Sea Affairs.*

At Whitstable, *a small Village on the Mouth of the East Swale of the River* Medway, *we are inform'd a Boat belonging to a* Hoy[21] *was taken up by the Violence of the Wind, clear off from the Water, and being bourn up in the Air, blew turning continually over and over in its progressive Motion, till it lodg'd against a rising Ground, above 50 Rod from the Water; in the passage it struck a Man, who was in the way, and broke his Knee to pieces.*

We content our selves with relating only the Fact, and giving Assurances of the Truth of what we Relate, we leave the needful Remarks on such Things to another place.

At a Town near Chartham, *the Lead of the Church rolled up together, and blown off from the Church above 20 Rod distance, and being taken up afterwards, and weigh'd it, appear'd to weigh above 2600 weight.*

At Brenchly *in the Western Parts of* Kent, *the Spire of the Steeple which was of an extraordinary hight was overturn'd; the particulars whereof you have in the following Letter, from the Minister of the place.*

SIR,

According to your request, and my promise, for the service of the publick, I have here given you an Account of the Effects of the late Tempestuous Winds in the Parish of *Brenchly*, in the County of *Kent*, as freely and impartially as can be consistent with the Damages sustained thereby, *viz.*

A stately Steeple, whose Altitude exceeded almost, if not all, in *Kent*, the height whereof, according to various Computations, it never in my knowledge being exactly measured, did amount at least to 10 Rods; some say 12, and others more; yet this strong and noble Structure by the Rage of the Winds was levelled with the Ground, and made the sport and pastime of Boys and Girls, who to future Ages, tho' perhaps incredibly, yet can boast they leaped over such a Steeple, the fall thereof beat down great part of the Church and Porch, the damage of which to repair, as before, will not amount to less than 800 or 1000 *l.* This is the publick loss; neither does private and particular much less bemoan their Condition, for some Houses, and some Barns, with other Buildings, are quite demolished; tho' Blessed be God, not many Lives or Limbs lost in the fall, and not one House, but what suffered greatly by the Tempest. Neither were Neighbouring Parishes much more favoured; but especially, a place called *Great Peckham*, whose Steeple also, almost as high as ours, was then

blown down, but not so much Damage to the Church, which God
preserve safe and sound for ever.

This is the nearest account that can be given,
by your unknown Servant,

Tho. Figg.

As the above Letter mentions the fall of the Spire of Great
Peckham, *we have omitted a particular Letter from the place.*

In or near Hawkhurst *in Sussex, a Waggon standing in a Field
loaden with Straw, and bound well down in order to be fetch't
away the next day, the Wind took the Waggon, drove it backward several Rods, force't it through a very thick Hedge into
the Road, and the way being dirty, drove it with that force into
the Mud or Clay of the Road, that six Horses could not pull it
out.*

*The Collector of these Accounts cannot but enter the Remarks
he made, having occasion to Traverse the County of* Kent *about
a Month after the Storm; and besides, the general Desolation
which in every Village gave almost the same prospect; he
declares, that he reckoned* 1107 *dwelling Houses, Out-houses
and Barns blown quite down, whole Orchards of Fruit Trees
laid flat upon the Ground, and of all other sorts of Trees such a
quantity, that tho' he attempted to take an Account of them, he
found 'twas impossible, and was oblig'd to give it over.*

From Monmouth *we have a Letter, that among a vast variety
of Ruins, in their own Houses and Barns; one whereof fell with
a quantity of Sheep in it, of which seven were kill'd: The Lead
of the great Church, tho' on the side from the Wind, was roll'd
up like a roll of Cloth, and blown off from the Church.*

*I chose to note this, because the Letter says, it was upon the
North-side of the Church, and which seems to confirm what I
have observ'd before, of the Eddies of the Wind, the Operation
whereof has been very strange in several places, and more Violent than the Storm it self.*

At Wallingford, *one* Robert Dowell, *and his Wife, being both
in Bed, the Chimney of the House fell in, demolish'd the House,
and the main Beam breaking fell upon the Bed, the* Woman

*receiv'd but little Damage, but the Man had his Thigh broke by
the Beam, and lay in a dangerous Condition when the Letter
was wrote, which was the 18th of* January *after.*

From Axminster *in* Somersetshire *take the following plain,
but honest Account.*

SIR,

The best account I can give of the Storm in these Parts is as
follows: Dr. *Towgood* had his Court Gate, with a piece of Wall
blown to the other side of the Road, and stands upright against
the Hedge, which was 12 Foot over, and it was as big as two
Horses could draw: A sheet of Lead which lay flat was carried
from Sir *William Drake*'s quite over a Wall into the Minister's
Court, near three-score Yards: There was a Tree which stood in
Mr. *John Whitty*'s Ground which broke in the middle, and the
top of it blew over the Hedge, and over a Wall, and over a top of
a House, and did not hurt the House: There was a Mow of Corn
that was blown off the Posts, and sate upright without hurt,
belonging to *William Oliver*, at an Estate of *Edward Seymour*'s,
called *Chappel Craft*: A Maiden Oke which stood in the *Quille*
more than a Man could fathom, was broke in the middle: Several
hundred of Apple-Trees, and other Trees blown down: Most
Houses damnify'd in the Tiles and Thatch, but no Houses blown
down, and no Person hurt nor killed; neither did the Church nor
Tower, nor the Trees in the Church-yard received much Damage:
Our loss in the Apple-Trees is the greatest; because we shall want
Liquor to make our Hearts merry; the Farmer's sate them up
again, but the Wind has blown them down since the Storm.

From Hartley *in the County of* Southampton, *an honest
Countryman brought the following Account by way of Certifi-
cate, from the Minister of the Parish.*

SIR,

I the Minister of the abovesaid Parish, in the County of *Southampton*, do hereby Certifie of the several Damages done by the
late great Wind in our own, and the Parish adjacent; several
dwelling Houses strip'd, and several Barns overturn'd, several

Sign Posts blown down, and many Trees, both Timber and Fruit; and particularly my own Dwelling House very much mortify'd, a Chimney fell down, and endanger'd both my own, and Families Lives. I am,

Sir, your humble Servant,

Nathan Kinsey.

From Okingham *in* Berkshire, *and from* Bagshot *in* Surrey, *as follows.*

SIR,

Great damage to the Houses, some Barns down, the Market-house very much shattred, the Clock therein spoiled, several hundreds of Trees torn up by the Roots, most of them Elms, nothing more remarkable than what was usual in other places. It is computed, that the damage amounts to 1000 *l.* And most of the Signs in the Town blown down, and some of the Leads on the Church torn up: Yet by the goodness of God, not one Person killed nor hurt.

Bagshot in *Surry.*

The Chimneys of the Mannor House, some of them blown down, and 400 Pannel of Pales,[22] with some of the Garden Walls blown down, and in and about the Town several great Elms torn up by the Roots, most of the Houses shatter'd, and the tops of Chimneys blown down.

In the Parish, a great many Chimneys, the tops of them blown down, and the Houses and Barns very much shatter'd, *&c.* the damage in all is supposed about 300 *l.* none killed.

This is all the Account I can give you concerning the damage done by the Tempest hereabouts. This is all at present from,

Your Humble Servant,

Bagshot,
Feb. 1. 1704.   Jo. Lewis.

At Becles *the Leads of the Church ript up, part of the Great Window blown down, and the whole Town exceedingly shatter'd.*

At Ewell *by* Epsome *in* Surry, *the Lead from the flat Roof of Mr.* Williams's *House was roll'd up by the Wind, and blown from the top of the House clear over a Brick Wall near* 10 *Foot high, without damnifying either the House or the Wall, the Lead was carried near* 6 *Rod from the House; and as our Relator says, was Computed to weigh near* 10 *Tun. This is Certified by Mr.* George Holdsworth *of* Epsome, *and sent for the Service of the present Collection, to the Post House at* London, *to whom we refer for the Truth of the Story.*

From Ely *in the County of* Cambridge, *we have the following Relation; also by a Letter from another Hand, and I the rather Transmit this Letter, because by other hands we had an account, that it was expected the Cathedral or Minster at* Ely, *being a very Ancient Building, and Crazy, would not have stood the fury of the Wind, and some People that lived within the reach of it, had Terrible Apprehensions of its falling, some shocks of the Wind gave it such a Motion, that any one that felt it, would have thought it was impossible it should have stood.*

SIR,

According to your request, I have made it my business to get the exactest and truest account (I am able) of the damages and losses sustain'd on this side the Country, by the late Violent Storm. The Cathedral Church of *Ely* by the Providence of God did, contrary to all Men's expectations, stand out the shock; but suffered very much in every part of it, especially that which is called the Body of it, the Lead being torn and rent up a considerable way together; about 40 lights[23] of Glass blown down, and shatter'd to pieces, one Ornamental Pinacle belonging to the North Isle demolish'd, and the Lead in divers other parts of it blown up into great heaps. Five Chimneys falling down in a place called the Colledge, the place where the Prebendaries Lodgings are, did no other damage (prais'd be God) then beat down some part of the Houses along with them; the loss which the Church and College of *Ely* sustain'd, being by computation near 2000 *l.* The Sufferers are the Reverend the Dean and Chapter of the said Cathedral. The Wind Mills belonging both to the Town and Country, felt a worse fate, being blown or burnt down by the Violence of the Wind, or else disabled to that degree, that they were wholy unable of answering the design they were made for; three of the aforesaid Mills belonging to one *Jeremiah Fouldsham* of *Ely,* a very Industrious Man of mean Substance, were burnt and blown down, to the almost Ruin and Impoverishment of the aforesaid Person, his particular loss being upward of a 100 *l.* these are the most remarkable disasters that befel this side of the Country. The Inhabitants both of the Town of *Ely* and Country general, receiv'd some small damages more or less in their Estates and Substance, *viz.* The Houses being stript of the Tiling, Barns and Out-houses laid even with the Ground, and several Stacks of Corn and Cocks of Hay being likewise much damaged, the general loss being about 20000 *l.* the escape of all Persons here from Death, being generally miraculous; none as we can hear of being kill'd, tho' some were in more imminent danger than others. This, Sir, is as true, and as faithful an account as we are able to collect.

I am Yours,

Ely, Jan. 21. 1703.   A. Armiger.

From Sudbury *in Suffolk, an honest plain Countryman gives us a Letter, in which telling us of a great many Barns blown down, Trees, Chimneys and Tiles, he tells us in the Close, that their Town fared better than they expected, but that for all the neighbouring Towns they are fearfully shatter'd.*

From Tunbridge, *a Letter to the Post Master, giving the following Account.*

SIR,

I cannot give you any great account of the particular damage the late great Winds has done, but at *Penchurst Park* there was above 500 Trees blown down, and the Grove at *Southborough* is almost blown down; and there is scarce a House in Town, but hath received some damage, and particularly the School-House. A

Stack of Chimnies blown down, but no body, God be thanked, have lost their Lives, a great many Houses have suffered very much, and several Barns have been blown down: At *East Peckam*, hard by us, the Spire of the Steeple was blown down: And at Sir *Thomas Twisden*'s in the same Parish, there was a Stable blown down, and 2 Horses killed: And at *Brenchly* the Spire of the Steeple was blown down; and at *Summer Hill Park* there were several Trees blown down; which is all at present from,

Your Servant to Command,

Elizabeth Luck.

At Laneloe *in the County of* Brecon *in* Wales, *a Poor Woman with a Child, was blown away by the Wind, and the Child being about* 10 *years old, was taken up in the Air two or three yards, and very much Wounded and Bruised in the fall.*

At Ledbury *in* Herefordshire, *we have an Account of two Wind Mills blown down, and four Stacks of Chimneys in a new built House at a Village near* Ledbury, *which Wounded a Maid Servant; and at another Gentleman's House near* Ledbury, *the Coachman fearing the Stable would fall, got his Master's Coach Horses out to save them, but leading them by a great Stack of Hay, the Wind blew down the Stack upon the Horses, killed one, and Maimed the other.*

From Medhurst *in* Sussex, *the following Letter is a short account of the loss of the Lord* Montacute, *in his Seat there, which is extraordinary great, tho' Abridg'd in the Letter.*

SIR,

I received a Letter from you, wherein you desire me to give you an account of what damage was done in and about our Town, I praise God we came off indifferent well; the greatest damage we received, was the untiling of Houses, and 3 Chimneys blown down, but 4 or 5 Stacks of Chimneys are blown down at my Lord *Montacute*'s House, within a quarter of a mile of us, one of them fell on part of the Great Hall, which did considerable damage; and the Church Steeple of *Osborn*, half a mile from us, was blown down at the same time; and my Lord had above 500 Trees torn up by the Roots, and near us several Barns blown down, one of Sir *John Mill*'s, a very large Tiled Barn.

Medhurst,   *Your humble Servant*
Jan. 18. 170¾.   John Prinke.

From Rigate *the particulars cannot be better related, than in the following Letter*

SIR,

In answer to the Letter you sent me, relating to the late great Wind, the Calamity was universal about us, great numbers of vast tall Trees were blown down, and some broken quite asunder in the middle, tho' of a very considerable bigness. Two Wind-mills were blown down, and in one there happened a remarkable Providence, and the Story thereof may perhaps be worth your observation, which is, *viz.* That the Miller of *Charlewood* Mill, not far from *Rigate* hearing in the night time the Wind blew very hard, arose from his Bed, and went to his Mill, resolving to turn it toward the Wind, and set it to work, as the only means to preserve it standing; but on the way feeling for the Key of the Mill, he found he had left it at his Dwelling House, and therefore returned thither to fetch it, and coming back again to the Mill, found it blown quite down, and by his lucky forgetfulness saved his Life, which otherwise he most inevitably had lost. Several Stacks of Corn and Hay were blown down and shattered a very great distance from the places where they stood. Many Barns were also blown down, and many Stacks of Chimneys; and in the Town and Parish of *Rigate*, scarce a House but suffered considerable damage, either in the Tyling or otherwise. In the Parish of *Capel* by *Darking* lived one *Charles Man*, who was in Bed with his Wife and two Children, and by a fall of part of his House, he and one Child were killed, and his Wife, and the other Child, miraculously preserved, I am

Rigate,   *Sir, Your humble Servant,*
Jan. 13. 170¾.   Tho. Foster.

From the City of Hereford, *this short Letter is very explicit.*

SIR,

The best account I can give of the Storm, is as follows; a Man and his Son was killed with the fall of his House, in the Parish of *Wormsle*, 2 miles off *Webly* in *Herefordshire*. My Lord *Skudamoor* had several great Oaks blown down in the Parish of *Hom*, 4 miles from *Hereford*; there were several great Elms blown down at a place called *Hinton*, on *Wye* side, half a mile off *Hereford*, and some hundreds of Fruit Trees in other Parts of this County, and two Stacks of Chimnies in this City, and abundance of Tiles off the old Houses,

Hereford,	*Yours*, &c.
Jan. 2. 1703.	Anne Watts.

At Hawkhurst, *on the Edge of* Sussex *and* Kent, 11 *Barnes were blown down, besides the Houses Shatter'd or Uncover'd.*
From Basingstoke *in* Hampshire, *the following Letter is our Authority for the Particulars.*

SIR,

I cannot pretend to give you a particular account concerning the great Wind, but here are a great many Houses blown down, many Barns, and abundance of Trees. A little Park, three Miles from *Basing Stoke*, belonging to Esq. *Waleps* has a great quantity of Timber blown down, there is 800 *l*'s worth of Oak sold, and 800 *l*'s worth of other Trees to be sold, and so proportionably all over the Country. Abundance of Houses until'd, and a great many Chimneys blown down; but I do not hear of any body kill'd about us. Most of the People were in great Fears and Consternation; insomuch, that they thought the World had been at an end. Sir,

Yours to Command
W. Nevill

At *Shoram* the Market House, an Antient and very strong building, was blown flat to the Ground, and all the Town shatter'd. *Brighthelmston* being an old built and poor, tho' populous Town, was most miserably torn to pieces, and made the very Picture of Desolation, that it lookt as if an Enemy had Sackt it.

The following Letter from a small Town near Helford *in* Cornwall *is very Authentick, and may be depended on.*

SIR,

According to your Request, in a late Advertisement, in which you desir'd an Impartial Account of what Accidents hapned by the late Dreadful Storm, in order to make a true and just Collection of the same, please to take the following Relation, *viz*. Between 8 and 9-a-Clock the Storm began, with the Wind at N. W. about 10-a-Clock it veer'd about from W. to S. W. and back to West again, and between 11 and 12-a-Clock it blew in a most violent and dreadful manner, that the Country hereabouts thought the great day of Judgment was coming.

It continued thus blowing till 5-a-Clock and then began to abate a little, but has done a Prodigious damage to almost all sorts of People, for either their Houses are blown down, or their Corn blown out of their tack-yards (some Furlongs[24] distance) from the same that the very fields look in a manner, as if they had shak'd the Sheaves of Corn over them. Several Barns blown down, and the Corn that was in the same carried clear away.

The Churches here abouts have suffered very much, the Roofs of several are torn in pieces, and blown a considerable Distance off.

The small Quantity of Fruit-Trees we had in the Neighbourhood about us are so dismember'd, and torn in pieces, that few or none are left fit for bearing Fruit.

The large Timber Trees, as Elm, Oak, and the like, are generally blown down, especially the largest and highest Trees suffered most; for few Gentlemen that had Trees about their Houses have any left; and it is generally observ'd here, that the Trees and Houses that stood in Valleys, and most out of the Wind, have suffered most. In short, the Damage has been so general, that both Rich and Poor have suffered much.

In *Helford*, a small Haven, not far from hence, there was a Tin Ship blown from her Anchors with only one Man, and two Boys on Board, without Anchor, Cable or Boat, and was forc'd out of

the said Haven about 12-a-Clock at Night; the next Morning by
8-a-Clock, the Ship miraculously Run in between two Rocks in
the *Isle of Wight*, where the Men and Goods were saved, but the
Ship lost: Such a Run, in so short a time, is almost Incredible, it
being near 80 Leagues in 8 hours time, I believe it to be very true,
for the Master of the said Ship I know very well, and some that
were concern'd in her Lading, which was Tin, &c.

From St. Keaverne Parish in Cornwall,

May 26. 1704.   *Yours &c.* W. T.

Thus far our Letters.

It has been impossible to give an exact relation in the matter of
publick Damage, either as to the particulars of what is remarke-
able, or an Estimate of the general loss.

The Abstract here given, as near as we could order it, is
so well taken, that we have, *generally speaking*, something
remarkable from every quarter of the Kingdom, to the South of
the *Trent*.

It has been observ'd, that tho' it blew a great Storm farther
Northward, yet nothing so furious as this way. At *Hull*, indeed,
as the Relation Expresses, it was violent, but even that violence
was moderate, compar'd to the Stupendious fury with which all
the Southern part of the Nation was Attack'd.

When the Reader finds an Account here from *Milford-haven*
in *Wales*, and from *Helford* in *Cornwall* West, from *Yarmouth*
and *Deal* in the East, from *Portsmouth* in the South, and *Hull*
in the North, I am not to imagine him so weak as to suppose all
the vast Interval had not the same, or proportion'd suffering,
when you find one Letter from a Town, and two from a County,
it is not to be supposed that was the whole damage in that
County, but, on the contrary, that every Town in the County
suffered the same thing in proportion; and it would have been
endless to the Collector, and tiresom to the Reader, to have
Enumerated all the Individuals of every County; 'twould be
endless to tell the the Desolation in the Parks, Groves, and fine
Walks of the Gentry, the general havock in the Orchards and

Gardens among the Fruit Trees, especially in the Counties of *Devon*, *Somerset*, *Hereford*, *Gloucester* and *Worcester*, where the making great quantities of Cyder and Perry, is the reason of numerous and large Orchards, among which, for several Miles together, there would be very few Trees left.

In *Kent* the Editor of this Book has seen several great Orchards, the Trees lying flat on the Ground, and perhaps one Tree standing in a place by it self, as a House might shelter it, perhaps none at all.

So many Trees were every where blown cross the Road, that till the People were call'd to saw them off, and remove them, the ways were not passable.

Stacks of Corn and Hay were in all places either blown down, or so torn, that they receiv'd great damage, and in this Article 'tis very observable, those which were only blown down receiv'd the least Injury; when the main body of a Stack of Hay stood safe, the top being loosen'd by the Violence of the Wind, the Hay was driven up into the Air, and flew about like Feathers; that it was entirely lost and hung about in the Neighbouring Trees, and spread on the Ground for a great distance and so perfectly seperated, that there was no gathering it together.

Barly and Oats suffered the same casualty, only that the weight of the Corn settled it sooner to the Ground than the Hay.

As to the Stacks of Wheat, the Accounts are very strange; from many places we have Letters, and some so incredible, that we dare not venture on the Readers faith to transmit them, least they should shock their belief in those very strange Relations already set down, and better Attested, as of a great Stack of Corn taken from the Hovel on which it stood, and without Dislocating the Sheaves, set upon another Hovel, from whence the Wind had just before remov'd another Stack of equal Dimensions; of a Stack of Wheat taken up with the Wind, and set down whole 16 Rod off, and the like. But as we have other Relations equally strange, their Truth considered, we refer the Reader to them, and assure the World we have several Accounts of Stacks of Wheat taken clear off from the Frame or Steddal, and set down whole, abundance more over-set, and thrown off from their standings, and others quite dispers'd, and in a great measure destroy'd.

'Tis true, Corn was exceeding cheap all the Winter after, but they who bring that as a reason to prove there was no great quantity destroy'd, are oblig'd to bear with me in telling them they are mistaken, for the true reason was as follows,

The Stacks of Corn in some Counties, the West chiefly, where the People generally lay up their Corn in Stacks, being so damnify'd as above, and the Barns in all parts being Universally uncovered, and a vast number of them overturn'd, and blown down, the Country People were under a necessity of Threshing out their Corn with all possible speed, least if a Rain had follow'd, as at that time of Year was not unlikely, it might ha' been all spoil'd.

And it was a special Providence to those People also, as well as to us in *London*; that it did not Rain, at least to any quantity, for near three Weeks after the Storm.

Besides this, the Country People were obliged to thresh out their Corn for the sake of the Straw, which they wanted to repair the Thatch, and covering of their Barns, in order to secure the rest.

All these Circumstances forc'd the Corn to Market in unusual quantities, and that by Consequence made it Cheaper than ordinary, and not the exceeding quantity then in Store.

The Seats of the Gentlemen in all places had an extraordinary share in the Damage; their Parks were in many places perfectly dismantled, the Trees before their Doors levelled, their Garden Walls blown down, and I could give a List, I believe, of a thousand Seats in *England*, within the compass of our Collected Papers, who had from 5 to 20 Stacks of Chimnies blown down, some more, some less, according to the several Dimentions of the Houses.

I am not obliging the Reader to comply with the Calculations here following, and it would have took up too much room in this small Tract to name particulars; but according to the best estimate I have been able to make from the general Accounts sent up by Persons forward to have this matter recorded, the following particulars are rather under than over the real Truth.

25 Parks in the several Counties, who have above 1000 Trees in each Park, blown down.

New Forest in *Hampshire* above 4000, and some of prodigious Bigness; above 450 Parks and Groves, who have from 200 large Trees to 1000 blown down in them.

Above 100 Churches covered with Lead, the Lead roll'd up, the Churches uncover'd; and on some of them, the Lead in prodigious Quantities blown to incredible Distances from the Church.

Above 400 Wind-mils overset, and broken to pieces; or the Sails so blown round, that the Timbers and Wheels have heat and set the rest on Fire, and so burnt them down, as particularly several were in the Isle of *Ely*.

Seven Steeples quite blown down, besides abundance of Pinacles and Battlements from those which stood; and the Churches where it happened most of them Demolish'd, or terribly Shattered.

Above 800 dwelling Houses blown down, in most of which the Inhabitants received some Bruise or Wounds, and many lost their Lives.

We have reckoned, including the City of *London*, about 123 People kill'd; besides such as we have had no account of; the Number of People drowned are not easily Guest; but by all the Calculations I have made and seen made, we are within compass, if we reckon 8000 Men lost, including what were lost on the Coast of *Holland*, what in Ships blown away, and never heard of, and what were drowned in the Flood of the *Severn*, and in the River of *Thames*.

What the Loss, how many poor Families ruin'd, is not to be Estimated, the Fire of *London* was an exceeding Loss, and was by some reckon'd at four Millions sterling; which, tho' it was a great Loss, and happened upon the spot, where vast Quantities of Goods being expos'd to the fury of the Flames, were destroy'd in a hurry, and 14000 dwelling Houses entirely consum'd.

Yet on the other Hand, that Desolation was confin'd to a small Space, the loss fell on the wealthiest part of the People; but this loss is Universal, and its extent general, not a House, not a Family that had any thing to lose, but have lost something by this Storm, the Sea, the Land, the Houses, the Churches, the Corn, the Trees, the Rivers, all have felt the fury of the Winds.

I cannot therefore think I speak too large, if I say, I am of the Opinion, that the Damage done by this Tempest far exceeded the Fire of *London*.

They tell us the Damages done by the Tide, on the Banks of the *Severn*, amounts to above 200000 pounds, 15000 Sheep drown'd in one Level, Multitudes of Cattle on all the sides, and the covering the Lands with Salt Water is a Damage cannot well be Estimated: The High Tide at *Bristol* spoil'd or damnify'd 1500 Hogsheds[25] of Sugars and Tobaccoes, besides great quantities of other Goods.

'Tis impossible to describe the general Calamity, and the most we can do is, to lead our Reader to supply by his Immagination what we omit; and to believe, that as the Head of the particulars is thus collected, an infinite Variety at the same time happened in every place, which cannot be expected to be found in this Relation.

There are some additional Remarks to be made as to this Tempests, which I cannot think improper to come in here: As,

1. That in some Parts of *England* it was join'd with terrible Lightnings and Flashings of Fire, and in other places none at all; as to Thunder the Noise the Wind made, was so Terrible, and so Unusual, that I will not say, People might not mistake it for Thunder; but I have not met with any, who will be positive that they heard it Thunder.

2. Others, as in many Letters we have received to that purpose insist upon it, that they felt an Earthquake; and this I am doubtful of for several Reasons.

1st. We find few People either in City or Country ventur'd out of their Houses, or at least till they were forced out, and I cannot find any Voucher to this opinion of an Earthquake, from those whose Feet stood upon the *Terra Firma*, felt it move, and will affirm it to be so.

2d. As to all those People who were in Houses, I cannot allow them to be competent Judges, for as no House was so strong as not to move and shake with the force of the Wind, so it must be impossible for them to distinguish whither that motion came from above or below: As to those in Ships, they will not pretend to be competent Judges in this case, and I think the People within doors as improper to decide, for what might not that motion they felt in their Houses, from the Wind do, that an Earthquake could do. We found it rockt the strongest Buildings, and in several places made the Bells in the Steeples strike, loosen'd the Foundations of the Houses, and in some below them quite down, but still if it had been an Earthquake, it must have been felt in every house, and every place; and whereas in those Streets of *London*, where the Houses stand thick and well Built, they could not be so shaken with the Wind as in opener places; yet there the other would have equally been felt, and better distinguisht; and this particularly by the Watch,[26] who stood on the Ground, under shelter of publick Buildings, as in St. *Paul*'s Church, the Exchange Gates, the Gates of the City, and such like; wherefore, as I am not for handing to Posterity any matter of Fact upon ill Evidence, so I cannot transmit what has its Foundation only in the Amazements of the People.

'Tis true, that there was an Earthquake felt in the *North East parts of the Kingdoms*, about a Month afterwards, of which several Letters here inserted make mention, and one very particularly from *Hull*; but that there was any such thing as an Earthquake during the Storm, I cannot agree.

Another remarkable thing I have observ'd, and have several Letters to show of the Water which fell in the Storm, being brackish, and at *Cranbrook* in *Kent*, which is at least 16 Miles from the Sea, and above 25 from any Part of the Sea to windward, from whence the Wind could bring any moisture, *for it could not be suppos'd to fly against the Wind*; the Grass was so salt, the Cattel would not eat for several Days, from whence the ignorant People suggested another Miracle, *viz*. that it rain'd salt Water.

The answer to this, I leave to two Letters printed in the *Philosophical Transactions*; as follows,

Part of a Letter from Mr. Denham *to the Royal Society,*

SIR,

I have just now, since my writing, receiv'd an account from a Clergy-man, an Intelligent Person at *Lewes* in *Sussex*, not only that the Storm made great desolations thereabouts, but also an odd Phænomenon occasioned by it, *viz.* 'That a Physician travelling soon after the Storm to *Tisehyrst*, about 20 Miles from *Lewes*, and as far from the Sea, as he rode he pluckt some tops of Hedges, and chawing them found them Salt. Some Ladies of *Lewes* hearing this, tasted some Grapes that were still on the Vines, and they also had the same relish. The Grass on the Downs in his Parish was so salt, that the Sheep in the Morning would not feed till hunger compelled them, and afterwards drank like Fishes, as the Shepherds report. This he attributeth to Saline Particles driven from the Sea. – He heareth also, that People about *Portsmouth* were much annoyed with sulphurous Fumes, complaining they were most suffocated therewith'.[27]

V. *Part of a Letter from Mr.* Anthony van Lauwenhoek, F. R. S.[28] *giving his Observations on the late Storm.*

Delft, Jan. 8. 1704. N. S.

SIR,

I affirmed in my Letter of the 3d of *November* last past, that Water may be so dash'd and beaten against the Banks and Dikes by a strong Wind, and divided into such small Particles, as to be carried far up into the Land.

Upon the 8th of *December*, 1703. N. S. We had a dreadful Storm from the South West, insomuch, that the Water mingled with small parts of Chalk and Stone, was so dasht against the Glass-windows, that many of them were darkned therewith, and the lower Windows of my House, which are made of very fine Glass, and always kept well scower'd, and were not open'd till 8-a-Clock that Morning, notwithstanding that they look to the North East, and consequently stood from the Wind; and moreover, were guarded from the Rain by a kind of Shelf or Pent-house over them; were yet so cover'd with the Particles of the Water which the Whirl-wind cast against them, that in less than half an hour they were deprived of most of their transparency, and, forasmuch as these Particles of Water were not quite exhaled, I concluded that it must be Sea-water, which the said Storm had not only dasht against our Windows, but spread also over the whole Country.

That I might be satisfied herein, I blow'd two small Glasses, such as I thought most proper to make my Observations with, concerning the Particles of Water that adhered to my Windows.

Pressing these Glasses gently against my Windows, that were covered with the suppos'd Particles of Sea-water, my Glasses were tinged with a few of the said Particles.

These Glasses, with the Water I had thus collected on them, I placed at about half a Foot distance from the Candle, I view'd them by my Microscope, reck'ning, that by the warmth of the Candle, and my Face together, the Particles of the said Water would be put into such a motion, that they would exhale for the most part, and the Salts that were in 'em would be expos'd naked to the sight, and so it happened; for in a little time a great many Salt Particles did, as it were, come out of the Water, having the Figure of our common Salt, but very small, because the Water was little, from whence those small Particles proceeded; and where the Water had lain very thin upon the Glass, there were indeed a great number of Salt Particles, but so exceeding fine, that they almost escaped the Sight through a very good Microscope.

From whence I concluded, that these Glass windows could not be brought to their former Lustre, but by washing them with a great deal of Water; for if the Air were very clear, and the Weather dry, the watry Particles would soon exhale, but the Salts would cleave fast to the Glass, which said Salts would be again dissolv'd in moist Weather, and sit like a Dew or Mist upon the Windows.

And accordingly my People found it when they came to wash the afore-mentioned lower Windows of my House: but as to the upper Windows, where the Rain had beat against them, there was little or no Salt to be found sticking upon that Glass.

Now, if we consider, what a quantity of Sea-water is spread all over the Country by such a terrible Storm, and consequently, how greatly impregnated the Air is with the same; we ought not to

wonder, that such a quantity of Water, being moved with so great
a force, should do so much mischief to Chimneys, tops of Houses,
&c. not to mention the Damages at Sea.

During the said Storm, and about 8-a-Clock in the Morning, I
cast my Eye upon my Barometer, and observ'd, that I had never
seen the Quick-silver[29] so low; but half an hour after the Quick-
silver began to rise, tho' the Storm was not at all abated, at least
to any appearance; from whence I concluded, and said it to those
that were about me, that the Storm would not last long; and so it
happened.

There are some that affirm, that the scattering of this Salt-water
by the Storm will do a great deal of harm to the Fruits of the
Earth; but for my part I am of a quite different Opinion, for I
believe that a little Salt spread over the surface of the Earth,
especially where it is heavy Clay-ground, does render it exceeding
Fruitful; and so it would be, if the Sand out of the Sea were made
use of to the same purpose.

These Letters are too well, and too judiciously Written to need
any comment of mine; 'tis plain, the watry Particles taken up
from the Sprye of the Sea into the Air, might by the impetuosity
of the Winds be carried a great way, and if it had been much
farther, it would have been no Miracle in my account; and this
is the reason, why I have not related these Things, among the
extraordinary Articles of the Storm.

That the Air was full of Meteors, and fiery Vapours, and that
the extraordinary Motion occasion'd the firing more of them
than usual, a small stock of Philosophy will make very rational;
and of these we have various Accounts, more in some places
than in others, and I am apt to believe these were the Lightnings
we have been told of; for I am of Opinion, that there was really
no Lightning, such as we call so in the common Acceptation
of it; for the Clouds that flew with so much Violence through
the Air, were not, as to my Observation, such as usually are
fraighted with Thunder and Lightning, the Hurries nature was
then in, do not consist with the System of Thunder, which is Air
pent in between the Clouds; and as for the Clouds that were
seen here flying in the Air, they were by the fury of the Winds

so seperated, and in such small Bodies, that there was no room for a Collection suitable, and necessary to the Case we speak of.

These Cautions I thought necessary to set down here, for the satisfaction of the Curious; and as they are only my Opinions, I submit them to the judgment of the Reader.

Of the Damages on the Water

As this might consist of several Parts, I was inclin'd to have divided it into Sections or Chapters, relating particularly to the publick Loss, and the private; to the Merchant, or the Navy, to Floods by the Tides, to the River Damage, and that of the Sea; but for brevity, I shall confine it to the following particulars.

First, *The Damage to Trade*.
Secondly, *The Damage to the Royal Navy*.
Thirdly, *The Damage by High Tides*.

First, *of the Damage to Trade*.

I might call it a Damage to Trade, that this Season was both for some time before and after the Tempest, so exceeding, and so continually Stormy, that the Seas were in a manner Unnavigable and Negoce,[1] at a kind of a general Stop, and when the Storm was over, and the Weather began to be tolerable; almost all the Shipping in *England* was more or less out of Repair, for there was very little Shipping in the Nation, but what had receiv'd some Damage or other.

It is impossible, but a Nation so full of Shipping as this, must be exceeding Sufferers in such a general Disaster, and who ever considers the Violence of this Storm by its other dreadful Effects will rather wonder, and be thankful that we receiv'd no farther Damage, than we shall be able to give an Account of by Sea.

I have already observ'd what Fleets were in the several Ports of this Nation, and from whence they came: As to Ships lost of whom we have no other Account than that they were never

heard of. I am not able to give any Perticulars, other than that
about three and forty Sail of all Sorts are reckon'd to have
perished in that manner. I mean of such Ships as were at Sea,
when the Storm began, and had no Shelter or Port to make for
their Safety: Of these, some were of the *Russia* Fleet, of whom
we had an Account of 20 Sail lost the Week before the great
Storm, but most of them reach'd the Ports of *Newcastle*,
Humber and *Yarmouth*, and some of the Men suffered in the
general Distress afterwards.

But to proceed to the most general Disasters, by the same
Method, as in the former Articles of Damages by Land. Several
Persons having given themselves the Trouble to further this
Design with Authentick Particulars from the respective Ports. I
conceive we cannot give the World a clearer and more Satisfac-
tory Relation than from their own Words.

*The first Account, and plac'd so, because 'tis very Authentick
and Particular, and the furthest Port Westward, and therefore
proper to begin our Relation, is from on Board her Majesty's
Ship the* Dolphin *in Milford Haven, and sent to us by Capt.
Soanes, the Commodore of a Squadron of Men of War then in
that Harbour, to whom the Public is very much oblig'd for the
Relation, and which we thought our selves bound there to
acknowledge. The Account is as follows,*

SIR,
Reading the Advertisement in the *Gazette*, of your intending to
Print the many sad Accidents in the late dreadful Storm, induced
me to let you know what this place felt, tho a very good Harbour.
Her Majesty's Ships the *Cumberland*, *Coventry*, *Loo*, *Hastings*
and *Hector*, being under my Command, with the *Rye* a Cruizer
on this Station, and under our Convoy about 130 Merchant Ships
bound about Land; the 26th of *November* at one in the Afternoon
the Wind came at S. by E. a hard Gale, between which and N. W.
by W. it came to a dreadful Storm, at three the next Morning was
the Violentest of the Weather, when the *Cumberland* broak her
Sheet Anchor,[2] the Ship driving near *this*, and the *Rye*, both
narrowly escap'd carrying away; she drove very near the Rocks,

having but one Anchor left, but in a little time they slung a Gun, with the broken Anchor fast to it, which they let go, and wonderfully preserv'd the Ship from the Shoar. Guns firing from one Ship or other all the Night for help, tho' 'twas impossible to assist each other, the Sea was so high, and the Darkness of the Night such, that we could not see where any one was, but by the Flashes of the Guns; when day light appear'd, it was a dismal sight to behold the Ships driving up and down one foul of another, without Masts, some sunk, and others upon the Rocks, the Wind blowing so hard, with Thunder, Lightning and Rain, that on the Deck a Man could not stand without holding. Some drove from *Dale*, where they were shelter'd under the Land, and split in pieces, the Men all drowned; two others drove out of a Creek, one on the Shoar so high up was saved, the other on the Rocks in another Creek, and Bulg'd; an *Irish* Ship that lay with a Rock thro' her, was lifted by the Sea clear away to the other side of the Creek on a safe place; one Ship forc'd 10 Miles up the River before she could be stop'd, and several strangely blown into holes, and on Banks; a Ketch of *Pembroke* was drove on the Rocks, the two Men and a Boy in her had no Boat to save their Lives; but in this great distress a Boat which broke from another Ship drove by them, without any in her, the two Men leap into her, and were sav'd, but the Boy drown'd; a Prize at *Pembroke* was lifted on the Bridge, whereon is a Mill, which the Water blew up, but the Vessel got off again; another Vessel carried almost into the Gateway which leads to the Bridge, and is a Road, the Tide flowing several Foot above its common Course. The Storm continu'd till the 27th about 3 in the Afternoon; that by Computation nigh 30 Merchant Ships and Vessels without Masts are lost, and what Men are lost is not known; 3 Ships are missing, that we suppose Men and all lost. None of her Majesty's Ships came to any harm; but the *Cumberland* breaking her Anchor in a Storm which happen'd the 18th at Night, lost another, which renders her uncapable of proceeding with us till supply'd. I saw several Trees and Houses which are blown down.

Your Humble Servant,
Jos. Soanes.

The next Account we have from the Reverend Mr. Tho. Chest, Minister *of* Chepstow, *whose Ingenious account being given in his own Words, gives the best Acknowledgement for his forwarding and approving this design.*

SIR,

Upon the Evening of *Friday, Nov.* 26. 1703, the Wind was very high; but about midnight it broke out with a more than wonted Violence, and so continued till near break of day. It ended a N. W. Wind, tho' about 3 in the Morning it was at S. W. The loudest cracks I observed of it, were somewhat before 4 of the Clock; we had here the common Calamity of Houses shatter'd and Trees thrown down.

But the Wind throwing the Tyde very strongly into the *Severn*, and so into the *Wye*, on which *Chepstow* is situated. And the Fresh in *Wye* meeting with a Rampant Tyde, overflowed the lower part of our Town. It came into several Houses about 4 foot high, rather more; the greatest damage sustained in Houses, was by the makers of Salt, perhaps their loss might amount to near 200 *l.*

But the Bridge was a strange sight; it stands partly in *Monmouthshire*, and partly in *Gloucestershire*, and is built mostly of Wood, with a Stone Peer in the midst, the Center of which divides the two Counties; there are also Stone Platforms in the bottom of the River to bear the Wood-work. I doubt not but those Stone Platforms were covered then by the great Fresh that came down the River. But over these there are Wooden Standards fram'd into Peers 42 Foot high; besides Groundsils, Cap-heads,[3] Sleepers, Planks, and (on each side of the Bridge) Rails which may make about 6 foot more, the Tyde came over them all: The length of the Wooden part of the Bridge in *Monmouthshire* is 60 yards exactly, and thereabout in *Gloucestershire*; the *Gloucestershire* side suffered but little, but in *Monmouthshire* side the Planks were most of them carried away, the Sleepers (about a Tun by measure each) were many of them carried away, and several removed, and 'tis not doubted but the great Wooden Peers would have gone too; but it was so, that the outward Sleepers on each side the Bridge were Pinn'd or Bolted to the Cap-heads, and so kept them in their places.

All the level Land on the South part of *Monmouthshire*, called the *Moors*, was overflow'd; it is a tract of Land about 20 miles long, all Level, save 2 little points of High-land, or 3; the Breadth of it is not all of one size, the broadest part is about 2 miles and $\frac{1}{2}$. This Tyde came 5 Tydes before the top of the Spring, according to the usual run, which surprized the People very much. Many of their Cattle got to shore, and some dy'd after they were landed. It is thought by a *Moderate Computation*, they might lose in Hay and Cattle between 3 and 4000 *l*. I cannot hear of any Person drowned, save only one Servant Man, that ventur'd in quest of his Master's Cattle. The People were carried off, some by Boats, some otherways, the days following; the last that came off (that I can hear of) were on *Tuesday* Evening, to be sure they were uneasy and astonished in that Interval. There are various reports about the height of this Tyde in the *Moors*, comparing it with that in *Jan.* 1606. But the account that seems likeliest to me, is, that the former Tyde ran somewhat higher than this. 'Tis thought most of their Land will be worth but little these 2 or 3 years, and 'tis known, that the repairing the Sea Walls will be very chargeable.

Gloucestershire too, that borders upon *Severne* hath suffered deeply on the Forrest of *Deane* side, but nothing in comparison of the other shore, from about *Harlingham* down to the mouth of *Bristol* River *Avon*, particularly from *Aust Cliffe* to the Rivers Mouth (about 8 miles) all that Flat, called the *Marsh* was drowned. They lost many Sheep and Cattle. About 70 Seamen were drown'd out of the *Canterbury* Storeship, and other Ships that were Stranded or Wreck'd. The *Arundel* Man of War, *Suffolk* and *Canterbury* Storeships, a *French* Prize, and a *Dane*, were driven ashore and damnified; but the *Arundel* and the *Danish* Ship are got off, the rest remain on Ground. The *Richard and John* of about 500 Tun, newly come into *King-road* from *Virginia*, was Staved. The *Shoram* rode it out in *King-road*; but I suppose you may have a perfecter account of these things from *Bristol*. But one thing yet is to be remembred, one *Nelms* of that Country, as I hear his Name, was carried away with his Wife and 4 Children, and House and all, and were all lost, save only one Girl, who caught hold of a Bough, and was preserved.

There was another unfortunate Accident yet in these parts, one Mr. *Churchman*, that keeps the Inns at *Betesley*, a passage over the *Severn*, and had a share in the passing Boats, seeing a single Man tossed in a Wood-buss[4] off in the River, prevailed with some belonging to the Customs, to carry himself and one of his Sons, and 2 Servants aboard the Boat, which they did, and the Officers desired Mr. *Churchman* to take out the Man, and come ashore with them in their Pinnace. But he, willing to save the Boat as well as the Man, tarried aboard, and sometime after hoisting Sail, the Boat overset, and they were all drowned, *viz.* the Man in the Boat, Mr. *Churchman*, his Son and 2 Servants, and much lamented, especially Mr. *Churchman*, and his Son, who were Persons very useful in their Neighbourhood. This happened on *Saturday* about 11 of the Clock.

Your Humble Servant,

Tho. Chest

Mr. Tho. Little *Minister of* — Church *in* Lyn, *in the County of* Norfolk, *being requested to give in the particulars of what happen'd thereabouts, gave the following, short but very pertinent Account.*

SIR,

I had answer'd yours sooner, but that I was willing to get the best Information I could of the effect of the late dismal Storm amongst us. I have advis'd with our Merchants, and Ship Masters, and find that we have lost from this Port 7 Ships, the damage whereof, at a modest Computation, amounts to 3000 *l.* the Men that perish'd in them are reckon'd about 20 in number. There is another Ship missing, tho we are not without hopes that she is gone Northward, the value of Ship and Cargo about 1500 *l.*

The Damage sustain'd in the Buildings of the Town is computed at 1000 *l.* at least.

I am your faithful Friend and Servant.

Lyn, *Jan.* 17. 1703.   Tho. Little.

We have had various Accounts from Bristol, *but as they all contain something of the Same in general, only differently Exprest, the following, as the most positively asserted, and best Exprest, is recorded for the publick Information.*

SIR,

Observing your desire (lately signify'd in the *Gazette*) to be further inform'd concerning the Effects of the late dreadful Tempest, in order to make a Collection thereof. I have presum'd to present you with the following particulars concerning *Bristol*, and the parts near Adjacent, being an Eye-witness of the same, or the Majority of it. On *Saturday* the 27th of *Novemb.* last, between the hours of one and two in the Morning, arose a most prodigious Storm of Wind, which continued with very little intermission for the space of 6 hours, in which time it very much shattered the Buildings, both publick and private, by uncovering the Houses, throwing down the Chimneys, breaking the Glass Windows, overthrowing the Pinnacles and Battlements of the Churches, and blowing off the Leads: The Churches in particular felt the fury of the Storm. St. *Stephen*'s Tower had three Pinnacles blown off, which beat down the greatest part of the Church. The Cathedral is likewise very much defac'd, two of its Windows, and several Battlements being blown away; and, indeed, most Churches in the City felt its force more or less; it also blew down abundance of great Trees in the Marsh, *College-Green*, St. *James*'s Church-yard, and other places in the City. And in the Country it blew down and scattered abundance of Hay and Corn Mows, besides almost Levelling many Orchards and Groves of stout Trees. But the greatest damage done to the City was, the violent over-flowing of the Tide, occasion'd by the force of the Wind, which flowed an extraordinary height, and did abundance of damage to the Merchants Cellers. It broke in with great fury over the Marsh Country, forcing down the Banks or Sea Walls, drowning abundance of Sheep, and other Cattle, washing some houses clear away, and breaking down part of others, in which many Persons lost their Lives. It likewise drove most of the Ships in *Kingroad* a considerable way upon the Land, some being much shatter'd, and one large Vessel broke all in pieces, and near all the Men lost, besides several lost out of other Vessels. To conclude, the Damage sustein'd by this City alone in Merchandise, Houses, &c. is Computed to an Hundred Thousand Pounds, besides the great Loss in the Country, of Cattel, Corn, &c. which has utterly ruined many Farmers, whose substance consisted in their Stock aforesaid. So having given you the most material Circumstances, and fatal Effects of this great Tempest in these Parts. I conclude

Your (unknown) Friend and Servant,

Danial James

From Huntspill *in* Somersetshire, *we have the following Account from, as we suppose, the Minister of the place, tho' unknown to the Collector of this Work.*

SIR,

The Parish of *Huntspill* hath receiv'd great Damage by the late Inundation of the Salt Water, particularly the West part thereof suffered most: For on the 27th Day of *November* last, about four of the Clock in the Morning, a mighty Southwest Wind blew so strong, as (in a little time) strangely tore our Sea Walls; insomuch, that a considerable part of the said Walls were laid smooth, after which the Sea coming in with great Violence, drove in five Vessels belonging to *Bridgewater Key* out of the Channel, upon a Wharf in our Parish, which lay some distance off from the Channel, and there they were all grounded; it is said, that the Seamen there fathom'd the depth and found it about nine Foot, which is taken notice to be four Foot above our Walls when standing; the Salt Water soon overflow'd all the West end of the Parish, forcing many of the Inhabitants from their Dwellings, and to shift for their Lives: The Water threw down several Houses, and in one an antient Woman was drown'd, being about fourscore Years old: Some Families shelter'd themselves in the Church, and there staid till the Waters were abated: Three Window Leaves of the Tower were blown down, and the Ruff-cast[5] scal'd off in many places: Much of the Lead of the Church was damnify'd; the Windows of the Church and Chancel much broken, and the Chancel a great part of it untiled: The Parsonage House, Barn and Walls received great Damage; as also, did some of the Neighbours in their Houses: At the West end of the Parsonage House stood a very large Elm, which was four Yards a quarter and half a quarter in the Circumference, it was broken off near the Ground by the Wind, without forcing any one of the Moars[6] above the Surface, but remain'd as they were before: The Inhabitants (many of them) have receiv'd great Losses in their Sheep, and their other Cattle; in their Corn and Hay there is great spoil made. This is what Information I can give of the Damage this Parish hath sustain'd by the late dreadful Tempest.

I am, Sir,

Huntspill,   *Your humble Servant,*
January 6, 170¾.   Sam. Wooddeson

From Minehead *in* Somersetshire, *and* Swanzy *in* Wales, *the following Accounts are to be depended upon.*

SIR,
I received yours, and in answer to it these are to acquaint you, that all the Ships in our Harbour except two (which were 23 or 24 in Number, besides Fishing Boats) were, through the Violence of the Storm, and the mooring Posts giving way, drove from their Anchors, one of them was stav'd to pieces, nine drove Ashoar; but 'tis hoped will be all got off again, though some of them are very much damnified: Several of the Fishing Boats likewise, with their Nets, and other Necessaries were destroy'd. Three Seamen were drowned in the Storm, and one Man was squeez'd to Death last *Wednesday*, by one of the Ships that was forc'd Ashoar, suddenly coming upon him, as they were digging round her, endeavouring to get her off.

Our Peer also was somewhat damaged, and 'tis thought, if the Storm had continued till another Tide, it would have been quite washed away, even level to the Ground; which if so, would infallibly have ruined our Harbour: Our Church likewise was almost all untiled, the neighbouring Churches also received much Damage: The Houses of our Town, and all the Country round about, were most of them damaged; some (as I am credibly informed) blown down, and several in a great Measure uncovered: Trees also of a very great Bigness were broken off in the middle, and vast Numbers blown down; one Gentleman, as he told me himself, having 2500 Trees blown down: I wish you good Success in these your Undertakings, and I pray God that this late great Calamity which was sent upon us as a punishment for our Sins, may be a warning to the whole Nation in general, and engage every one of us to a hearty and sincere Repentance; otherwise, I'm afraid we must expect greater Evils than this was to fall upon us.

From your unknown Friend and Servant,

Frist. Chave.

Swanzy, January 24, 170¾.

SIR,

I receiv'd yours and accordingly have made an enquiry in our Neighbourhood what damage might be done in the late Storm, thro Mercy we escap'd indifferently, but you will find underwritten as much as I can learn to be certainly true.

The Storm began here about 12 at Night, but the most violent part of it was about 4 the next Morning, about which time the greatest part of the Houses in the Town were uncovered more or less, and one House clearly blown down; the damage sustain'd to the Houses is modestly computed at 200 *l.* the South Isle of the Church was wholly uncovered, and considerable damage done to the other Isles, and 4 large Stones weighing about One Hundred and Fifty or Two Hundred Pound each, was blown down from the end of the Church, three of the four Iron Spears, that stood with Vanes on the corners of the Tower, were broke short off in the middle, and the Vanes not to be found, and the Tail of the Weather Cock, which stood in the middle of the Tower was blown off, and found in a Court near 400 yards distant from the Tower. In *Cline* Wood belonging to the Duke of *Beaufort* near this Town, there is about 100 large Trees blown down; as also in a Wood on our River belonging to Mr. *Thomas Mansell* of

Brittonferry about 80 large Oakes. The Tydes did not much damage, but two Ships were blown off our Bar, and by Providence one came aground on the Salt House point near our Harbour, else the Ship and Men had perished; the other came on shore, but was saved. I hear further, that there are several Stacks of Corn over-turn'd by the violence of the Wind, in the Parishes of *Roysily* and *Largenny* in *Gower*; most of the Thatcht Houses in this Neighbourhood was uncovered. Sir, this you may rely on to be true,

Yours, &c.

William Jones

From Grimsby *in* Lincolnshire, *the following Account is taken for favourable.*

SIR,

The late dreadful Tempest did not (Blessed be God) much affect us on shore, so far was it from having any events more than common, that the usual marks of ordinary Storms are not to be met with in these parts upon the Land. I wish I could give as good an Account of the Ships then at Anchor in our Road, the whole Fleet consisted of about an hundred Sail, fifty whereof were wanting after the Storm. The Wrecks of four are to be seen in the Road at low Water their Men all lost, three more were sunk near the *Spurn*, all the Men but one saved, six or seven were driven ashoar, and got off again with little or no damage. A small Hoy, not having a Man on Board, was taken at Sea, by a Merchant Ship, what became of the rest, we are yet to learn. This is all the Account I am able to give of the effects of the late Storm, which was so favourable to us. I am

Sir, Your most Humble Servant,

Tho. Fairweather

From Newport *and* Hastings *the following Accounts are chiefly mentioned to confirm what we have from other Inland parts,*

and particularly in the Letter Printed in the Philosophical Trans-
actions, concerning the Salt being found on the Grass and
Trees, at great distance from the Sea, of which there are very
Authentick Relations.

SIR,

I received yours, and do hereby give you the best account of what
hapned by the late Storm in our Island; we have had several Trees
blown down, and many Houses in our Town, and all parts of the
Island partly uncovered, but Blessed be God not one Person
perisht that I know or have heard of; nor one Ship or Vessel
stranded on our shores in that dreadful Storm, but only one Vessel
laden with Tin, which was driven from her Anchors in *Cornwal*,
but was not stranded here till the *Tuesday* after, having spent her
Main-mast and all her Sails. On *Sunday* night last we had several
Ships and Vessels stranded on the South and South West parts of
our Island; but reports are so various, that I cannot tell you how
many, some say 7, others 8, 12, and some say 15; one or two
laden with Cork, and two or three with *Portugal* Wine, Oranges
and Lemons, one with Hides and Butter, one with Sugar, one
with Pork, Beef and Oatmeal, and one with Slates. *Monday* night,
Tuesday and *Wednesday* came on the back of our Island, and
some in at the *Needles*, the Fleet that went out with the King of
Spain, but it has been here such a dreadful Storm, and such dark
weather till this Afternoon, that we can give no true account of
them; some say that have been at the Wrecks this Afternoon, that
there were several great Ships coming in then: There is one thing
I had almost forgotten, and I think is very remarkable, that there
was found on the Hedges and Twigs of Trees, knobs of Salt
Congeal'd, which must come from the South and South West
parts of our Sea Coast, and was seen and tasted at the distance of
6 and 10 miles from those Seas, and this account I had my self
from the mouths of several Gentlemen of undeniable Reputation,

Yours,

Tho. Reade.

Hastings in *Sussex, Jan.* 25. 1703.

SIR,

You desire to know what effect the late dreadful Storm of Wind had upon this Town; in answer to your desire, take the following Account. This Town consists of at least 600 Houses, besides two great Churches, some Publick Buildings, and many Shops standing upon the Beach near the Sea, and yet by the special Blessing and Providence of God, the whole Town suffered not above 30 or 40 *l.* damage in their Houses, Churches, Publick Building and Shops, and neither Man, Woman or Child suffered the least hurt by the said Terrible Storm. The Town stands upon the Sea shore, but God be thanked the Sea did us no damage; and the Tydes were not so great as we have seen upon far less Storms. The Wind was exceeding Boisterous, which might drive the Froth and Sea moisture six or seven miles up the Country, for at that distances from the Sea, the Leaves of the Trees and Bushes, were as Salt as if they had been dipped in the Sea, which can be imputed to nothing else, but the Violent Winds carrying the Froth and Moisture so far. I believe it may be esteemed almost Miraculous that our Town escaped so well in the late terrible Storm, and therefore I have given you this Account. I am

Sir, your Friend,

Stephen Gawen.

The following melancholy Account from the Town of Brighthemstone *in* Sussex *is sent us.*

SIR,

The late dreadful Tempest in *Novemb.* 27. 1703. last, had very terrible Effects in this Town. It began here much about One of the Clock in the Morning, the violence of the Wind stript a great many Houses, turn'd up the Leads off the Church, over-threw two Windmills, and laid them flat on the ground, the Town in general (upon the approach of Day-light) looking as if it had been Bombarded. Several Vessels belonging to this Town were lost, others stranded, and driven ashoar, others forced over to *Holland*

and *Hamborough*, to the great Impoverishment of the Place. *Derick Pain*, Junior, Master of the *Elizabeth* Ketch of this Town lost, with all his Company. *George Taylor*, Master of the Ketch call'd the *Happy Entrance*, lost, and his Company, excepting *Walter Street*, who swiming three days on a Mast between the *Downs* and *North Yarmouth*, was at last taken up. *Richard Webb*, Master of the Ketch call'd the *Richard* and *Rose* of *Bright-helmston*, lost, and all his Company near St. *Hellens*. *Edward Friend*, Master of the Ketch call'd *Thomas and Francis*, stranded near *Portsmouth*. *Edward Glover*, Master of the Pink[7] call'd *Richard and Benjamin*, stranded near *Chichester*, lost one of his Men, and he, and the rest of his Company, forced to hang in the Shrouds[8] several hours. *George Beach*, Junior, Master of the Pink call'd *Mary*, driven over to *Hamborough* from the *Downes*, having lost his Anchor, Cables and Sails. *Robert Kichener*, Master of the *Cholmley* Pink of *Brighton*, lost near the *Roseant* with nine Men, five Men and a Boy saved by another Vessel. This is all out of this Town, besides the loss of several other able Seamen belonging to this Place, aboard of her Majesty's Ships, Transports and Tenders.

From Lymington *and* Lyme *we have the following Letters:*

SIR,

I receiv'd your Letter, and have made Enquiry concerning what Disasters happen'd during the late Storm; what I can learn at present, and that may be credited, are these. That a *Guernsey* Privateer lost his Fore-top-mast, and cut his main Mast by the Board, had 12 Men wash'd over board, and by the toss of another immediate Sea three of them was put on board again, and did very well; this was coming within the *Needles*. That six Stacks of Chimneys were, by the violence of the Wind, blown from a great House call'd *New Park* in the *Forrest*, some that stood directly to Windward, were blown clear off the House without injuring the Roof, or damaging the House, or any mischief to the Inhabitants, and fell some Yards from the House. Almost 4000 Trees were torn up by the roots within her Majesty's Forrest call'd *New*

Forrest, some of them of very great bulk, others small, *&c.* A Ship of about 200 Tun, from *Maryland*, laden with Tobacco, call'd the *Assistance*, was Cast away upon *Hurst Beach*, one of the Mates, and 4 Sailors, were lost. By the flowing of the Sea over *Hurst Beach*, two Salt-terns[9] were almost ruin'd belonging to one Mr. *Perkins*. A new Barn, nigh this Town, was blown quite down. The Town receiv'd not much damage, only some Houses being stript of the Healing,[10] Windows broke, and a Chimney or two blown down. Considerable damages amongst the Farmers in the adjacent Places, by over-turning Barns, Out-houses, Stacks of Corn and Hay, and also amongst poor Families, and small Houses, and likewise abundance of Trees of all sorts, especially Elms and Apple-Trees, has been destroy'd upon the several Gentlemen's, and others Estates hereabouts. These are the most remarkable Accidents that I can Collect at present; if any thing occur, it shall be sent you by

Your humble Servant,

Lymington, *Feb.* 1704.   *James Baker.*

A True and exact Account of the Damages done by the late great Wind in the Town of Lyme Regis, *and parts adjacent in the County of* Dorset, *as followeth,*

SIR

Impri. Five Boats drove out of the Cob[11] and one Vessel lost, broke loose all but one Cabel, and swung out of the Cob, but was got in again with little Damage; and had that Hurricane happened here at High Water, the Cob must without doubt have been destroyed, and all the Vessels in it been lost, most of the Houses had some Damage: But a great many Trees blown up by the Roots in our Neighbourhood, and four Miles to the Eastward of this Town: A *Guernsey* Privateer of eight Guns, and 43 Men drove Ashoar, and but three Men saved of the 43; the place where the said Privateer run Ashoar, is call'd *Sea Town*, half a Mile from *Chidock*, where most of there Houses were uncovered, and one Man killed as he lay in Bed: This is the true

Account here, but all Villages suffered extreamly in Houses, Trees, both Elm and Apples without Number.

Sir, I am your humble Servant,

Stephen Bowdidge.

From Margate, *and the Island of* Thanet *in Kent, the following is an honest Account.*

SIR,

The following Account is what I can give you, of what Damage is done in this Island in the late great Storm; in this Town hardly a House escaped without Damage, and for the most part of them the Tiles blown totally off from the Roof, and several Chimneys blown down, that broke through part of the Houses to the Ground; and several Families very narrowly escaped being kill'd in their Beds, being by Providence just got up, so that they escaped, and none was kill'd; the like Damages being done in most little Towns and Villages upon this Island, as likewise Barns, Stables and Out-housing blown down to the Ground in a great many Farm-houses and Villages within the Island, part of the Leads of our Church blown clear off, and a great deal of Damage to the Church it self; likewise a great deal of Damage to the Churches of St. *Lawrance Minster, Mounton* and St. *Nichola*: In this Road was blown out one *Latchford* of *Sandwich* bound home from *London*, with divers Men and Women passengers all totally lost: And another little Pink that is not heard of blown away at the same time, but where it belonged is not known; here rid out the Storm the Princess *Anne*, Captain *Charles Gye*, and the *Swan*, both Hospital Ships, had no Damage, only Captain *Gye* was parted from one of his Anchors, and part of a Cable which was weigh'd and carry'd after him to the River, by one of our Hookers.[12] All from

Yours to Command,

P. H.

From Malden *in Essex, and from* Southampton, *the following Accounts.*

SIR,

By the late great Storm our Damages were considerable. A Spire of a Steeple blown down: Several Vessels in this Harbour were much shatter'd, particularly one Corn Vessel laden for *London*, stranded, and the Corn lost to the Value of about 500 *l.* and the Persons narrowly escaped by a small Boat that relieved them next Day: Many Houses ript up, and some blown down: The Churches shatter'd, and the principal Inn of this Town thirty or forty pound Damage in Tiling: At a Gentleman's House (one Mr. *Moses Bourton*) near us, a Stack of Chimneys blown down, fell through the Roof upon a Bed, where his Children was, who were drag'd out, and they narrowly escaped; many other Chimney's blown down here, and much Mischief done.

Southampton, February the 7th 170$\frac{3}{4}$.

SIR,

Yours I have receiv'd, in which you desire me to give you an Account of what remarkable Damage the late violent Storm hath done at this place; in answer, We had most of the Ships in our River, and those that laid off from our Keys blown Ashoar, some partly torn to Wrecks, and three or four blown so far on Shoar with the Violence of the Wind, that the Owners have been at the Charges of unlading them, and dig large Channels for the Spring Tides to float them off, and with much a do have got them off, it being on a soft Sand or Mud, had but little Damage; we had, God be prais'd no body drowned, tho' some narrowly Escape't: As to our Town it being most part old Building, we have suffer'd much, few or no Houses have escape't: Several Stacks of Chimneys blown down, other Houses most part untiled: Several People bruis'd, but none kill'd: Abundance of Trees round about us, especially in the New Forest blown down; others with their Limbs of a great bigness torn; it being what we had most Material. I rest.

Sir, your humble Servant,

Geo. Powell.

*We have abundance of strange Accounts from other Parts, and
particularly the following Letter from the* Downs, *and tho' every
Circumstance in this Letter is not litterally True, as to the
Number of Ships, or Lives lost, and the stile Coarse, and Sailor
like; yet I have inserted this Letter, because it seems to describe
the Horror and Consternation the poor Sailors were in at that
time. And because this is Written from one, who was as near an
Eye Witness as any could possible be, and be safe,*

SIR,

These Lines I hope in God will find you in good Health, we are
all left here in a dismal Condition, expecting every moment to be
all drowned: For here is a great Storm, and is very likely to
continue; we have here the Rear Admiral of the Blew[13] in the Ship,
call'd the *Mary*, a third Rate, the very next Ship to ours, sunk,
with Admiral *Beaumont*, and above 500 Men drowned: The Ship
call'd the *Northumberland*, a third Rate, about 500 Men all sunk
and drowned: The Ship call'd the *Sterling Castle*, a third Rate, all
sunk and drowned above 500 Souls: And the Ship call'd the
Restoration, a third Rate, all sunk and drowned: These Ships
were all close by us which I saw; these Ships fired their Guns all
Night and Day long, poor Souls, for help, but the Storm being so
fierce and raging, could have none to save them: The Ship call'd
the *Shrewsberry* that we are in, broke two Anchors, and did run
mighty fierce backwards, within 60 or 80 Yards of the Sands, and
as God Almighty would have it, we flung our sheet Anchor down,
which is the biggest, and so stopt: Here we all pray'd to God to
forgive us our Sins, and to save us, or else to receive us into his
Heavenly Kingdom. If our sheet Anchor had given way, we had
been all drown'd: But I humbly thank God, it was his gracious
Mercy that saved us. There's one Captain *Fanel*'s Ship, three
Hospital Ships, all split, some sunk, and most of the Men drown'd.

There are above 40 Merchant Ships cast away and sunk: To see
Admiral *Beaumont*, that was next us, and all the rest of his Men,
how they climed up the main Mast, hundreds at a time crying out

for help, and thinking to save their Lives, and in the twinkling of an Eye were drown'd: I can give you no Account, but of these four Men of War aforesaid, which I saw with my own Eyes, and those Hospital Ships, at present, by reason the Storm hath drove us far distant from one another: Captain *Crow*, of our Ship, believes we have lost several more Ships of War, by reason we see so few; we lye here in great danger, and waiting for a North Easterly Wind to bring us to *Portsmouth*, and it is our Prayers to God for it; for we know not how soon this Storm may arise, and cut us all off, for it is a dismal Place to Anchor in. I have not had my Cloaths off, nor a wink of Sleep these four Nights, and have got my Death with cold almost.

Yours to Command,

Miles Norcliffe.

I send this, having opportunity by our Botes, that went Ashoar to carry some poor Men off, that were almost dead, and were taken up Swimming.

The following Letter is yet more Particular and Authentick, and being better exprest, may further describe the Terror of the Night in this place.

SIR,

I understand you are a Person concerned in making up a Collection of some remarkable accidents that happened by the Violence of the late dreadful Storm. I here present you with one of the like. I presume you never heard before, nor hope may never hear again of a Ship that was blown from her Anchors out of *Helford Haven* to the *Isle of Wight*, in less than eight hours, *viz*. The Ship lay in *Helford Haven* about two Leagues and a half Westward of *Falmouth*, being laden with Tin, which was taken on Board from *Guague* Wharf, about five or six miles up *Helford* River, the Commanders name was *Anthony Jenkins*, who lives at *Falmouth*. About eight Clock in the Evening before the Storm begun, the said Commander and Mate came on Board and ordered the Crew that he left on Board, which was but one Man and 2 Boys; that if the Wind should chance to blow hard (which he had some apprehension of) to carry out the small Bower Anchor,[14] and moor the Ship by 2 Anchors, and gave them some other orders, and his Mate and he went ashoar, and left the Crew aforesaid on Board; about nine a Clock the Wind began to blow, then they carried out the small Bower (as directed) it continued blowing harder and harder at West North West, at last the Ship began to drive, then they were forced to let go the best Bower Anchor which brought the Ship up. The Storm increasing more, they let go the Kedge Anchor,[15] which was all they had to let go, so that the Ship rid with four Anchors a head: Between eleven and twelve a Clock the Wind came about West and by South in a most Terrible and Violent manner, that notwithstanding a very high Hill just to Windward of the Ship, and four Anchors ahead, she was drove from all her Anchors; and about twelve a Clock drove out of the Harbour without Anchor or Cable, nor so much as a Boat left in case they could put into any Harbour. In dreadful condition the Ship drove out clear of the Rocks to Sea, where the Man with the two Boys consulted what to do, at last resolved to keep her far enough to Sea, for fear of *Deadman*'s *Head*, being a point of Land between *Falmouth* and *Plimouth*, the latter of which places they designed to run her in, if possible, to save their Lives; the next morning in this frighted condition they steer'd her clear of the Land (to the best of their skill) sometimes almost under Water, and sometimes a top, with only the bonet[16] of her Foresail out, and the Fore yard almost lower'd to the Deck; but instead of getting into *Plymouth* next day as intended, they were far enough off that Port, for the next morning they saw Land, which proved to be *Peverel* Point, a little to the Westward of the *Isle of Wight*; so that they were in a worse Consternation then before, for over-running their designed Port by seven a Clock, they found themselves off the *Isle of Wight*; where they consulted again what to do to save their Lives, one of the Boys was for running her into the *Downs*, but that was objected against, by reason they had no Anchors nor Boat, and the Storm blowing off shore in the *Downs*, they should be blown on the unfortunate *Goodwin Sands* and lost. Now comes the last consultation for their lives, there was one of the Boys said he had been in a certain

Creek in the *Isle of Wight*, where between the Rocks he believed there was room enough to run the Ship in and save their Lives, and desired to have the Helm from the Man, and he would venture to steer the Ship into the said place, which he according did, where there was only just room between Rock and Rock for the Ship to come in, where she gave one blow or two against the Rocks, and sunk immediately, but the Man and two Boys jumpt ashore, and all the Lading being Tin was saved, (and for their Conduct and Risk they run) they were all very well gratified, and the Merchants well satisfied.

Your Friend and Servant,

May 28. 1704.   R. P.

And here I cannot omit that great Notice has been taken of the Towns-people of *Deal* who are blam'd, and I doubt not with too much Reason for their great Barbarity in neglecting to save the Lives of abundance of poor Wretches; who having hung upon the Masts and Rigging of the Ships, or floated upon the broken Pieces of Wrecks, had gotten a Shore upon the *Goodwin Sands* when the Tide was out.

It was, without doubt, a sad Spectacle to behold the poor Seamen walking too and fro upon the Sands, to view their Postures, and the Signals they made for help, which, by the Assistance of Glasses was easily seen from the Shore.

Here they had a few Hours Reprieve, but had neither present Refreshment, nor any hopes of Life, for they were sure to be all wash'd into another World at the Reflux of the Tide. Some Boats are said to come very near them in quest of Booty, and in search of Plunder, and to carry off what they could get, but no Body concern'd themselves for the Lives of these miserable Creatures.

And yet I cannot but incert what I have receiv'd from very good Hands in behalf of one Person in that Town, whose Humanity deserves this remembrance, and I am glad of the Opportunity of doing some Justice in this Case to a Man of so much Charity in a Town of so little.

Mr. *Thomas Powell*, of *Deal*, a Slop-Seller[17] by Trade, and at

that time Mayor of the Town. The Character of his Person I
need not dwell upon here, other than the ensuing Accounts will
describe, for when I have said he is a Man of Charity and
Courage, there is little I need to add to it, to move the Reader
to value both his Person, and his Memory; and tho' I am otherwise a perfect Stranger to him, I am very well pleased to transmit
to Posterity the Account of his Behaviour, as an Example to all
good Christians to imitate on the like Occasions.

He found himself mov'd with Compasion at the Distresses of
the poor Creatures, whom he saw as aforesaid in that miserable
Condition upon the Sands, and the first Thing he did, he made
Application to the Custom-House Officers for the Assistance of
their Boats and Men, to save the Lives of as many as they could
come at, the Custom House Men rudely refus'd, either to send
their Men, or to part with their Boats.

Provoked with the unnatural Carriage of the Custom House
Officers, he calls the People about him; and finding some of the
Common People began to be more than ordinarily affected with
the Distresses of their Countrymen, and as he thought a little
enclin'd to venture; he made a general Offer to all that would
venture out, that he would pay them out of his own Pocket 5s.
per head for all the Men whose Lives they could save, upon this
Proposal several offered themselves to go, if he would furnish
'em with Boats.

Finding the main Point clear, and that he had brought the
Men to be willing, he with their Assistance took away the
Custom House Boats by Force; and tho' he knew he could
not justify it, and might be brought into Trouble for it, and
particularly if it were lost, might be oblig'd to pay for it, yet he
resolv'd to venture that, rather than hazard the loss of his
Design, for the saving so many poor Men's Lives, and having
Mann'd their Boat with a Crew of stout honest Fellows, he with
them took away several other Boats from other Persons, who
made use of them only to Plunder and Rob, not regarding the
Distresses of the poor Men.

Being thus provided both with Men and Boats he sent them
off, and by this means brought on Shore above 200 Men, whose
Lives a few Minutes after, must infallibly ha' been lost.

Nor was this the End of his Care, for when the Tide came in, and 'twas too late to go off again, for that all that were left were swallow'd up with the Raging of the Sea, his Care was then to relieve the poor Creatures, who he had sav'd, and who almost dead with Hunger and Cold, were naked and starving.

And first he applied himself to the Queen's Agent *for Sick and Wounded Seamen*, but he would not relieve them with One Penny, whereupon, at his own Charge, he furnish'd them with Meat, Drink and Lodging.

The next Day several of them died, the Extremities they had suffer'd, having too much Master'd their Spirits, these he was forc'd to bury also at his own Charge, the Agent still refusing to Disburse one Penny.

After their Refreshment the poor Men assisted by the Mayor, made a fresh Application to the Agent for Conduct Money to help them up to *London*, but he answer'd he had no Order, and would Disburse nothing, whereupon the Mayor gave them all Money in their Pockets, and Passes to *Graves-End*.

I wish I could say with the same Freedom, that he receiv'd the Thanks of the Government, and Reimbursement of his Money as he deserv'd, but in this I have been inform'd, he met with great Obstructions and Delays, tho' at last, after long Attendance, upon a right Application I am inform'd he obtain'd the repayment of his Money, and some small Allowance for his Time spent in solliciting for it.

Nor can the Damage suffered in the River of *Thames* be forgot. It was a strange sight to see all the Ships in the River blown away, the Pool was so clear, that as I remember, not above 4 Ships were left between the Upper part of *Wapping*, and *Ratcliff Cross*, for the Tide being up at the Time when the Storm blew with the greatest violence. No Anchors or Landfast, no Cables or Moorings would hold them, the Chains which lay cross the River for the mooring of Ships, all gave way.

The Ships breaking loose thus, it must be a strange sight to see the Hurry and Confusion of it, and as some Ships had no Body at all on Board, and a great many had none but a Man or Boy left on Board just to look after the Vessel, there was nothing to be done, but to let every Vessel drive whither and how she would.

Those who know the Reaches of the River, and how they lye, know well enough, that the Wind being at South West Westerly, the Vessels would naturally drive into the Bite or Bay from *Ratcliff Cross* to *Lime-house Hole*, for that the River winding about again from thence towards the New Dock at *Deptford*, runs almost due South West, so that the Wind blew down one Reach, and up another, and the Ships must of necessity drive into the bottom of the Angle between both.

This was the Case, and as the Place is not large, and the Number of Ships very great, the force of the Wind had driven them so into one another, and laid them so upon one another as it were in heaps, that I think a Man may safely defy all the World to do the like.

The Author of this Collection had the curiosity the next day to view the place and to observe the posture they lay in, which nevertheless 'tis impossible to describe; there lay, by the best Account he could take, few less than 700 sail of Ships, some very great ones between *Shadwel* and *Limehouse* inclusive, the posture is not to be imagined, but by them that saw it, some Vessels lay heeling off with the Bow of another Ship over her Waste, and the Stem of another upon her Fore-Castle, the Bolt-sprits[18] of some drove into the Cabbin Windows of others; some lay with their Sterns tossed up so high, that the Tide flowed into their Fore-Castles before they cou'd come to Rights; some lay so leaning upon others, that the undermost Vessels wou'd sink before the other could float; the numbers of Masts, Boltsprits and Yards split and broke, the staving the Heads, and Sterns and Carved Work, the tearing and destruction of Rigging, and the squeezing of Boats to pieces between the Ships, is not to be reckoned; but there was hardly a Vessel to be seen that had not suffer'd some damage or other in one or all of these Articles.

There was several Vessels sunk in this hurry, but as they were generally light Ships, the damage was chiefly to the Vessels; but there were two Ships sunk with great quantity of Goods on Board, the *Russel* Galley was sunk at *Lime-house*, being a great part laden with Bale Goods for the *Streights*, and the *Sarah*

Gally lading for *Leghorn*, sunk at an Anchor at *Blackwall*; and though she was afterwards weighed and brought on shore, yet her back was broke, or so otherwise disabled, as she was never fit for the Sea; there were several Men drown'd in these last two Vessels, but we could never come to have the particular number.

Near *Gravesend* several Ships drove on shoar below *Tilbury* Fort, and among them five bound for the *West Indies*, but as the shoar is ouzy and soft, the Vessels sat upright and easy, and here the high Tides which follow'd, and which were the ruin of so many in other places, were the deliverance of all these Ships whose lading and value was very great, for the Tide rising to an unusual height, floated them all off, and the damage was not so great as was expected.

If it be expected I should give an account of the loss, and the particulars relating to small Craft, *as the Sailors call it*, in the River it is to look for what is impossible, other than by generals.

The Watermen[19] tell us of above 500 Wheries lost, most of which were not sunk only but dasht to pieces one against another, or against the Shores and Ships, where they lay: Ship Boats without number were driven about in every corner, sunk and staved, and about 300 of them is supposed to be lost. Above 60 Barges and Lighters[20] were found driven foul of the *Bridge*: some Printed accounts tell us of sixty more sunk or staved between the *Bridge* and *Hammersmith*.

Abundance of Lighters and Barges drove quite thro' the *Bridge*, and took their fate below, whereof many were lost, so that we Reckon by a modest account above 100 Lighters and Barges lost and spoil'd in the whole, not reckoning such as with small damage were recovered.

In all this confusion it could not be, but that many Lives were lost, but as the *Thames* often times Buries those it drowns, there has been no account taken. Two Watermen at *Black Fryars* were drowned, endeavouring to save their Boat; and a Boat was said to be Overset near *Fulham*, and five People drown'd: According to the best account I have seen, about 22 People were drown'd in the River upon this sad occasion, which considering all circumstances is not a great many, and the damage to Shipping computed with the vast number of Ships then in the River, the Violence of the Storm, and the heighth of the Tide, confirms me in the Truth of that Opinion, which I have heard many skilful Men own, *viz*. that the River of *Thames* is the best Harbour of *Europe*.

The heighth of the Tide, as I have already observ'd, did no great damage in the River of *Thames*, and I find none of the Levels or Marshes, which lye on both sides the River overflowed with it, it fill'd the Cellars indeed at *Gravesend*, and on both sides in *London*, and the Alehouse-keepers suffered some loss as to their Beer, but this damage is not worth mentioning with what our Accounts give us from the *Severn*; which, besides the particular Letters we have already quoted, the Reader may observe in the following, what our general intelligence furnishes us with.

The Damages in the City of *Gloucester* they compute at 12000 *l.* above 15000 Sheep drown'd in the Levels on the side of the *Severne*, and the Sea Walls will cost, as these Accounts tell us, 5000 *l.* to repair, all the Country lyes under Water for 20 or 30 Miles together on both sides, and the Tide rose three Foot higher than the tops of the Banks.

At *Bristol* they tell us, The Tide fill'd their Cellars, spoil'd 1000 Hogsheads of Sugar, 1500 Hogsheds of Tobacco, and the Damage they reckon at 100000 *l.* Above 80 People drown'd in the Marshes and River, Several whole Families perishing together.

The Harbour at *Plimouth*, the Castle at *Pendennis*, the Cathederal at *Gloucester*, the great Church at *Berkely*, the Church of St. *Stephen's* at *Bristol*; the Churches at *Blandford*, at *Bridgewater*, at *Cambridge*, and generally the Churches all over *England* have had a great share of the Damage.

In *King Road* at *Bristol*, the Damage by Sea is also very great; the *Canterbury* store Ship was driven on Shoar, and twenty-five of her Men drown'd, as by our account of the Navy will more particularly appear, the *Richard* and *John*, the *George*, and the *Grace* sunk, and the number of People lost is variously reported.

These Accounts in the four last Paragraphs being abstracted from the publick Prints, and what other Persons collect, I desire the Reader will observe, are not particularly vouch'd, but as they are all true in substance, they are so far to be depended upon, and if there is any mistake it relates to Numbers, and quantity only.

From *Yarmouth* we expected terrible News, and every one was impatient till they saw the Accounts from thence, for as there was a very great Fleet there, both of laden Colliers, *Russia* Men, and others, there was nothing to be expected but a dreadful Destruction among them.

But it pleas'd God to order Things there, that the loss was not in Proportion like what it was in other Places, not but that it was very great too.

The *Reserve* Man of War was come in but a day or two before, Convoy to the great Fleet from *Russia*, and the Captain, Surgeon and Clerk, who after so long a Voyage went on Shoar with two Boats to refresh themselves, and buy Provisions, had the Mortification to stand on Shoar, and see the Ship sink before their Faces; she foundred about 11-a-Clock, and as the Sea went too high for any help to go off from the Shoar to them, so their own Boats being both on Shoar, there was not one Man sav'd; one *Russia* Ship driving from her Anchors, and running foul of a laden Collier sunk by his side, but some of her Men were sav'd by getting on Board the Collier; three or four small Vessels were driven out to Sea, and never heard of more; as for the Colliers, tho' most of them were driven from their Anchors, yet going away to Sea, we have not an account of many lost.

This next to the Providence of God, I give this reason for, first by all Relations it appears that the Storm was not so violent farther Northward, as it was there; and as it was not so Violent, so neither did it continue so long: Now those Ships, who found they could not ride it out in *Yarmouth* Roads, but slipping their Cables went away to Sea, possibly as they went away to the Northward, found the Weather more moderate at least, not so violent, but it might be borne with, to this may be added, that 'tis well known to such as use the Coast after they had run the length of *Flambro*,[21] they had the benefit of the Weather Shoar, and pretty high land, which if they took shelter under might help them very much; these, with other Circumstances, made the Damage much less than every Body expected, and yet as it was, it was bad enough as our Letter from *Hull* gives an Account. At *Grimsby* it was still worse as to the Ships, where almost all the Vessels were blown out of the Road, and a great many lost.

At *Plymouth* they felt a full Proportion of the Storm in its utmost fury, the *Edystone* has been mention'd already, but it was a double loss in that, the light House had not been long down, when the *Winchelsea*, a homeward bound *Virginia* Man was split upon the Rock, where that Building stood, and most of her Men drowned.

Three other Merchant Ships were cast away in *Plimouth* Road, and most of their Men lost: The *Monk* Man of War rode it out, but was oblig'd to cut all her Masts by the Board, as several Men of War did in other places.

At *Portsmouth* was a great Fleet, as has been noted already, several of the Ships were blown quite out to Sea, whereof some were never heard of more; the *Newcastle* was heard off upon the Coast of *Sussex*, where she was lost with all their Men but 23; the *Resolution*, the *Eagle* advice Boat,[22] and the *Litchfield* Prize felt the same fate, only sav'd their Men: From *Cows* several Ships were driven out to Sea, whereof one run on Shoar in *Stokes-bay*, one full of Soldiers, and two Merchant Men have never heard off, as I could ever learn, abundance of the Ships sav'd themselves by cutting down their Masts, and others Stranded, but by the help of the ensuing Tides got off again.

Portsmouth, *Plymouth*, *Weymouth*, and most of our Sea Port Towns look'd as if they had been Bombarded, and the Damage of them is not easily computed.

Several Ships from the *Downs* were driven over to the Coast of *Holland*, and some sav'd themselves there; but several others were lost there.

At *Falmouth* 11 Sail of Ships were stranded on the Shoar, but most of them got off again.

In *Barstable* Harbour, a Merchant Ship outward bound was over-set, and the express advice Boat very much shatter'd, and the Quay of the Town almost destroy'd.

'Tis endless to attempt any farther Description of Losses, no place was free either by Land or by Sea, every thing that was capable felt the fury of the Storm; and 'tis hard to say, whether was greater the loss by Sea, or by Land; the Multitude of brave stout Sailors is a melancholy subject, and if there be any difference gives the sad Ballance to the Account of the Damage by Sea.

We had an Account of about 11 or 12 Ships droven over for the Coast of *Holland*, most of which were lost, but the Men saved, so that by the best Calculation I can make, we have not lost less than 150 sail of Vessels of all sorts by the Storm; the number of Men and other damages, are Calculated elsewhere.

We have several Branches of this Story which at first were too easily credited, and put in Print, but upon more strict examination, and by the discoveries of Time, appear'd otherwise, and therefore are not set down.

It was in the design to have Collected the several Accounts of the fatal effects of the Tempest abroad in Foreign Parts; but as our Accounts came in from thence too imperfect to be depended upon; the Collector of these Papers could not be satisfied to offer them to the World, being willing to keep as much as possible to the Terms of his Preface.

We are told there is an Abstract to the same purpose with this in *France*, Printed at *Paris*, and which contains a strange variety of Accidents in that Country.

If a particular of this can be obtained, the Author Promises to put it into *English*, and adding to them the other Accounts, which the rest of the World can afford, together with some other Additions of the *English* Affairs, which could not be obtain'd in time here shall make up the second part of this Work.

In the mean time the Reader may observe, *France* felt the general shock, the Peers, and Ricebank[23] at *Dunkirk*, the Harbour at *Haver de Grace*, the Towns of *Calais* and *Bulloign* give us strange Accounts.

All the Vessels in the Road before *Dunkirk*, being 23 or 27, I am not certain, were dasht in pieces against the Peer Heads, not one excepted, that side being a Lee shoar, the reason is plain, there was no going off to Sea; and had it been so with us in the *Downs* or *Yarmouth* Roads, it would have fared with us in the same manner, for had there been no going off to Sea, 300 sail in *Yarmouth* Roads had inevitably perisht.

At *Diepe* the like mischief happened, and in proportion *Paris* felt the effects of it, as bad as *London*, and as a Gentleman who came from thence since that time, affirmed it to me it was much worse.

All the N. East Countries felt it, in *Holland* our accounts in general are very dismal, but the Wind not being N. W. as at former Storms, the Tyde did not drown them, nor beat so directly upon their Sea Wall.

It is not very irrational to Judge, that had the Storm beat more to the North West, it must have driven the Sea upon them in such a manner, that all their Dikes and Dams could not have sustained it, and what the consequence of such an Inundation might ha' been they can best judge, who remember the last terrible Irruption of the Sea there, which drowned several thousand People, and Cattle without number.

But as our Foreign Accounts were not satisfactory enough to put into this Collection, where we have promised to limit our selves by just Vouchers, we purposely refer it all to a farther description as before.

Several of our Ships were driven over to those parts, and some lost there, and the story of our great Ships which rid it out, at or near the *Gunfleet*, should have come in here, if the Collector could have met with any Person that was in any of the said Vessels, but as the accounts he expected did not come in the time for the Impression, they were of necessity left out.

The *Association*, a Second Rate, on Board whereof was Sir *Stafford Fairborn*,[24] was one of these, and was blown from the Mouth of the *Thames* to the Coast of *Norway*, a particular whereof as Printed in the Annals of the Reign of Queen *Ann*'s is as follows.[25]

An Account of Sir Stafford Fairborne's Distress in the late Storm.

SIR,

Her Majesty's Ship *Association*, a second Rate of 96 Guns, commanded by Sir *Stafford Fairborne*, Vice-Admiral of the Red, and under him Captain *Richard Canning*, sailed from the *Downs* the 24th of *November* last, in Company with seven other Capital

Ships, under the Command of the Honourable Sir *Cloudesley Shovel*, Admiral of the White, in their return from *Leghorn* up the River. They anchored that Night off of the *Long-sand-head*. The next Day struck Yards and Top-Masts. The 27th about three in the Morning, the Wind at West South West, encreased to a Hurricane, which drove the *Association* from her Anchors. The Night was exceeding dark, but what was more Dreadful, the *Galloper*, a very dangerous Sand, was under her Lee; so that she was in Danger of striking upon it, beyond the Power of Man to avoid it. Driving thus at the Mercy of the Waves, it pleased God, that about five a Clock she passed over the tail of the *Galloper* in seven Fathom of Water. The Sea boisterous and angry, all in a Foam, was ready to swallow her up; and the Ship received at that time a Sea on her Starboard-side, which beat over all, broke and washed several half Ports, and forced in the entering Port.[26] She took in such a vast quantity of Water, that it kept her down upon her side, and every Body believ'd, that she could not have risen again, had not the Water been speedily let down into the hold by scuttling the Decks. During this Consternation two of the Lower-Gun-Deck-Ports were pressed open by this mighty weight of Water, the most hazardous Accident, next to touching the Ground, that could have happened to us. But the Port, that had been forced open, being readily secured by the Direction and Command of the Vice-Admiral, who, though much indisposed, was upon Deck all that time, prevented any farther Mischief. As the Ship still drove with the Wind, she was not long in this Shoal, (where it was impossible for any Ship to have lived at that time) but came into deeper Water, and then she had a smoother Sea. However the Hurricane did not abate, but rather seemed to gather Strength. For Words were no sooner uttered, but they were carried away by the Wind, so that although those upon Deck spoke loud and close to one another, yet they could not often distinguish what was said; and when they opened their Mouths, their Breath was almost taken away. Part of the Sprit Sail, tho' fast furled, was blown away from the Yard. A Ten-Oar-Boat, that was lashed on her Starboard-side, was often hove up by the Strength of the Wind, and over-set upon her Gun-Wale.[27] We plainly saw the Wind skimming up the Water, as if it had been Sand, carrying it

up into the Air, which was then so thick and gloomy, that Day
light, which should have been comfortable to us, did, but make it
appear more ghastly. The Sun by intervals peeped through the
corner of a Cloud, but soon disappearing, gave us a more melan-
cholick Prospect of the Weather. About 11 a Clock it dispersed
the Clouds, and the Hurricane abated into a more moderate
Storm, which drove us over to the Bank of *Flanders*, and thence
along the Coast of *Holland* and *Friesland* to the entrance of the
Elb, where the 4th of *December* we had almost as violent a Storm,
as when we drove from our Anchors, the Wind at North West,
driving us directly upon the Shoar. So that we must all have
inevitably perished, had not God mercifully favoured us about 10
a Clock at night with a South West Wind, which gave us an
opportunity to put to Sea. But being afterwards driven near the
Coast of *Norway*, the Ship wanting Anchors and Cables, our
Wood and Candles wholly expended; no Beer on Board, nor any
thing else in lieu; every one reduced to one quart of Water *per*
Day, the Men, who had been harrassed at *Belle Isle*;[28] and in our
Mediterranean Voyage, now jaded by the continual Fatigues of
the Storms, falling sick every Day, the Vice-Admiral in this exi-
gency thought it advisable to put into *Gottenbourgh*, the only
Port where we could hope to be supplied. We arrived there the
11th of *December*, and having without lost of time got Anchors
and Cables from *Copenhagen*, and Provisions from *Gotten-*
bourgh, we sailed thence the Third of *January*, with twelve Merchant Men under our Convoy, all loaden with Stores for her
Majesty's Navy. The Eleventh following we prevented four
French Privateers[29] from taking four of our Store-Ships. At Night
we anchored off the *Long-Sand-Head*. Weighed again the next
Day, but soon came to an Anchor, because it was very hazy
Weather. Here we rid against a violent Storm, which was like to
have put us to Sea. But after three Days very bad Weather, we
weighed and arrived to the *Buoy of the Nore* the 23d of *January*,
having run very great Risks among the Sands. For we had not
only contrary Winds, but also very tempestuous Winds. We lost
28 Men by Sickness, contracted by the Hardships which they
endur'd in the bad Weather; and had not Sir *Stafford Fairborne*
by his great care and diligence, got the Ship out of *Gottenbourgh*,

A LIST of such of Her Majesty's Ships, with their Commanders Names, as were cast away by the Violent Storm on Friday Night the 26th of November 1703. the Wind having been from the S. W. to W. S. W. and the Storm continuing from about Midnight to past Six in the Morning.

Rates.	Ships.	Number of Men before the Storm.	Guns.	Commanders.	Places where lost.	
Fourth	Reserve	258	54	John Anderson	Yarmouth Roads	Her Captain, Purser, Master, Chyrsurgeon, Clerk and Sixteen Men were Ashoar, the rest drowned.
Third	Northumberland	253	70	James Greenway		All their Men lost.
	Restoration	386	70	Fleetwood Emes		
	Sterling Castle	349	70	John Johnson	Goodwin Sands	Third Lieutenant, Chaplain, Cook Chyrsurgeon's Mate; four Marine Captains, and sixty-two Men saved.
Fourth	Mary	273	64	Rear Admiral Beaumont, Edward Hopson		Only one Man saved by Swimming from Wreck to Wreck, and getting to the Sterling Castle; the Captain Ashoar, as also the Purser.

Rates.	Ships.	Number of Men before the Storm.	Guns.	Commanders.	Places where lost.	
Fourth – cont.	Vigo ——	212	54	Thomas Long ——	Holland ——	Her Company saved except four.
Bomb. Vessel	Mortar ——	59	12	Raymond Raymond ——	Selsey ——	Their Officers and Men saved.
Advice Boat	Eagle ——	42	10	Nathan Bostock ——	Pemsey ——	
Third ——	Resolution ——	211	70	Thomas Liell ——		
Fourth ——	Newcastle ——	233	46	William Carter ——	Drove from Spithead, and lost upon the Coast near Chichester.	Carpenter and twenty-three Men saved.
Storeship ——	Canterbury ——	31	8	Thomas Blake ——	Bristol ——	Captain and twenty-five Men drown'd; the Ship recover'd, and order'd to be sold.
Bomb-Vessel	Portsmouth ——	44	4	George Hawes ——	Nore ——	Officers and Men lost.

The Van Guard, a Second Rate, was over-set at Chatham, but no Men lost, the Ship not being fitted out.

and by that prevented her being frozen up, most part of the Sailers had perished afterwards by the severity of the Winter, which is intolerable Cold in those parts.

Of the Damage to the Navy

This is a short but terrible Article, there was one Ship called the *York*, which was lost about 3 days before the great Storm off of *Harwich*, but most of the Men were saved.

The loss immediately sustain'd in the Royal Navy during the Storm, is included in the List hereunto annex'd, as appears from the Navy Books.

The damage done to the Ships that were sav'd, is past our Power to compute. The Admiral, Sir *Cloudesley Shovel* with the great Ships, had made sail but the day before out of the *Downs*, and were taken with the Storm as they lay at or near the *Gunfleet*, where they being well provided with Anchors and Cables, rid it out, tho' in great extremity, expecting death every minute.

The loss of small Vessels hir'd into the Service, and tending the Fleet, is not included in this, nor can well be, several such Vessels, and some with Soldiers on Board, being driven away to Sea, and never heard of more.

The loss of the *Light-House*, call'd the *Eddystone* at *Plymouth*, is another Article, of which we never heard any particulars other than this; that at Night it was standing, and in the Morning all the upper part from the Gallery was blown down, and all the People in it perished, and by a particular Misfortune, Mr. *Winstanly*,[1] the Contriver of it, a Person whose loss is very much regreted by such as knew him, as a very useful Man to his Country: The loss of that *Light-House* is also a considerable Damage, as 'tis very doubtful whether it will be ever attempted again, and as it was a great Security to the Sailors, many a good Ship having been lost there in former Times.

It was very remarkable, that, as we are inform'd, at the same time the *Light-House* abovesaid was blown down, the Model of it in Mr. *Windstanly*'s House at *Littlebury* in *Essex*, above 200 Miles from the *Light-House*, fell down, and was broken to pieces.

There are infinite Stories of like nature with these, the Disasters at Sea are full of a vast variety, what we have recommended to the view of the World in this History, may stand as an Abridgment; and the Reader is only to observe that these are the short Representations, by which he may guess at the most dreadful Night, these parts of the World ever saw.

To relate all Things, that report Furnishes us with, would be to make the story exceed common probability, and look like Romance.

Tis a sad and serious Truth, and this part of it is preserv'd to Posterity to assist them in reflecting on the Judgments of God, and handing them on for the Ages to come.

Of the Earthquake

Tho' this was some time after the Storm, yet as the Accounts of the Storm bring it with them in the following Letters, we cannot omit it.

The two following Letters are from the respective Ministers of *Boston* and *Hull*, and relate to the Account of the Earthquake, which was felt over most part of the County of *Lincoln* and the East Riding of *Yorkshire*.

The Letter from *Hull*, from the Reverend Mr. *Banks*, Minister of the Place, is very particular, and deserves intire Credit, both from the extraordinary Character of the worthy Gentleman who writes it, and from its exact Correspondence with other Accounts.

SIR,

I receiv'd yours, wherein you acquaint me with a Design that (I doubt not) will meet with that Applause and Acceptance from the World which it deserves; but am in no capacity to be any way serviceable to it my self, the late Hurricane having more frighted than hurt us in these Parts. I doubt not but your Intelligence in general from the Northern Parts of the Nation, supplies you with as little Matter as what you have from these hereabouts, it having been less violent and mischievous that way. Some Stacks of Chimneys were over-turn'd here, and from one of them a little Child of my own was (thanks be to God) almost miraculously preserv'd, with a Maid that lay in the Room with him. I hear of none else this way that was so much as in danger, the Storm beginning here later than I perceive it did in some other Places, its greatest Violence being betwixt 7 and 8 in the Morning, when most People were stirring.

The Earthquake, which the Publick Accounts mention to have happen'd at *Hull* and *Lincoln* upon the 28th *ult.* was felt here by some People about 6 in the Evening, at the same time that People there, as well as at *Grantham* and other Places, perceived it. We have some flying Stories about it which look like fabulous, whose Credit therefore I wou'd not be answerable for; as, that upon *Lincoln-Heath* the Ground was seen to open, and Flashes of Fire to issue out of the Chasm.

I doubt this Account will hardly be thought worth the Charge of Passage: Had there been any thing else of note, you had been very readily serv'd by,

SIR, Your Humble Servant,

Boston, Jan. 8. 1703.   E. K.

SIR,

I am afraid that you will believe me very rude, that yours, which I receiv'd the 12th of *April*, has not sooner receiv'd such an Answer as you expect and desire, and truly I think deserve; for, a Design so generous, as to undertake to transmit to Posterity, A Memorial of the dreadful Effects of the late terrible Tempest (that when God's Judgments are in the World, they may be made so publick, as to ingage the Inhabitants of the Earth to learn Righteousness) ought to receive all possible Encouragement.

But the true Reason why I writ no sooner, was, Because, by the most diligent Enquiries I cou'd make, I cou'd not learn what

Harm that dreadful Tempest did in the *Humber*; neither indeed can I yet give you any exact Account of it: for, the great Mischief was done in the Night; which was so Pitch-dark, that of above 80 Ships that then rid in the *Humber*, about *Grimsby* Road, very few escap'd some Loss or other, and none of 'em were able to give a Relation of any body but themselves.

The best Account of the Effects of the Storm in the *Humber*, that I have yet met with, I received but Yesterday, from Mr. *Peter Walls*, who is Master of that Watch-Tower, call'd the *Spurn-Light*, at the *Humber* Mouth, and was present there on the Night of the 26th of *November*, the fatal Night of the Storm.

He did verily believe that his Pharos[1] (which is above 20 Yards high) wou'd have been blown down; and the Tempest made the Fire in it burn so vehemently, that it melted down the Iron-bars on which it laid, like Lead; so that they were forced, when the Fire was by this means almost extinguished, to put in new Bars, and kindle the Fire a-fresh, which they kept in till the Morning Light appear'd: And then *Peter Walls* observed about six or seven and twenty Sail of Ships, all driving about the *Spurn-Head*, some having cut, others broke their Cables, but all disabled, and render'd helpless. These were a part of the two Fleets that then lay in the *Humber*, being put in there by stress of Weather a day or two before, some from *Russia*, and the rest of 'em *Colliers*, to and from *Newcastle*. Of these, three were driven upon an Island call'd the *Den*, within the *Spurn* in the Mouth of the *Humber*.

The first of these no sooner touch'd Ground, but she over-set, and turn'd up her Bottom; out of which, only one of six (the Number of that Ship's Company) was lost, being in the Shrowds: the other five were taken up by the second Ship, who had sav'd their Boat. In this Boat were saved all the Men of the three Ships aforementioned (except as before excepted) and came to Mr. *Walls*'s House, at the *Spurn-Head*, who got them good Fires, and all Accommodations necessary for them in such a Distress. The second Ship having no body aboard, was driven to Sea, with the Violence of the Tempest, and never seen or heard of more. The third, which was then a-ground, was (as he supposes) broken up and driven; for nothing, but some Coals that were in her, was to be seen the next Morning.

Another Ship, the Day after, *viz.* the 27th of *November*, was riding in *Grimsby* Road, and the Ships Company (except two Boys) being gone a-shore, the Ship, with the two Lads in her, drive directly out of *Humber*, and was lost, tho' 'tis verily believ'd the two Boys were saved by one of the *Russia* Ships, or Convoys.

The same Day, in the Morning, one *John Baines*, a *Yarmouth* Master, was in his Ship, riding in *Grimsby* Road, and by the Violence of the Storm, some other Ships coming foul upon him, part of his Ship was broken down, and was driven towards Sea; whereupon he anchored under *Kilnsey-Land*, and with his Crew came safe a-shore, in his Boat, but the Ship was never seen more.

The remainder of the six or seven and twenty Sail aforesaid, being (as was before observed) driven out of the *Humber*, very few, if any of 'em, were ever heard of; and 'tis rationally believ'd, that all, or the most of them, perished. And indeed, altho' the Storm was not so violent here as it was about *Portsmouth*, *Yarmouth* Roads, and the Southern Coast, yet the Crews of the three Ships above-mentioned declare, that they were never out in so dismal a Night as that was of the 26th of *November*, in which the considerable Fleet aforesaid rid in *Grimsby* Road in the *Humber*; for most of the 80 Sail broke from their Anchors, and run foul one upon another; but by reason of the Darkness of the Night, they cou'd see very little of the Mischief that was done.

This is the best Account I can give you at present of the Effects of the Tempest in the *Humber*; whereas had the Enquiry been made immediately after the Storm was over, a great many more of remarkable Particulars might have been discover'd.

As to the Earthquake here, tho' I perceiv'd it not my self (being then walking to visit a sick Parishoner) yet it was so sensibly felt by so many Hundreds, that I cannot in the least question the Truth and Certainty of it.

It happen'd here, and in these Parts, upon *Innocent*'s Day,[2] the 28th of *December*, being *Tuesday*, about Five of the Clock in the Evening, or thereabout. Soon after I gave as particular Account as I cou'd learn of it, to that ingenious Antiquary Mr. *Thorsby* of *Leeds* in *Yorkshire*,[3] but had no time to keep a Copy of my Letter to him, nor have I leisure to transcribe a Copy of this to you, having so constant a Fatigue of Parochial business to attend; nor will my Memory serve me to recollect all the Circumstances of that Earthquake, as I sent them to Mr. *Thoresby*; and possibly he may have communicated that Letter to you, or will upon your least intimation, being a generous Person, who loves to communicate any thing that may be serviceable to the Publick.

However, lest I shou'd seem to decline the gratifying your Request, I will recollect, and here set down, such of the Circumstances of that Earthquake as do at present occur to my Memory.

It came with a Noise like that of a Coach in the Streets, and mightily shak'd both the Glass Windows, Pewter, *China* Pots and Dishes, and in some places threw them down off the Shelves on which they stood. It did very little Mischief in this Town, except the throwing down a Piece of one Chimney. Several Persons thought that a great Dog was got under the Chair they sat upon; and others fell from their Seats, for fear of falling. It frighted several Persons, and caus'd 'em for a while to break off their Reading, or Writing, or what they were doing.

They felt but one Shake here: but a Gentleman in *Nottingham-shire* told me, that being then lame upon his Bed, he felt three Shakes, like the three Rocks of a Cradle, to and again.

At *Laceby* in *Lincolnshire*, and in several other Parts of that County, as well as of the Counties of *York* and *Nottingham*, the Earthquake was felt very sensibly; and particularly at *Laceby* aforesaid. There happen'd this remarkable Story.

On *Innocent*'s Day, in the Afternoon, several Morrice-Dancers came thither from *Grimsby*; and after they had Danc'd and play'd their Tricks, they went towards *Alesby*, a little Town not far off: and as they were going about Five a Clock, they felt two such terrible Shocks of the Earth, that they had much ado to hold their Feet, and thought the Ground was ready to open, and swallow 'em up. Whereupon thinking that God was angry at 'em for playing the Fool, they return'd immediately to *Laceby* in a great Fright, and the next Day home, not daring to pursue their intended Circuit and Dancing.

I think 'tis the Observation of Dr. *Willis*, that upon an Earthquake the Earth sends forth noisome Vapours which infect the Air, as the Air does our Bodies: and accordingly it has prov'd here, where we have ever since had a most sickly time, and the greatest Mortality that has been in this Place for 15 Years last past: and so I believe it has been over the greatest part of *England*. This, SIR, is the best Account I can give you of the Earthquake, which had com'd sooner, but that I was desirous to get likewise the best Account I cou'd of the Effects of the Storm in the *Humber*. My humble Service to the Undertakers: and if in any thing I am capable to serve them or you, please freely to command,

SIR, *Your most humble Servant*,

Ro. Banks.

We have a farther Account of this in two Letters from Mr. *Thoresby*, F.R.S. and written to the Publisher of the Philosophical Transactions, and printed in their Monthly Collection, No. 289. as follows, which is the same mentioned by Mr. *Banks*.

Part of two Letters from Mr. Thoresby, F. R. S. *to the Publisher, concerning an Earthquake, which happen'd in some Places of the North of* England, *the 28th of* December 1703.[4]

You have heard, no doubt, of the late *Earthquake* that affected some part of the North, as the dreadful Storm did the South. It being most observable at *Hull*, I was desirous of an Account from thence that might be depended upon; and therefore writ to the very obliging Mr. *Banks*, Prebendary of *York*, who being Vicar of *Hull*, was the most suitable Person I knew to address my self unto: and he being pleased to favour me with a judicious Account of it, I will venture to communicate it to you, with his pious Reflection thereupon. 'As to the Earthquake you mention, it was felt here on *Tuesday* the 28th of the last Month, which was *Childermas* Day, about three or four Minutes after Five in the Evening. I confess I did not feel it my self; for I was at that moment walking to visit a sick Gentleman, and the Noise in the Streets, and my quick Motion, made it impossible, I believe, for me to feel it: but it was so almost universally felt, that there can be no manner of doubt of the Truth of it.

Mr. *Peers*, my Reader, (who is an ingenious good Man) was then at his Study, and Writing; but the heaving up of his Chair and his Desk, the Shake of his Chamber, and the rattling of his Windows, did so amaze him, that he was really affrighted, and was forc'd for a while to give over his Work: and there are twenty such Instances amongst Tradesmen, too tedious to repeat. My Wife was then in her Closet, and thought her *China* would have come about her Ears, and my Family felt the Chairs mov'd, in which they were sitting by the Kitchen Fire-side, and heard such a Rattle of the Pewter and Windows as almost affrighted them. A Gentlewoman not far off said, her Chair lifted so high, that she thought the great Dog had got under it, and to save her self from falling, slipt off her Chair. I sent to a House where part of a Chimney was shak'd down, to enquire of the particulars; they kept Ale, and being pretty full of Company that they were merry, they did not perceive the Shock, only heard the Pewter and Glass-windows dance; but the Landlady's Mother, who was in a Chamber by her self, felt the Shock so violent, that she verily believed the House to be coming down (as part of the Chimney afore mention'd did at the same Moment) and cried out in a Fright, and had fall'n, but that she catched hold of a Table. It came and went suddenly, and was attended with a Noise like the Wind, though there was then a perfect Calm.'

From other Hands I have an Account that it was felt in *Beverly*, and other Places; at *South Dalton* particularly, where the Parson's Wife (my own Sister) being alone in her Chamber, was sadly frighted with the heaving up of the Chair she sat in, and the very sensible Shake of the Room, especially the Windows, *&c.* A Relation of mine, who is a Minister near *Lincoln*, being then at a Gentleman's House in the Neighbourhood, was amaz'd at the Moving of the Chairs they sat upon, which was so violent, he writes every Limb of him was shaken; I am told also from a true Hand, that so nigh us as *Selby*, where Mr. *Travers*, a Minister, being in his Study writing, was interrupted much as Mr. *Peers* above-mentioned; which minds me of worthy Mr. *Bank*'s serious Conclusion. 'And now I hope you will not think it unbecoming my Character to make this Reflection upon it, *viz.* that Famines, Pestilences and Earthquakes, are joyned by our Blessed Saviour, as portending future Calamities, and particularly the Destruction of *Jerusalem* and the *Jewish* State; if not the End of the World,

St. *Matth*. 24. 7. And if, as Philosophers observe, those gentler Convulsions within the Bowels of the Earth, which give the Inhabitants but an easie Jog, do usually portend the Approach of some more dreadful Earthquake; then surely we have Reason to fear the worst, because I fear we so well deserve it, and pray God of his infinite Mercy to avert his future Judgments.'

Since my former Account of the Earthquake at *Hull*, my Cousin *Cookson* has procured to me the following Account from his Brother, who is a Clergyman near *Lincoln*, viz, That he, being about Five in the Evening, *December* the 20th past, set with a neighbouring Minister at his House about a Mile from *Navenby*, they were surpriz'd with a sudden Noise, as if it had been of two or three Coaches driven furiously down the Yard, whereupon the Servant was sent to the Door, in Expectation of some Strangers; but they quickly perceived what it was, by the shaking of the Chairs they sat upon; they could perceive the very Stones move: the greatest Damage was to the Gentlewoman of the House, who was put into such a Fright, that she miscarried two Days after. He writes, they were put into a greater Fright upon the Fast-day; when there was so violent a Storm, they verily thought the Church would have fallen upon them. We had also at *Leedes* a much greater Storm the Night preceding the Fast, and a stronger Wind that Day, than when the fatal Storm was in the South; but a good Providence timed this well, to quicken our too cold Devotions.

Of remarkable Deliverances

As the sad and remarkable Disasters of this Terrible Night were full of a Dismal Variety, so the Goodness of Providence, in the many remarkable Deliverances both by Sea and Land, have their Share in this Account, as they claim an equal Variety and Wonder.

The Sense of extraordinary Deliverances, as it is a Mark of Generous Christianity, so I presume 'tis the best Token, that a good Use is made of the Mercies receiv'd.

The Persons, who desire a thankful Acknowledgement should be made to their Merciful Deliverer, and the Wonders of his Providence remitted to Posterity, shall never have it to say, that the Editor of this Book refus'd to admit so great a Subject a Place in these Memoirs; and therefore, with all imaginable Freedom, he gives the World the Particulars from their own Mouths, and under their own Hands.

The first Account we have from the Reverend Mr. *King*, Lecturer at St. *Martins* in the Fields, as follows.

SIR,

The short Account I now send to shew the Providence of God in the late Dreadful Storm, (if yet it comes not too late) I had from the Mouth of the Gentleman himself, Mr. *Woodgate Gisser* by Name, who is a Neighbour of mine, living in St. *Martin's-street* in the Parish of St. *Martins* in the Fields, and a Sufferer in the common Calamity; is as follows, *viz.*

Between Two and Three of the Clock in the Morning, my Neighbour's Stack of Chimneys fell, and broke down the Roof of my Garret into the Passage going up and down Stairs; upon which, I thought it convenient to retire into the Kitchen with my Family; where we had not been above a Quarter of an Hour, before my Wife sent her Maid to fetch some Necessaries out of a Back Parlour Closet, and as she had shut the Door, and was upon her Return, the very same Instant my Neighbour's Stack of Chimneys, on the other Side of the House, fell upon my Stack, and beat in the Roof, and so drove down the several Floors through the Parlour into the Kitchen, where the Maid was buried near Five Hours in the Rubbish, without the least Damage or Hurt whatsoever: This her miraculous Preservation was occasion'd (as, I afterwards with Surprize found) by her falling into a small Cavity near the Bed, and afterwards (as she declar'd) by her creeping under the Tester that lay hollow by Reason of some Joices that lay athwart each other, which prevented her perishing in the said Rubbish: About Eight in the Morning, when I helped her out of the Ruins, and asked her how she did, and why she did not cry out for Assistance, since she was not (as I suppos'd she had been) dead, and so to let me know she was alive; her Answer was, that truly she for her Part had felt no Hurt, and was not the least affrighted, but lay quiet; and which is more, even slumbred until then.

The Preservation of my self, and the rest of my Family, about Eleven in Number, was, next to the Providence of God, occasion'd by our running into a Vault almost level with the Kitchen upon the Noise and Alarm of the Falling of the Chimneys, which breaking through three Floors, and about two Minutes in passing, gave us the Opportunities of that Retreat. Pray accept of this short Account from

Your Humble Servant, and Lecturer,

Feb. 12. 1703.   James King, *M.A.*

Another is from a Reverend Minister at — whose Name is to his Letter as follows.

SIR,

I thank you for your charitable Visit not long since; I could have heartily wish'd your Business would have permitted you to have made a little longer Stay at the parsonage, and then you might have taken a stricter View of the Ruins by the late terrible Wind. Seeing you are pleas'd to desire from me a more particular Account of that sad Disaster; I have for your fuller Satisfaction sent you the best I am able to give; and if it be not so perfect, and so exact a one, as you may expect, you may rely upon me it is a true, and a faithful one, and that I do not impose upon you, or the World in the least in any Part of the following Relation. I shall not trouble you with the Uneasiness the Family was under all the fore Part of the Evening, even to a Fault, as I thought, and told them, I did not then apprehend the Wind to be much higher than it had been often on other Times; but went to Bed, hoping we were more afraid than we needed to have been: when in Bed, we began to be more sensible of it, and lay most of the Night awake, dreading every Blast till about Four of the Clock in the Morning, when to our thinking it seemed a little to abate; and then we fell asleep, and slept till about Six of the Clock, at which Time my Wife waking, and calling one of her Maids to rise, and come to the Children, the Maid rose, and hasten'd to her; she had not been up above Half an Hour, but all on the sudden we heard a prodigious Noise, as if part of the House had been fallen down; I need not tell you the Consternation we were all in upon this Alarm; in a Minutes Time, I am sure, I was surrounded with all my Infantry, that I thought I should have been overlay'd; I had not even Power to stir one Limb of me, much less to rise, though I could not tell how to lie in Bed. The Shrieks and the Cries of my dear Babes perfectly stun'd me; I think I hear them still in my Ears, I shall not easily, I am confident, if ever, forget them. There I lay preaching Patience to those little Innocent Creatures, till the Day began to appear.

Preces & Lachrimæ, Prayers and Tears, the Primitive Christians Weapons, we had great Plenty of to defend us withal; but had the House all fallen upon our Heads, we were in that Fright as we could scarce have had Power to rise for the present, or do any thing for our Security. Upon our rising, and sending a Servant to view what she could discover, we soon understood that the Chimney was fallen down, and that with its Fall it had beaten down a great part of that End of the House, *viz.* the Upper Chamber, and the Room under it, which was the Room I chose for my Study: The Chimney was thought as strong, and as well built as most in the Neighbourhood; and it surpriz'd the Mason (whom I immediately sent for to view it) to see it down: but that which was most surprizing to me, was the Manner of its Falling; had it fallen almost any other Way than that it did, it must in all Likelihood have killed the much greater part of my Family, for no less than Nine of us lay at that End of the House, my Wife and Self, and Five Children, and Two Servants, a Maid, and a Man then in my Pay, and so a Servant, though not by the Year: The Bed my Eldest Daughter and the Maid lay in joyned as near as possible to the Chimney, and it was within a very few Yards of the Bed that we lay in; so that as *David* said to *Jonathan*, there seem'd to be but one single Step between Death and us, to all outward Appearance.[1] One Thing I cannot omit, which was very remarkable and surprizing: It pleased God so to order it, that in the Fall of the House two great Spars seem'd to fall so as to pitch themselves on an End, and by that Means to support that other

Part of the House which adjoined to the Upper Chamber; or else in all Likelihood, that must also have fallen too at the same Time. The Carpenter (whom we sent for forthwith) when he came, ask'd who plac'd those two Supporters, supposing somebody had been there before him; and when he was told, those two Spars in the Fall so plac'd themselves, he could scarce believe it possible; it was done so artificially, that he declar'd, they scarce needed to have been removed.

In short, Sir, it is impossible to describe the Danger we were in; you your self was an Eye-witness of some Part of what is here related; and I once more assure you, the whole Account I have here given you is true, and what can be attested by the whole Family. None of all those unfortunate Persons who are said to have been killed with the Fall of a Chimney, could well be much more expos'd to Danger than we were; it is owing wholly to that watchful Providence to whom we all are indebted for every Minute of our Lives, that any of us escaped; none but he who never sleeps nor slumbers could have secured us. I beseech Almighty God to give us All that due Sense as we ought to have of so great and so general Calamity; that we truly repent us of those Sins that have so long provoked his Wrath against us, and brought down so heavy a Judgment as this upon us. O that we were so wise as to consider it, and to *sin no more lest a worse thing come upon us!* That it may have this happy Effect upon all the sinful Inhabitants of this Land is, and shall be, the Dayly Prayer of Dear Sir,

Your real Friend and Servant,

John Gipps.

Another Account from a Reverend Minister in *Dorsetshire*, take as follows, *viz.*

SIR,

As you have desired an Account of the Disasters occasion'd by the late Tempest, (which I can assure you was in these Parts very Terrible) so I think my self oblig'd to let you know, that there was a great Mixture of Mercy with it: For though the Hurricane was frightful, and very mischievous, yet God's gracious Providence was therein very remarkable, in restraining its Violence from an universal Destruction: for then there was a Commotion of the Elements of Air, Earth and Water, which then seemed to outvie each other in Mischief; for (in *David*'s Expression, 2 *Sam*. 22. 8.) *The Earth trembled and quak'd, the Foundations of the Heavens mov'd and shook, because God was angry*: and yet, when all was given over for lost, we found our selves more scar'd than hurt; for our Lives was given us for a Prey, and the Tempest did us only so much Damage, as to make us sensible that it might have done us a great deal more, had it not been rebuk'd by the God of Mercy; the Care of whose Providence has been visibly seen in our wonderful Preservations. My Self and Three more of this Parish were then strangely rescued from the Grave: I narrowly escaped with my Life, where I apprehended nothing of Danger; for going out about Midnight to give Orders to my Servants to secure the House, and Reeks[2] of Corn and Furses from being blown all away; as soon as I mov'd out of the Place were I stood, I heard something of a great Weight fall close behind me, and a little after going out with a Light, to see what it was, I found it to be the great Stone which covered the Top of my Chimney to keep out the Wet; it was almost a Yard square, and very thick, weighing about an Hundred and Fifty Pound. It was blown about a Yard off from the Chimney, and fell Edge-long, and cut the Earth, about four Inches deep, exactly between my Foot-steps; and a little after, whilst sitting under the Clavel[3] of my Kitchen Chimney, and reaching out my Arm for some Fewel to mend the Fire, I was again strangely preserved from being knock'd on the Head by a Stone of great Weight; it being about a Foot long, Half a Foot broad, and two Inches thick: for as soon as I had drawn in my Arm, I felt something brush against my Elbow, and presently I heard the Stone fall close by my Foot, a third Part of which was broken off by the Violence of the Fall, and skarr'd my Ancle, but did not break the Skin; it had certainly killed me, had it fallen while my Arm was extended. The Top of my Wheat Rick was blown off, and some of the Sheaves were carried a Stones Cast, and with that Violence, that one of them, at that Distance, struck down one *Daniel Fookes* a late Servant of the Lady *Napier*, and so forceably, that he was taken up dead, and to all Appearance remain'd so a great while; but at last was happily recover'd to Life again. His Mother, poor Widow, was at the same time more fatally threatned at Home, and her Bed had certainly prov'd her Grave, had not the first Noise awaken'd and scar'd her out of Bed; and she was scarce gotten to the Door, when the House fell all in: The Smith's Wife likewise being scar'd at such a Rate, leapt out of Bed, with the little Child in her Arms, and ran hastily out of Doors naked, without Hose or Shooes, to a Neighbour's House; and by that hasty Flight, both their Lives were wonderfully preserved. The Sheets of Lead on *Lytton* Church, were rolled up like Sheets of Parchment, and blown off to a great Distance. At *Strode*, a large Apple Tree, being about a Foot in Square, was broken off cleverly like a Stick, about four Foot from the Root, and carried over an Hedge about ten Foot high; and cast, as if darted, (with the Trunk forward) above fourteen Yards off. And I am credibly inform'd, that at *Ellwood* in the Parish of *Abbotsbury*, a large Wheat Rick (belonging to one *Jolyffe*) was cleverly blown, with its Staddle, off from the Stones, and set down on the Ground in very good Order. I would fain know of the Atheist what mov'd his *Omnipotent Matter* to do such Mischief, &c.

> SIR, *I am*,
> *Your Affectionate Friend and Servant,*
> *though unknown,*

Jacob Cole, *Rect. of* Swyre in County of *Dorset*.

This Account is very remarkable, and well attested, and the Editor of this Collection can vouch to the Reputation of the Relators, tho' not to the Particulars of the Story.

A great Preservation in the late Storm

About Three of the Clock in the Morning, the Violence of the Wind blew down a Stack of Chimneys belonging to the dwelling House of Dr. *Gideon Harvey*, (situate in St. *Martin*'s Lane over against the Street End) on the back Part of the next House, wherein dwells Mr. *Robert Richards* an Apothecary, at the Sign

of the Unicorn; and Capt. *Theodore Collier* and his Family lodges
in the same. The Chimney fell with that Force as made them
pierce thro' the Roofs and all the Floors, carrying them down
quite to the Ground. The two Families, consisting of Fourteen,
Men, Women, and Children, besides Three that came in from
the next House, were at that Instant dispos'd of as follows, a
Footman that us'd to lie in the back Garret, had not a Quarter of
an Hour before remov'd himself into the fore Garret, by which
means he escap'd the Danger: In the Room under that lay Capt.
Collier's Child, of Two Months old, in Bed with the Nurse, and
a Servant Maid lay on the Bed by her; the Nurse's Child lying in
a Cribb by the Bed-side, which was found, with the Child safe in
it, in the Kitchen, where the Nurse and Maid likewise found
themselves; their Bed being shatter'd in Pieces, and they a little
bruis'd by falling down Three Stories: Capt. *Collier*'s Child was
in about Two Hours found unhurt in some Pieces of the Bed
and Curtains, which had fallen through Two Floors only, and
hung on some broken Rafters in that Place, which was the
Parlour: In the Room under This, being one Pair of Stairs from
the Street, and two from the Kitchen, was Capt. *Collier* in his
Bed, and his Wife just by the Bed-side, and her Maid a little
behind her, who likewise found her self in the Kitchin a little
bruis'd, and ran out to cry for Help for her Master and Mistress,
who lay buried under the Ruins: Mrs. *Collier* was, by the timely
Aid of Neighbours who remov'd the Rubbish from her, taken out
in about Half an Hours Time, having receiv'd no Hurt but the
Fright, and an Arm a little bruis'd: Capt. *Collier* in about Half an
Hour more was likewise taken out unhurt. In the Parlour were
sitting Mr. *Richards* with his Wife, the Three Neighbours, and
the rest of his Family, a little Boy of about a Year old lying in the
Cradle, they all run out at the first Noise, and escap'd, Mrs.
Richards staying a little longer than the rest, to pull the Cradle
with her child in it along with her, but the House fell too sud-
denly on it, and buried the Child under the Ruins, a Rafter fell on
her Foot, and bruis'd it a little, at which she likewise made her
Escape, and brought in the Neighbours, who soon uncovered the
Head of the Cradle, and cutting it off, took the Child out alive

and well. This wonderful Preservation being worthy to be transmitted to Posterity, we do attest to be true in every Particular.
Witness our Hands,

                                                            Gideon Harvey.
London,   *Theo. Collier.*
Nov. 27. 1703.   *Robert Richards.*

These Accounts of like Nature are particularly attested by
Persons of known Reputation and Integrity.

SIR,

In order to promote the good Design of your Book, in perpetuating
the Memory of God's signal Judgment on this Nation, by the late
dreadful Tempest of Wind, which has hurl'd so many Souls into
Eternity; and likewise his Providence in the miraculous Preservation of several Persons Lives, who were expos'd to the utmost
Hazards in that Hurricane: I shall here give you a short but true
Instance of the latter, which several Persons can witness besides
my self; and if you think proper may insert the same in the Book
you design for that Purpose; which is as follows. At the *Saracen's*
Head in *Friday* Street, a Country Lad lodging three Pair of Stairs
next the Roof of the House, was wonderfully preserv'd from
Death; for about Two a Clock that *Saturday* Morning the
27th of *November*, (which prov'd fatal to so many) there fell a
Chimney upon the Roof, under which he lay, and beat it down
through the Ceiling (the Weight of the Tiles, Bricks, *&c.* being
judged by a Workman to be about Five Hundred Weight) into
the Room, fell exactly between the Beds Feet and Door of the
Room, which are not Two Yards distance from each other, it
being but small: the sudden Noise awaking the Lad, he jumps out
of Bed endeavouring to find the Door, but was stopt by the
great Dust and falling of more Bricks, *&c.* and finding himself
prevented, in this Fear he got into Bed again, and remain'd there
till the Day Light, (the Bricks and Tiles still falling between-whiles
about his Bed) and then got up without any Hurt, or so much as
a Tile or Brick falling on the Bed; the only thing he complain'd of
to me, was his being almost choak'd with Dust when he got out

of Bed, or put his Head out from under the Cloaths: There was a great Weight of Tiles and Bricks, which did not break through, as the Workmen inform me, just over the Beds Tester, enough to have crush'd him to Death, if they had fallen: Thus he lay safe among the Dangers that threatned him, whilst wakeful Providence preserv'd him. And SIR, if this be worthy your taking Notice of, I am ready to justify the same. In Witness whereof, here is my Name,

Dec. 3. 1703.   *Henry Mayers.*

A great Preservation in the late Storm

William Phelps and *Frances* his Wife, living at the Corner of *Old Southampton Buildings*, over against *Gray's-Inn Gate* in *Holborn*, they lying up three pair of Stairs, in the Backroom, that was only lath'd and plaister'd, he being then very ill, she was forc'd to lie in a Table-Bed in the same Room: about One a Clock in the Morning, on the 27th of *November* last, the Wind blew down a Stack of Chimneys of seven Funnels[4] that stood very high; which broke through the Roof, and fell into the Room, on her Bed; so that she was buried alive, as one may say: she crying out, *Mr.* Phelps, *Mr.* Phelps, *the House is fall'n upon me*, there being so much on her that one could but just hear her speak; a Coachman and a Footman lying on the same Floor, I soon call'd them to my Assistance. We all fell to work, tho' we stood in the greatest Danger; and through the Goodness of God we did take her out, without the least hurt; neither was any of us hurt, tho' there was much fell after we took her out. And when we took the Bricks off the Bed the next Morning, we found the Frame of the Bed on which she lay broke all to pieces.

William Phelps.

Another great Preservation

Mr. *John Hanson*, Register of *Eaton College*, being at *London* about his Affairs, and lying that dreadful Night, *Nov.* 26, at the *Bell-Savage Inn* on *Ludgate Hill*, was, by the Fall of a Stack of Chimneys (which broke through the Roof, and beat down two

Floors above him, and also that in which he lay) carried in his
Bed down to the Ground, without the least hurt, his Cloaths,
and every thing besides in the Room, being buried in the Rubbish; it having pleased God so to order it, that just so much of
the Floor and Ceiling of the Room (from which he fell) as
covered his Bed, was not broken down. Of this great Mercy he
prays he may live for ever mindful, and be for ever thankful to
Almighty God.

SIR,

The Design of your Collecting the remarkable Accidents of the
late Storm coming to my Hands, I thought my self obliged to take
this Opportunity of making a publick Acknowledgment of the
wonderful Providence of Heaven to me, namely, the Preservation
of my only Child from imminent Danger.

Two large Stacks of Chimneys, containing each five Funnels,
beat through the Roof, in upon the Bed where she lay, without
doing her the least Harm, the Servant who lay with her being very
much bruised. There were several Loads of Rubbish upon the Bed
before my Child was taken out of it.

This extraordinary Deliverance I desire always thankfully to
remember.

I was so nearly touch'd by this Accident, that I could not take
so much notice as I intended of this Storm; yet I observ'd the
Wind gradually to encrease from One a Clock till a Quarter after
Five, or thereabouts: at which time it seem'd to be at the highest;
when every Gust did not only return with greater Celerity, but
also with more Force.

From about a Quarter before Six it sensibly decreas'd. I went
often to the Door, at which times I observ'd, that every Gust was
preceded by small Flashes, which, to my Observation, did not
dart perpendicularly, but seem'd rather to skim along the Surface
of the Ground; nor did they appear to be of the same kind with
the common Light'ning Flashes.

I must confess I cannot help thinking that the Earth it self
suffer'd some Convulsion; and that for this Reason, because
several Springs, for the space of 48 Hours afterwards, were very

muddy, which were never known to be so by any Storm of Wind or Rain before: nor indeed is it possible, they lying so low, could be affected by any thing less than a Concussion of the Earth it self.

How far these small Hints may be of use to the more ingenious Enquirers into this matter, I shall humbly leave to their Consideration, and subscribe my self,

SIR, *Your humble Servant,*

Joseph Clench,

Apothecary in Jermyn *Street,*
Dec. 8, 1703.   *near* St. James's.

SIR,

This comes to let you know that I received yours in the *Downs,* for which I thank you. I expected to have seen you in *London* before now, had we not met with a most violent Storm in our way to *Chatham.* On the 27th of the last Month, about Three of the Clock in the Morning, we lost all our Anchors and drove to Sea: about Six we lost our Rother,[5] and were left in a most deplorable condition to the merciless Rage of the Wind and Seas: we also sprung a Leak, and drove 48 Hours expecting to perish. But it pleased God to give us a wonderful Deliverance, scarce to be parallell'd in History; for about Midnight we were drove into shoul Water,[6] and soon after our Ship struck upon the Sands: the Sea broke over us, we expected every minute that she would drop to pieces, and that we should all be swallowed up in the Deep; but in less than two hours time we drove over the Sands, and got (without Rother or Pilot, or any Help but Almighty God's) into this Place, where we run our Ship on shore, in order to save our Lives: but it has pleased God also, far beyond our expectation, to save our Ship, and bring us safe off again last Night. We shall remain here a considerable while to refit our Ship, and get a new Rother. Our Deliverance is most remarkable, that in the middle of a dark Night we should drive over a Sand where a Ship that was not half our Bigness durst not venture to come in the Day; and then, without knowing where we were, drive into a narrow place where we have saved both Lives and Ship. I pray God give us all Grace to be thankful, and never forget so great a mercy.

I am,

Your affectionate Friend and humble Servant,

Russell, at *Helversluce* in
Holland, Dec. 16. 1703.   Henry Barclay.

SIR

According to the publick Notice, I send you two or three Observations of mine upon the late dreadful Tempest: As,

1. In the Parish of St. *Mary Cray, Kent*, a poor Man, with his Wife and Child, were but just gone out of their Bed, when the Head of their House fell in upon it; which must have kill'd them.

2. A great long Stable in the Town, near the Church, was blown off the Foundation entirely at one sudden Blast, from the West-side to the East, and cast out into the High-way, over the Heads of five Horses, and a Carter feeding them at the same time, and not one of them hurt, nor the Rack or Manger touch'd, which are yet standing to the Admiration of all Beholders.

3. As the Church at *Heyes* received great Damage, so the Spire, with one Bell in it, were blown away over the Church yard.

4. The Minister of *South-Ash* had a great Deliverance from a Chimney falling in upon his Bed just as he rose, and hurt only his Feet; as blessed be God, our Lives have been all very miraculously preserv'd, tho' our Buildings every where damag'd. You may depend on all, as certify'd by me,

Thomas Watts,

Vicar of Orpington *and St.* Mary Cray.

There are an innumerable variety of Deliverances, besides these, which deserve a Memorial to future Ages; but these are noted from the Letters, and at the Request of the Persons particularly concern'd.

Particularly, 'tis a most remarkable Story of a Man belonging to the *Mary*, a fourth Rate Man of War, lost upon the *Goodwin*

Sands; and all the Ship's Company but himself being lost, he, by the help of a piece of the broken Ship, got a-board the *Northumberland*; but the Violence of the Storm continuing, the *Northumberland* ran the same fate with the *Mary*, and coming on shore upon the same Sand, was split to pieces by the Violence of the Sea: and yet this Person, by a singular Providence, was one of the 64 that were delivered by a *Deal Hooker* out of that Ship, all the rest perishing in the Sea.

A poor Sailor of *Brighthelmston* was taken up after he had hung by his Hands and Feet on the top of a Mast 48 hours, the Sea raging so high, that no Boat durst go near him.

A Hoy run on shore on the Rocks in *Milford* Haven, and just splitting to pieces (as by Captain *Soam*'s Letter) a Boat drove by, being broke from another Vessel, with no body in it, and came so near the Vessel, as that two Men jumpt into it, and sav'd their Lives: the Boy could not jump so far, and was drowned.

Five Sailors shifted three Vessels on an Island near the *Humber* and were at last sav'd by a Long-boat out of the fourth.

A Waterman in the River of *Thames* lying asleep in the Cabbin of a Barge, at or near *Black-Fryers*, was driven thro' Bridge in the Storm, and the Barge went of her self into the *Tower-Dock*, and lay safe on shore; the Man never wak'd, nor heard the Storm, till 'twas Day; and, to his great Astonishment, he found himself safe as above.

Two Boys in the *Poultry* lodging in a Garret or Upper-room, were, by the Fall of Chimneys, which broke thro' the Floors, carried quite to the bottom of the Cellar, and receiv'd no Damage at all.

SIR,

At my Return home on *Saturday* at Night, I receiv'd yours: and having said nothing in my last concerning the Storm, I send this to tell you, that I hear of nothing done by it in this Country that may seem to deserve a particular Remark. Several Houses and Barns were stript of their Thatch, some Chimneys and Gables blown down, and several Stacks of Corn and Hay very much dispers'd; but I hear not of any Persons either kill'd or maim'd. A

Neighbour of ours was upon the Ridge of his Barn endeavouring
to secure the Thatch, and the Barn at that instant was overturn'd
by the Storm; but by the good Providence of God, the Man
received little or no harm. I say no more, not knowing of any
thing more remarkable. I am sorry that other Places were such
great Sufferers, and I pray God avert the like Judgments for the
future. I am

Your real Friend to serve you,

Orby, Dec. 18. 1703.   Hen. Marshal.

SIR,

I have no particular Relation to make to you of any Deliverance in
the late Storm, more than was common with me to all the rest
that were in it: but having, to divert melancholly Thoughts while it
lasted, turn'd into Verse the CXLVIII Psalm to the 9th, and afterwards all the Psalm; I give you leave to publish it with the rest of
those Memoirs on that Occasion you are preparing for the Press.

SIR, Your, &c.

Henry Squier.

I. Verse 1, 2

Hallelujah: From Heav'n
The tuneful Praise begin;
Let Praise to God be giv'n
Beyond the Starry Scene:
Ye Angels sing
His joyful Praise;
Your Voices raise
Ye swift of Wing.

II. 3, 4

Praise him, thou radiant Sun,
The Spring of all thy Light;
Praise him thou changing Moon,
And all the Stars of Night:

Ye Heav'ns declare
   His glorious Fame;
   And waves that swim
Above the Sphere.

III. 5, 6

Let all his Praises sing,
   His Goodness and his Power,
For at his Call they spring,
   And by his Grace endure;
      That joins 'em fast,
         The Chain is fram'd,
         Their Bounds are nam'd,
      And never past.

IV. 7, 8

Thou Earth his Praise proclaim,
   Devouring Gulfs and Deeps;
Ye Fires, and fire-like Flame,
   That o'er the Meadows sweeps;
      Thou rattling Hail,
         And flaky Snow,
         And Winds that blow
      To do his Will.

V. 9, 10

Ye Prodigies of Earth,
   And Hills of lesser size,
Cedars of nobler Birth,
   And all ye fruitful Trees;
      His Praises show
         All things that move,
         That fly above,
      Or creep below.

VI. 11, 12

Monarchs, and ye their Praise,
  The num'rous Multitude;
Ye Judges, Triumphs raise;
And all of nobler Blood:
    Of ev'ry kind,
      And ev'ry Age,
        Your Hearts engage,
    In Praises join'd.

VII. 13, 14

Let all his glorious Name
    Unite to celebrate;
Above the Heaven's his Fame;
His Fame that's only great:
    His Peoples Stay
      And Praise is He,
        And e're will be:
    Hallelujah.[7]

The two following Letters, coming from Persons in as great
Danger as any could be, are plac'd here, as proper to be call'd
Deliverances of the greatest and strangest kind.

From on board a Ship blown out of the Downs *to* Norway.

SIR,
I cannot but write to you of the Particulars of our sad and terrible
Voyage to this Place. You know we were, by my last, riding safe
in the *Downs*, waiting a fair Wind, to make the best of our way
to *Portsmouth*, and there to expect the *Lisbon* Convoy.

We had had two terrible Storms, one on the *Friday* before,
and one on *Thursday*; the one the 18th, the other the 25th of
November: In the last I expected we shou'd have founder'd at an
Anchor; for our Ground Tackle[8] being new and very good held

us fast, but the Sea broke upon us so heavy and quick, that we were in danger two or three times of Foundring as we rode but, as it pleas'd God we rid it out, we began to think all was over, and the Bitterness of Death was past.

There was a great Fleet with us in the *Downs*, and several of them were driven from their Anchors, and made the best of their way out to Sea for fear of going on shore upon the *Goodwin*. the Grand Fleet was just come in from the *Streights*, under Sir *Cloudsly Shovel*; and the Great Ships being design'd for the River, lay to Leeward: Most of the Ships that went out in the Night appear'd in the Morning; and I think there was none known to be lost, but one *Dutch* Vessel upon the *Goodwin*.

But the next Day, being *Friday*, in the Evening, it began to gather to Windward; and as it had blown very hard all Day, at Night the Wind freshen'd, and we all expected a stormy Night. We saw the Men of War struck their Top-masts, and rode with two Cables an-end: so we made all as *snug* as we could, and prepar'd for the worst.

In this condition we rid it out till about 12 a-clock; when, the Fury of the Wind encreasing, we began to see Destruction before us: the Objects were very dreadful on every side; and tho' it was very dark, we had Light enough to see our own Danger, and the Danger of those near us. About One-a-clock the Ships began to drive, and we saw several come by us without a Mast standing, and in the utmost Distress.

By Two a-clock we could hear Guns firing in several Parts of this Road, as Signals of Distress; and tho' the Noise was very great with the Sea and Wind, yet we could distinguish plainly, in some short Intervals, the Cries of poor Souls in Extremities.

By Four-a-clock we miss'd the *Mary* and the *Northumberland*, who rid not far from us, and found they were driven from their Anchors; but what became of them, God knows: and soon after a large Man of War came driving down upon us, all her Masts gone, and in a dreadful Condition. We were in the utmost Despair at this sight, for we saw no avoiding her coming thwart *our Haiser*:[9] she drove at last so near us, that I was just gowing to order the Mate to cut away, when it pleas'd God the Ship sheer'd contrary to our Expectation to Windward, and the Man of War, which we found to be the *Sterling Castle*, drove clear off us, not two Ships Lengths to Leeward.

It was a Sight full of terrible Particulars, to see a Ship of Eighty Guns and about Six Hundred Men in that dismal Case; she had cut away all her Masts, the Men were all in the Confusions of Death and Despair; she had neither Anchor, nor Cable, nor Boat to help her; the Sea breaking over her in a terrible Manner, that sometimes she seem'd all under Water; and they knew, as well as we that saw her, that they drove by the Tempest directly for the *Goodwin*, where they could expect nothing but Destruction: The Cries of the Men, and the firing their Guns, One by One, every Half Minute for Help, terrified us in such a Manner, that I think we were half dead with the Horror of it.

All this while we rid with two Anchors a-head, and in great Distress: To fire Guns for Help, I saw was to no Purpose, for if any Help was to be had, there were so many other Objects for it, that we could not expect it, and the Storm still encreasing.

Two Ships, a-head of us, had rid it out till now, which was towards Five in the Morning, when they both drove from their Anchors, and one of them coming foul of a small *Pink*, they both sunk together; the other drove by us, and having one Mast standing, I think it was her Main-Mast, she attempted to spread a little Peak of her Sail, and so stood away before it; I suppose she went away to Sea.

At this time, the Raging of the Sea was so violent, and the Tempest doubled its Fury in such a Manner, that my Mate told me, we had better go away to Sea, for 'twould be impossible to ride it out; I was not of his Opinion, but was for cutting my Masts by the Board,[10] which at last we did, and parted with them with as little Damage as could be expected, and we thought she rid easier for it by a great deal; and I believe, had it blown two Hours longer, we should have rid it out, having two new Cables out, and our best Bower and Sheet Anchor down: But about Half an Hour after Five to Six, it blew, if it be possible to conceive it so, as hard again as it had done before, and first our best Bower Anchor came Home, the Mate, who felt it give way, cried out, we are all undone, for the Ship drove; I found it too true, and, upon as short a Consultation as the Time would admit, we concluded to put out to Sea before we were driven too far to Leeward, when it would be impossible to avoid the *Goodwin*.

So we slipt our Sheet Cable, and sheering the Ship towards the Shore, got her Head about, and stood away afore it; Sail we had none, nor Mast standing: Our Mate had set up a Jury Missen[11] but no Canvass could bear the Fury of the Wind, yet he fasten'd an old Tarpaulin so as that it did the Office of a Missen and kept us from driving too fast to Leeward.

In this Condition we drove out of the *Downs*, and past so near the *Goodwin*, that we could see several great Ships fast a ground, and beating to Pieces. We drove in this desperate Condition till Day-break, without any Abatement of the Storm, and our Men heartless and dispirited, tir'd with the Service of the Night, and every Minute expecting Death.

About 8 a Clock, my Mate told me, he perceiv'd the Wind to abate; but it blew still such a Storm, that if we had not had a very tite Ship, she must have founder'd, as we were now farther off at Sea, and by my Guess might be in the mid Way between *Harwich* and the *Brill*,[12] the Sea we found run longer, and did not break so quick upon us as before, but it ran exceeding high, and we having no Sail to keep us to rights, we lay wallowing in the Trough of the Sea in a miserable Condition: We saw several Ships in the same Condition with our selves, but could neither help them, nor they us; and one we saw founder before our Eyes, and all the People perish'd.

Another dismal Object we met with, which was an open Boat full of Men, who, as we may suppose, had lost their Ship; any Man may suppose, what Condition a Boat must be in, if we were in so bad a Case in a good Ship: we were soon tost out of their Sight, and what became of them any one may guess; if they had been within Cables Length of us we could not have help'd them.

About Two a Clock in the Afternoon, the Wind encreased again, and we made no doubt it would prove as bad a Night as before; but that Gust held not above Half an Hour.

All Night it blew excessive hard, and the next Day, which was Sabbath Day, about Eleven a Clock it abated, but still blew hard: about three it blew something moderately, compar'd with the former; and we got up a Jury Main-Mast, and rigg'd it as well as we could, and with a Main Sail lower'd almost to the Deck, stood at a great Rate afore it all Night and the next Day, and on *Tuesday* Morning we saw Land, but could not tell where it was; but being not in a Condition to keep the Sea, we run in, and made Signals of Distress; some Pilots came off to us, by whom we were inform'd we had reached the Coast of *Norway*, and having neither Anchor nor Cable on board capable to ride the Ship, a *Norweigian* Pilot came on board, and brought us into a Creek where we had smooth Water, and lay by till we got Help, Cables, and Anchors, by which means we are safe in Place.

Your Humble Servant,

J. Adams.

From on board the John and Mary, riding in Yarmouth Roads during the great Storm, but now in the River of Thames.

SIR,

Hearing of your good Design of preserving the Memory of the late Dreadful Storm for the Benefit of Posterity, I cannot let you want the Particulars as happen'd to us on board our Ship.

We came over the Bar of *Tinmouth* about the — having had terrible blowing Weather for almost a Week, insomuch that we were twice driven back almost the Length of *Newcastle*, with much Difficulty and Danger we got well over that, and made the *High-land* about *Cromer* on the North-side of *Norfolk*; here it blew so hard the *Wednesday* Night before, that we could not keep the Sea, nor fetch the Roads of *Yarmouth*; but as the Coast of *Norfolk* was a Weather-shore,[13] we hall'd as close *Cromer* as we durst lie, the Shore there being very flat; here we rode *Wednesday* and *Thursday*, the 24th and 25th of *November*.

We could not reckon our selves safe here, for as this is the most dangerous Place between *London* and *Newcastle*, and has been particularly fatal to our Colliers, so we were very uneasy; I considered that when such Tempestuous Weather happen'd, as this seem'd to threaten, nothing is more frequent than for the Wind to shift Points; and if it should have blown half the Wind from the South East, as now blew from the South West, we must have gone a-shore there, and been all lost for being embayed; there we should have had no putting out to Sea, nor staying there.

This Consideration made me resolve to be gon, and thinking on *Friday* Morning the Wind slacken'd a little, I weigh'd and stood away for *Yarmouth* Roads; and with great Boating and Labour got into the Roads about One in the Afternoon, being a little after Flood, we found a very great Fleet in the Roads; there was above Three Hundred Sail of Colliers, not reckoning above Thirty Sail which I left behind me, that rode it out thereabouts, and there was a great Fleet just come from *Russia*, under the Convoy of the *Reserve* Frigate, and Two other Men of War; and about a Hundred Sail of Coasters, *Hull*-Men, and such small Craft.

We had not got to an Anchor, moor'd, and set all to Rights, but I found the Wind freshen'd, the Clouds gather'd, and all look'd very black to Windward; and my Mate told me, he wish'd he had staid where we were, for he would warrant it we had a blowing Night of it.

We did what we could to prepare for it, struck our Top-mast, and slung our Yards, made all tite and fast upon Deck; the Night prov'd very dark, and the Wind blew a Storm about Eight a Clock, and held till Ten, when we thought it abated a little, but at Eleven it freshen'd again, and blew very hard; we rid it out very well till Twelve, when we veer'd out more Cable, and in about Half an Hour after, the Wind encreasing, let go our Sheet Anchor; by One a Clock it blew a dreadful Storm, and though our Anchors held very well, the Sea came over us in such a vast Quantity, that we was every Hour in Danger of Foundring: About Two a Clock the Sea fill'd our Boat as she lay upon the Deck, and we was glad to let her go over board for Fear of staving in our Decks: Our Mate would then have cut our Mast by the Board, but I was not willing, and told him, I thought we had better slip our Cables, and go out to Sea, he argued she was a deep Ship, and would not live in the Sea, and was very eager for cutting away the Mast; but I was loth to part with my Mast, and could not tell where to run for Shelter if I lost them.

About Three a Clock abundance of Ships drove away, and came by us; some with all their Masts gone, and foul of one another; in a sad Condition my Men said they saw Two founder'd together, but I was in the Cabin, and cannot say I saw it. I saw a *Russia* Ship come foul of a Collier, and both drove away together out of our Sight, but I am told since the *Russia* Man sunk by her Side.

In this Condition we rid till about Three a Clock, the *Russia* Ships which lay a-head of me, and the Men of War, who lay a-head of them, fir'd their Guns for Help, but 'twas in vain to expect it; the Sea went too high for any Boat to live. About Five, the Wind blew at that prodigious Rate, that there was no Possibility of riding it out, and all the Ships in the Road seem'd to us to drive: Yet still our Anchors held it, and I began to think we should ride it out there, or founder; when a Ship's long Boat came driving against us, and gave such a Shock on the Bow that I thought it must have been a Ship come foul of us, and expected to sink all at once; our Men said there was some people in the Boat, but as the Sea went so high no Man dust stand upon the Fore-castle, so no Body could be sure of it; the Boat stav'd to pieces with the Blow, and went away, some on One Side of us and some on the other; but whether our Cable receiv'd any Damage by it or not we cannot tell, but our Sheet Cable gave Way immediately, and as the other was not able to hold us alone, we immediately drove; we had then no more to do, but to put afore the Wind, which we did: it pleased God by this Time the Tide of Ebb was begun, which something abated the Height of the Sea, but still it went exceeding high; we saw a great many Ships in the same Condition with our selves, and expecting every Moment to sink in the Sea. In this Extremity we drove till Daylight when we found the Wind abated, and we stood in for the Shore, and coming under the Lee of the *Cliff* near *Scarbro*, we got so much Shelter, as that our small Bower Anchors would ride us.

I can give you no Account but this; but sure such a Tempest never was in the World. They say here, that of Eighty Sail in *Grimsby* Road, they can hear of but Sixteen; yet the rest are all blown away, Here is about Twelve or Fourteen Sail of Ships come in to this Place, and more are standing in for the Shore.

Yours, &c.

Abundance of other strange Deliverances have been related, but with so small Authority as we dare not convey them into the World under the same Character with the rest; and have therefore chose to omit them.

The Conclusion

The Editor of this Book has labour'd under some Difficulties in this Account: and one of the chief has been, how to avoid too many Particulars, the Crowds of Relations which he has been oblig'd to lay by to bring the Story into a Compass tolerable to the Reader.

And tho' some of the Letters inserted are written in a homely Stile, and exprest after the Country Fashion from whence they came, the Author chose to make them speak their own Language, rather than by dressing them in other Words make the Authors forget they were their own.

We receiv'd a Letter, very particular, relating to the Bishop of *Bath* and *Wells*, and reflecting upon his Lordship for some Words he spoke, *That he had rather have his Brains knock'd out, than* &c. relating to his Inferiour Clergy. The Gentleman takes the Disaster for a Judgment of God on him: But as in his Letter the Person owns himself the Bishop's Enemy, fills his Letter with some Reflexions indecent, at least for us: and at last, tho' he dates from *Somerton*, yet baulks setting his Name to his Letter: for these Reasons we could not satisfie to record the Matter, and leave a Charge on the Name of that unfortunate Gentleman, which, he being dead, could not answer, and we alive could not prove. And on these Accounts hope the Reverend Gentleman who sent the Letter will excuse Us.[14]

Also we have omitted, tho' our List of Particulars promis'd such a thing, An Account of some unthinking Wretches, who pass'd over this dreadful Judgment with Banter, Scoffing, and Contempt. 'Tis a Subject ungrateful to recite, and full of Horror to read; and we had much rather cover such Actions with a general Blank in Charity to the Offenders, and in hopes of their Amendment.

One unhappy Accident I cannot omit, and which is brought us from good Hands, and happen'd in a Ship homeward bound from the *West-Indies*. The Ship was in the utmost Danger of Foundring; and when the Master saw all, as he thought, lost, his Masts gone, the Ship leaky, and expecting her every moment to sink under him, fill'd with Despair, he calls to him the Surgeon of the Ship, and by a fatal Contract, as soon made as hastily executed, they resolv'd to prevent the Death they fear'd by one more certain; and going into the Cabbin, they both shot themselves with their Pistols. It pleas'd God the Ship recover'd the Distress, was driven safe into — and the Captain just liv'd to see the desperate Course he took might have been spar'd; the Surgeon died immediately.

There are several very remarkable Cases come to our Hands since the finishing this Book, and several have been promis'd which are not come in; and the Book having been so long promis'd, and so earnestly desir'd by several Gentlemen that have already assisted that way, the Undertakers could not prevail with themselves to delay it any longer.

FINIS.

THE

Lay-Man's
SERMON
UPON THE
LATE STORM;

Held forth at an Honest

Coffee-House-Conventicle.

𝔑𝔬𝔱 𝔰𝔬 𝔪𝔲𝔠𝔥 𝔞 𝔍𝔢𝔰𝔱 𝔞𝔰 '𝔱𝔦𝔰 𝔱𝔥𝔬𝔲𝔤𝔥𝔱 𝔱𝔬 𝔟𝔢.

Printed in the Year 1704.

NAHUM. I. III

The Lord has his way in the Whirle-Wind and in the Storm, and the Clouds are the Dust of his Feet.

This Text is not chosen more for the Suitableness to the present Callamity, which has been the Portion of this Place, than for the aptness of the Circumstances, 'twas spoken of God going to Chastise, a Powerful, Populous, Wealthy and most reprobate City.

Nineveh[1] was the Seat of a mighty Empire, a Wealthy Encreasing People, Opulent in Trade, Flourishing in Power and Proud in Proportion.

The Prophet does not seem to deliver these words, to the *Ninevites*, to convince them, or encline them to consider their own Circumstances and repent, but he seems to speak, it to the *Israelites* inviteing them to Triumph and Insult over the Heathen adversary, by setting forth the Power of their God, in the most exalted Terms.

And that this is a just Exposition of this Text, seems plain from the words Imediately going before, *the Lord is slow to Anger, and Great in Power and will not at all acquit the wicked.*[2] These words could have no Connexion with the Text, tho' they are joyn'd with them in the same Verse, if it were not meant of his being slow to Anger, to his own People, and Terrible to the Heathen World, and this being spoken as an Expression of his being not easily provoked as to his Church, the Subsequent part of the Verse tells them how his power and Vengance is matter of particular Satisfaction to his People as being exercis'd in Revenging the affront put upon his Glory by his Enemies, *God is Jealous, and the Lord Revengeth, the Lord Revengeth and is Furious, the Lord will take Vengeance on his adversaries and he reserveth wrath for his Enemies.*[3] Tis plain this is meant of his Enemies, but as if brought in with a Parenthesis, tis spoken for the comfort of his Church, the Lord is slow to Anger as to them, and to lift up their hearts in a further confidence that their Enemies are all in his hand, he goes on discribing the Terrors of his Judgement.

The Lord has his way in the Whirl-wind and in the Storm, and the Clouds are the Dust of his Feet. Eloquent Flourishes upon the Omnipotence of God.

The short Exposition I shall make of the words, Tends only to remind us that the Whirl-wind and Storm which are here made use of, to express the Magnipotent power of God are acted by his Direction, *he has his way in them*, it may note indeed the Invisible secrecy and swiftness of his providences, but to avoid long Paraphrases, I confine my self to my own Construction, as that which, as it is a just inference from the matter of the Text, so 'tis most suitable to the design of this discourse.

And as this Sermon may be a little Immethodical, because I purpose to make it almost all Aplication so I shall advance some Conclusions from the Premises which I lay down, as the Geneuine sence of the Words.

1. The Omnipotence of God gives Christians sufficient ground to Insult their Enemies, *wherefore do the Heathen Mock thy People and say unto them where is now your God? Behold our God is in the Heavens, and doeth whatsoever he pleaseth*; as the Prophet *Elija*, Banter'd the Heathen Priest of *Baal*, with the Impotence of their Gods, Cry aloud for *he is a God, either he is talking or he is Pursuing, or he is in a Journey, or Peradventure he Sleepeth and must be awakned*, so he insulted them about the power of the true God, *let it be known O Lord says he this day that thou art God in Israel.*[4]

2. As God in all the works of his Providence, makes use of the subserviency of means, so the whole Creation is Subordinate to the Execution of his Divine will, *the Clouds are the Dust of his Feet and he rides upon the Wings of the Wind*, the most Powerful Elements are so subjected to his almighty power that the Clouds are but as Dust under his feet, tis as easy for him to Govern and mannage them; as it is for a man to shake off the

Dust from his feet, or he can as easily subdue the fury of them as a man Tramples the Dust, they are small and Triffling things, in his Eyes.

3. The ways of God are unsearchable, the Methods of his Providence are secret and powerfull; his way is in the Whirle-wind, and in the Storm, tis invisible and iresistible, invisible as the Wind, and iresistible as the Storm.

But waving these and abundance more usefull observations which might be justly drawn from so rich a Text, I shall proceed upon one which tho' it favours something more of private authority, and I have not so Authentick Opinion of the Learned Commentators, on my side, yet I shall endeavour not to Merit much Censure, in the Improvement of it, even from those who perhaps may not joyn with me in the Exposition.

According therefore to my own private opinion of these words; I shall for the present occasion only Paraphrase them thus, that *the Lord has a way* or an end *in the Whirle-wind, and in the Storm*, nor is this a very unusual Method of expressing things in Scripture, where the way is Exprest, to signify the design, or end of a thing.

And from this Exposition I advance this head.

That as God by his power Governs the elements, so in all their Extraordinary Motions, they are in a Perticular manner acted by his Soveraignity. And,

2. When the Creation is put into any Violent or Supernatural Agitation, God has always some Extraordinary thing to bring to pass, *he has a meaning in all the Remarkables of Nature*.

3. We ought dilligently to observe the extraordinary actings of Providence, in order to discover and Deprecate the displeasure of Almighty God, Providences are never Dumb, and if we can not discern the signals of his Anger, we must be very blind. The Voice of his Judgements is heard in the Voice of Nature, and if we make our selves Deaf, he is pleas'd to make them speak the Louder, to awaken the stupifyed sences, and startle the World, which seem'd rather Amus'd than Amas'd, with the common Course of things. This I take to be some of the true meaning of the way of God, in the Whirle-wind, and in the Storm.

The design of this Discourse therefore, is to put the Nation in general upon proper Resolutions; if we pretend to believe that there is any such thing as a Collateral Sympathy, a Communication of Circumstances, between a Nations Follies, and her Fate. Any Harmony between Merit and Mischief, between the Crimes of Men and the Vengeance of Heaven; we cannot but allow this *Extra*-Pulpit admonition to be just.

And let not any man Object against this being call'd a Sermon, and its being introduc'd from a Text of Scripture while the remainer of this Discourse, seems wholly Civil and Political.

If all our Measures in Civil affairs were deduc'd as Inferences from sacred Texts, I am of the Opinion the Text would be well improv'd, and Publick matters never the worse Guided.

And for this reason, tho' the Subject be not Treated, with the Gravity of a Sermon, nor in so serious a manner, as would become a Pulpit, yet it may be not the less suitable to the occasion and for the manner, it must be placed to the Authors account.

Besides the Title I think has provided for the Method and If so he that expected it otherwise than it is tis his Fault, and not Mine.

The Term Sermon which is but *Sermo*, a Speech, may Justify all the Novelty of my Method if those who find fault please to give themselves leave to allow it, and since it has never profain'd the Pulpit, I believe the Text will receive no Prejudice by it, I wish every Sermon equally Improv'd.

And what tho' your Humble Servant be no Man of the Text; if he be a Man of Honesty, he may have a hand in making you all Men of Application.

In publick Callamities, every Circumstance is a Sermon, and every thing we see a Preacher.

The trembling Habitations of an Unthinking People Preach to us, and might have made any Nation in the World tremble but us; when we were rock'd out of our Sleep as Children are Rock'd into it; and when the terrible Hand of Soveraign Power rock'd many a Wretch from one Sleep to another, and made a Grave of the Bed, without the Ceremony of waking in the Passage.

The shatter'd Palaces of our Princes Preach to us, and tell us aloud, that without respect to Dignity, he is able to put that Dreadful Text in Execution; *That if a Nation does wickedly they shall be destroy'd both they and their King.*[5]

The fallen Oaks, which stood before to tell us they were the longest liv'd of all God's Creatures, Preach to us, and tell us that the most towring object of humane Beauty and strength must lye humble and prostrate, when he is pleased to give a Check to that Splendor which was deriv'd from his Power.

The Wrecks of our Navies and Fleets Preach to us, that 'tis in vain we pretend to be Wall'd about by the Ocean, and ride Masters of the Sea: And that, if he who bestow'd that Scituation upon us thinks fit, he can make that Element which has been our Strength, and the Encreaser of our Wealth, be the Grave of our Treasure, and the Enemy of our Commerce; he can put it into so violent Agitation, by the blast of his Mouth, that all our Defence and the Naval Strength we have vallued our selves so much upon, shall at once be swallow'd up in the Mouth of our Friend the Sea; and we shall find our Destruction in the very thing from which we expected our Defence.

Our Seamen and Soldiers, whose Dead Bodies Embrace the *English* Shores, Preach aloud to us, that whenever we think fit to Embark them on any Design, which Heaven approves not of, he can blast the Embrio, and devour those People whose Hands are lifted up against Justice and Right.

Also they Preach to us, Not to build our hopes of Success upon the multitude of Ships or Men, who are thus easily reduc'd, and the Strength of a whole Nation brought to Ruine in a Moment.

These are the Monitors of our Missfortunes, and some of these admonitions would be well preach'd from the Mouths of those whose Tallent as well as Office gives them reason to do it, and us to expect it.

But since the Sons of the Prophets have not yet thought it proper to enter very far into this Matter, not doubting but they will in due time find it as suitable to their Inclination as 'tis to their Duty,

In the mean time let us see if no uncommon Application may be made of so uncommon a Circumstance.

First, 'tis matter of wonder that any Man can be so senceless, as to suppose there is nothing extraordinary in so signal an Instance of a Supream Power; but 'tis much more remarkable that those who have Religion enough to own it a Judgment, are yet at a loss how to appropriate it's signification.

Every one thinks it to be a Judgment upon the Person or Parties they see touch'd with it. W— the Carpenter was knock'd on the head with a Stack of Chimneys, and his Wife saved; all the Neighbours cried out 'twas a Judgment upon him for keeping a Whore; but if Stacks of Chimnies were to have fallen on the Heads of all that keep Whores, *Miserere Dei*.[6]

S— was kill'd by the like Accident, and he must be singl'd out for Extortion; But think ye that he was a Sinner above all the *Gallileans*?

The *Jacobites* and *Non-Jurants*[7] shall rise up in Judgment against this Generation, and shall condemn them, for they tell us, this Storm is a Judgment on the whole Nation, for Excluding their Lawful Soveraign, and Abjuring his Posterity: Upon this head they have been preaching up Repentance, and Humiliation to us; and some of them are willing to reduce all to a very practical Exhortation, and tell us, we ought to look upon it as a Loud Call to Restore the Right Owner (as they call him) to the Possession of his own again; that is, in short, to rebel against a Mild, Gentle, Just and Protestant Queen, and call in the Popish Posterity of an abdicated Tyrant.

These Gentlemen are Men of Uses and Application, and know very well how to make an Advantage of God's Judgments, when they serve their turn.

The *Whigs* and *Occasional Conformists*[8] shall rise up in Judgment against this Generation; for they are sensible of the present severe Stroke of Providence, and think 'tis a mark of Heavens Displeasure upon the Nation, for the violent methods made use of by some People against them, for their Religion, contrary to their Native Right, and the Liberty of their Consciences.

Some think a general Blast follows all the Endeavours of this Nation against the Common Enemy, for their slighting and reproaching the Glorious Memory of the late King *William*,[9] whose Gallant Endeavours for the general good of *Europe*, and of *England* in particular, were Treacherously thwarted and disappointed while he was alive, and are Basely and Scandalously undervalued and slighted now he is Dead; and of this sort I confess my self enclined to be one.

From these general Observations we may descend to particulars, and every one judges according to their own Fancy.

Some will have it, that the Slaughter and Destruction among the Fleet, is a Judgment upon them, for going into the *Streights*,[10] and coming home again without doing any business; but those forget, that if they did all they were ordered to do, the Fault lies in those who sent them, and not in they that went.

Some will have the Damage among the Colliers to be a Judgment, upon those who have Engross'd the Trade, and made the Poor pay so dear for Coals;[11] not enquiring whether those Engrossers of the Coals are not left safe on Shore, while the poor Seamen are drown'd, who know nothing of the matter.

'Tis plain to me, who ever are Punish'd by the Storm, we that are left have a share in the Judgment, and a Trebble concern in the Cause.

If it could be said that those who are destroy'd, or who have suffered the loss of Lives, Limbs or Goods, were the only People who gave any occasion to the Divine Justice thus severely to Revenge it self, then all admonition to the rest of Mankind would be useless, any farther than it directed them to be Cautious how they provoked him in like manner; but have we not all had a hand in the general provocation, though not an equal share in the general Calamity.

Sometimes the Judgements of Heaven, bear so much Analogy to the Crimes, that the Punishment points out the Offence, and 'tis easy to distinguish what it is the perticular hand of Justice points at.

And if we will seek for a Perticular case, in which Heaven seems to have singled out this way of Punishment on the Nation, as best proportion'd to the general National Crime we are all guilty of? what seems more Rational than to Judge that tis a severe Animadversion upon the Feuds and Storms of parties kept up among us in this Nation, with such unnatural Heat, and such unaccountable Fury, that no man, who has the least Compassion for his Native Country, but must with more than Common Grief, be concerned for it, since unless some speedy course be taken to bring a general Composure upon the minds of Men, the general ruin seems Inevitable.

If the matters in Debate were of Extraordinary Consequence, there might be some pretence for Espousing contrary parties with unusual heat; but while the difference lies in small, and, in some cases, indifferent things, tis a most inexcusable Madness that the Feuds shou'd be run up so high, that all manner of Charity should Perish and be lost among us.

We have had an Extraordinary Bustle in the World about Moderation, and all Parties pretend to it, and now we are as busy about Peace, and every one lays in a Loud Claim to it.

I have seen, with some regret, the strange Mysterious Management of this Age about Moderation, and tho' some late Authors have Published that Moderation is a Vertue, It begins to be a question whether it is or no.

I wish some Body would make enquiry after the occasion that has brought this Blessed Word into so much Contempt in the World; tis very hard that a word expressive of the most Glorious Principle in the World, should become the Brand of reproach, and a Badge of Infamy to Parties; be a Nick-name it self, and be Nick-nam'd on every side; and that at a time when the Vertue it self, is perhaps the only thing left in the World, that can preserve this Nation from Destruction.

'Tis too unhappy for *England*, that Men of immoderate Principles are so powerfull as they are. Let the Party be which it will, tis Destruction even to themselves, to run up all their Niceties and all their Scruples to the Extremes. Every Dispute becomes a Feud, every Spark a Flame, every word a Blow, every Blow, a Civil-War, and by this Intestine Confusion of Principles, Backt with the Passion and Fury of Men, this unhappy Nation is Subdivided into an Infinite Number of Parties, Factions, Intrests and seperate Opinions.

Every Man being thus bent upon the propagation of his own Notion, for want of this healing Spirit of Moderation, falls foul upon his Neighbour because he has not the same Heat, and if he finds him better Temper'd than himself, if he finds him less Violent, less Furious, than himself, he is Imediately Branded with the Scandal of Moderation.

Since then the Change of times has made this Practice, which in its very Nature is a Foundation of Vertue, become a Crime, Let us examine who are, and who are not Guilty of it.

For the Negatives of this Vice of Moderation they are something Easier to be discover'd than ordinary, both in Principles and in Practice; and, without the Scandal of a Censorious Writer, I may be allowed to say all the following Instances may stand clear of this Crime.

1. If Mr. *Sachaverell*, with his Bloody Flag, and Banner of Defiance, were Indicted for Moderation, I verily believe no Jury would bring him in Guilty.[12]

2. If Dr. *J—ne*, Author of the Character of a Low-Churchman, Mr. — Author of the New Association, if a famous Bishop who told us, 'twould never be well with *England* till all the Dissenters were serv'd like the *Hugonots* in *France*, if any of these were Indicted for Moderation, they might safely plead not Guilty.[13]

3. If Sir *John Friend* and Sir *William Parkins*, had been only accus'd for Moderation, they had never been Hanged, nor *Collyer* and *Cook* had never absolv'd them at the Gallows without Repentance.[14]

4. If he were Hang'd for Moderation, who ask'd the Question, *whether if the Play-house in Dorset-Garden, were let for a Meeting-house, 'twould not do more harm than tis like to do as a Theatre*, he would certainly Dye Innocently.

5. If *Fuller*[15] had been Voted an Incorrigible Rogue only for the Vice of Moderation, I should have thought the House of Commons had done him wrong.

6. If the Councellors of the late King, such as Father *P—*, my Lord *S—*[16] and all those that betray'd their Master, by hurrying on his ruin and their own. If those Gentlemen were Charged with Moderation, I doubt we should wrong them.

7. If some of the Members of our Late Convocation shou'd be accused for Moderation, I believe it might be no Difficult task to Vindicate them.

8. If this Crime should be Charged higher than we dare to mention, I am perswaded some Persons of Note would think themselves abused.

9. In short all those Gentlemen, by whatsoever Names or Titles Distinguish'd, who repine at the Settlement,[17] who reproach the Tolleration, and who Blame the Queen for her promises of Maintaining it, these abhor the thoughts of this Scandalous Crime of Moderation, and are as Innocent of it as the Child unborne.

10. Tis the Opinion of some People, That there are some of our beloved Friends in *Scotland*, may be Vindicated in this case, nay others are of the Opinion, tis not a National Crime in that Country, that is, 'tis not a sin the *Scots* are much adicted to.

11. Lastly, Take our English Clergy in general, some are ready to say they have no great cause of Repentance for the sin of Moderation.

On the other hand, some People have so home a Charge of this Error laid upon them, that 'twill be very hard to clear themselves of it, and I am afraid they would be brought in Guilty by a Jury, almost without going away from the Bar. as,

1. Our Observator,[18] they say, is Guilty of Moderation, with Relation to his Wit, and Especially as concerning his good Manners; I hope he wont be prosecuted for it the next Sessions, if he should, I doubt, 'twill go hard with him.

2. If our News-writers should be Indited for Moderation, as to Truth of Fact, I would advise them to plead Guilty, and throw themselves upon the Mercy of the Court.

3. Some of our Captains, they say, are addicted to Fight but Moderately; I hope all the rest wont be Infected, but I know not what to say to it.

4. Some of our Lawyers are apt to be very Moderate in their Justice, but being well read in the Law are cunning enough to keep off an Indictment, so there is no fear of them.

5. Some of our General Receivers, when they got the Publick Money in their hands, were apt to be very Moderate in paying it out again.

6. Some have been very Moderate in giving in their accounts

too, as may appear in former Reigns, and perhaps in time to come too.

Some Moderately Wise, some Moderatly Honest, but most Immoderately adicted to think themselves Both.

Tho' I might be a little more serious upon the matter, yet this way of talking is not so much a Jest neither as it looks like; and has its Moral, in it self, which a Wise man may see, and for the Fool tis no matter whether he does or no. Custome has prevailed upon us to such a degree, that almost in every part the very Practice seem a Scandal, and the Word passes for a Reproach.

To say, among the Sons of *Levy*,[19] such a man is a Moderate Church-man is to say he is no Church-man, and some of our present Bishops from the Practice of Moderation have been boldly call'd Presbiterians in the Pamphlets of our less Moderate writers.

In short, 'tis hard to find any party or profession of Men among us, that care for the Title; and those who but Moderately espouse an Intrest, are generally suspected by those who are of that side, as Persons Favouring their Enemies.

These Moderate Men, said a Gentleman whose Gown and Band had given us reason to expect better Language, they will Ruin the Church, this Damn'd Moderation, says he, spoils all, we should deal well enough with the Dissenters, if it were not for these men of Moderation, they are worse than Dissenters, for they seem to be among us, and yet wont Joyn heartily to do the Work.

Moderation seems to be cast off on every side, and is used as a Badge of reproach in every Class, or degree of Men in the World.

In the Church of *England*, 'tis call'd Low-Church.

In the Court, 'tis call'd Whiggism.

In the Dissenters, 'tis call'd Occasional Conformity.

In Parties, 'tis call'd Trimming.[20]

In Religion, 'tis call'd Latitudinarian.

In Opinion, 'tis call'd Indifference,

In the Church of *Scotland*, 'tis call'd Prelacy.[21]

While Moderation of principles seems thus the general Sin of Parties, Let them consider whether Heaven it self has not declar'd War against us all on this Head, and fill'd us with immoderate Judgements.

Where's all our prospect of success Abroad, or prosperity at home? Since our late Thanksgiveing for Victories,[22] how has Heaven Treated us, but like a Nation, that being puff'd up and exalted with prosperity, began to slight Forreign Judgements, and leaving Providence to Work by it self fell to making War at home with one another, as if we would prove that the Scripture was not true *and that a Kingdom might stand tho' it were divided against it self.*[23]

How has Heaven declar'd that he is resolv'd not to bless this immoderate Generation? How has all their Measures been disappointed both abroad and at home, all their designes been blasted, and the Anger of Heaven so remarkably bent against them, that even the little success we have had, has been pre-scrib'd by Providence to those few hands who Act from Prin-ciples of Honesty and Temper, as if God did thereby point out to us who they are he delights to bless.

The *D—* of *M—* is a Whig *say some of our People who Hate all Moderation*, he is so *Dutchify'd*, we shall never have any Good of him, why that may be, but yet you see there is not one Article of our Conduct has succeeded but what has been under his Mannagement.[24]

And Heaven has declar'd so Eminently against all other Branches of our Affaires, that I wish I am mistaken when I say 'tis plain either he seems to mislike the Cause or the Persons employ'd, and that however severe he was pleas'd to Anminad-vert upon the Publick affaires in the late Violent Tempest, it seems that *for all this his Anger is not turned away but his hand is Stretched out still.*[25]

But what has a Sermon to do to enquire, may some say, and if it had, how shall it make appear whether God is displeased with our designs or the Persons employed, with the cause or the Carryers of it on.

As to the cause, all men are Judges of the Justice of it, and all men know the Foot of the present Confederacy, at least our part must be Just as it is to Maintain our just Rights, Liberty, Trade and Religion.

It must then be the Persons, the *R—s*, the Sir *G—s*, *G—ns*, the *R—ks* of this War;[26] that Heaven is resolv'd shall not be the men, whom he will honour with the Deliverance of his People.

All wise Princes in the World have made it a constant Maxim in their Governments, that when any of their great Generals prove Unfortunate, tho' never so Wise, they lay them by, as Persons that God does not think fit to bless with success, and 'tis not needful to examine whether it were not their fault, but to be Unfortunate is to be told from Heaven, that such a one is not the Man, and a Nation ought to understand it so.

But sure when Heaven Singles men out by Crossing their attempts *and Marks them for unfortunate*, and we can give our selves good reasons why they are thus Mark'd by the Divine displeasure; when we can see their false steps, their General designs against God and their Countries Intrests, 'tis high time then for those who sit at the Helm of Government, to Change hands and put their affaires into such Persons Conduct, against whom Heaven has not declar'd so plainly its Displeasure, nor the Nation its Dislike.

Why shou'd the Queen be desir'd to Chain down her own Happiness and the Nations Interest, to the Missfortune of a few Men. Perhaps God may Bless the Fleet under one Admiral, when he will not under another. I know nothing against Admiral *Callemburgh*, he may be an Honest and worthy-man, and ready enough to Fight for the cause, for indeed most of the *Dutch* Captains of Ships are so, but since Heaven has now 'twice refus'd to let him go, and driven him back again, if I were the Governour of his Masters affairs, he should not be sent a Third time, least we should seem obstinately to Employ somebody that God himself had declar'd against and had three times from Heaven forbid to go.

I hope no Body will Construe this to be a Personal Satyr upon *Myn Heer Callemburgh*, But *take it among ye*, let it go, where it Fitts best.

If these are not the Generation of Men that must do the Nations business, then 'tis plain our Deliverance will never be wrought while they are employ'd; If God will not bless them he will never bless us till they are dismist.

I doubt not we shall be deliver'd, and this Nation shall yet Triumph over her Enemies; but while wrong Instruments are Employ'd the Work will be delay'd. *God would have a House built him* But *David* was not the Man and therefore the Work was put off till *Solomon* was in the Throne.[27]

God would have *Israel* go into the Land of *Canaan* and possess it, but those Generals and those Captains were not the Men; *Moses* and *Aaron*, and the great Men of the Camp were not such as God approv'd off and therefore *Israel* could not go over *Joardan* till they had laid their Bones in the Wilderness.

England is hardly ever to pass over the *Jourdan* before her, till these Immoderate Men of Strife and Storms are laid by.

If any man ask me why these men shou'd not perfect the Nation Peace as well as other men? *I do not say which Men nor who*, but let them be who the enquirer please, I answer the Question, with a question *How shou'd men of no Moderaion bring us to Peace*.

How shou'd Men of strife bring us Peace and Union: Contraries may Illustrate but Contraries never Incorporate; Men of Temper, are the safe men for this Nation. Men of heat are fit to Embroil it, but not to Cure it: they are something like our Sea Surgeons who fly to Amputation of Members upon every slight Fracture, when a more proper Application would effect the Cure and save the Joynt.

'Tis an ill sign especially for *England* when Wars abroad wont make us Friends at home. Foreign dangers us'd to Unite us from whence Queen *Elizabeth*, has been said to leave this Character of the Nation behind her, that they were much easier to be Govern'd in a time of War than in Peace.

But when This, which us'd to be the only Cure of all our diseases, fails us, 'tis a sign the Distemper is Grown very strong, and there is some more than usual Room for despair.

The only Way left the Nation is to obtain from those in power, that Moderation may cease being the pretence and be really the practice.

It would be well all men would at least *be Occasional Conformists*, to this Extraordinary principle; and when there is such a Loud call to Peace both from Heaven and from the Throne, they would do well to consider who are the Men of Peace and who are not: For certainly those Immoderate Gentlemen, who slight the Proposals for a general Union of Charity, cannot pretend to be Friends to the present Intrest of their Native Country.

These men, 'tis true, Cry out of the danger of the Church, but can they make it appear that the Church is in any danger from Moderation and Temper; can they pretend that there is no way to secure her, but by pulling down all that differ with them, no way to save her but by the ruin of her Protestant Brethren; there are Thousands of Loyal honest Church-men, who are not of this mind; who believe that Moderation and Charity to Protestant Dissenters is very Consistant with the safety of the Church and with the present general Union which they Earnestly desire.

As to Persons we have nothing to say to them, but this, without pretending to prophesy, may be safely advanced, that Heaven it self, has Eminently declared it self against the Fury and Immoderate Zeal of those Gentlemen, and told us as plainly as possible, unless we would Expect a Voice from on high, that he neither Has nor Designs to bless this Generation nor their proceedings.

When ever our rulers think fit to see it, and to employ the Men and the Methods which Heaven approves, then we may expect success from abroad, Peace at home, prosperity in Trade, Victory in War, plenty in the Field, Mild and Comfortable Seasons, Calm Air, Smooth Seas, and safe Habitations.

Till then we are to expect our Houses Blown down, our Pallaces Shatter'd, our Voyages broken, our Navys Shipwreck'd, our Saylors Drown'd, our Confedrates Beaten, our Trade ruin'd, our Money spent and our Enemies encreased.

The Grand dispute in this Quarrelsome Age, is against our Brethren who Dissent from the Church; and from what principle do we act? it is not safe say they to let any of them be entrusted in the Government, that is, it is not profitable to let any Body enjoy great Places but themselves.

This is the Bottom of the pretence, as to the safety of it. These are the People who Cry out of the Danger from the Dissenters, but are not concerned at our Danger from the *French*; that are frighted at the Dissenters who as they pretend grow too Formidable for the Church, but are not disturb'd at the Threatning Growth of a Conquering *Popish* Enemy; that Deprecate the Clouds of Whiggism and Phanaticism, but apprehend nothing of the Black Clouds of God's Threatning Judgements, which plainly tell them *if they would suffer themselves to think*, that there is somthing in the general practice of the Nation which does not please him, and for which the hand of his Judgements is extended against us.

These are strange dull-sighted men, whose Intrest stands so directly between them and their understanding that they can see nothing but what that represents to them; God may Thunder from Heaven with Storms upon Storms, Ruin our Fleets, Drown our Sailors and Blow us back from the best Contriv'd Expeditions in the World, but they will never believe the case affects them, never look into their own Conduct to see if they have not help'd to bring these heavy Strokes upon the Nation.

How many Thousands have we in *England*, who if the whole *Navy* of *England* had been at Stake; had rather have lost it than the *Bill against Occasional Conformity*; that had rather the *French* should have taken *Landau* and Beat the Prince of *Hess Cassell*, than the Queen should have made such a *Speech for Peace and Union*; that had rather the *Duke* of *Bavaria* should have taken *Ausburgh*, than that there should not have been *some Affront put upon the House of Lords*.[28]

And if such Zealots, such Christian Furies are met with by Providence, and see both the *Fleet* and the *Occasional Bill* lost together is it not plain, what Providence meant in it. He that can not see that God from on high has Punish'd them in their own way and pointed out the Crime in the Vengeance must be more blind than usual, and must shut their Eyes against their own Consciences.

'Tis plain Heaven has suited his Punishment to the Offence, has Punish'd the Stormy Temper of this Party of Men with *Storms of his Vengeance*, *Storms on their Navies*, *Storms on their Houses*, *Storms on their Confederates*, and I question not will at last with *Storms in their Consciences*.

If there be any Use to be made of this matter, 'tis to excite the

Nation to Spue out from among them these Men of Storms, that Peace, Love, Charity and a General Union may succeed, and God may Bless us, Return to us and delight to dwell among us, that the Favour of Heaven may Return to us, and the Queen who has heartily declared her Eyes open to this needful happiness, may enjoy the Blessing of Wise Counsellors and Faithful Servants, that Constant Victory may Crown all our Enterprizes, and the General Peace of Europe may be Established.

If any one can tell us a way to bring all these Blessed ends to pass, without a General Peace of Parties and Interests at home, he is Wellcome to do it, for I profess It is hid from my Eyes.

FINIS.

THE

STORM.

AN

ESSAY.

THE STORM. AN ESSAY

I'm told, *for we have News among the Dead*,
   Heaven lately spoke, but few knew what it said;
   The Voice, in loudest Tempests spoke,
And Storms, which Nature's strong Foundation shook.
I felt it hither, and I'd have you know
I heard the Voice, and knew the Language too.
   Think it not strange I heard it here,
No Place is so remote, but when *he speaks*, they hear.
   Besides, tho' I am dead in Fame,
   I never told you where I am.   10

   Tho' I have lost Pœtick Breath,
   I'm not in perfect State of Death:
From whence this *Popish Consequence* I draw,
   I'm in the Limbus[1] *of the Law*.
Let me be where I will I heard the Storm,
From every Blast *it eccho'd thus, REFORM*;
I felt the mighty Shock, and saw the Night,
When Guilt look'd pale, and own'd the Fright;
   And every Time the raging Element
Shook *London*'s lofty Towers, at every Rent   20
The falling Timbers gave, *they cry'd, REPENT*.

I saw, when all the stormy Crew,
   Newly commission'd from on high,
Newly instructed what to do,
   In Lowring, Cloudy, Troops drew nigh:

They hover'd o'er the guilty Land,
As if they had been backward to obey;
As if they wondred at the sad Command,
    And pity'd those they shou'd destroy.
But Heaven, that long had gentler Methods tried,   30
And saw those gentler Methods all defied,
    Had now resolv'd to be obey'd.
The Queen, an Emblem of the *soft, still, Voice*,
Had told the Nation how to make their Choice;
    Told them the only Way to Happiness
    Was by the Blessed Door of Peace.
But the unhappy Genius of the Land,
Deaf to the Blessing, as to the Command,
    Scorn the high Caution, and contemn the News,
    And all the blessed Thoughts of Peace refuse.   40
Since Storms are then the Nation's Choice,
Be Storms their Portion, said the Heavenly Voice:
    He said, and I could hear no more,
So soon th' obedient Troops began to roar:
    So soon the blackning Clouds drew near,
And fill'd with loudest Storms the trembling Air:
    I thought I felt the World's Foundation shake,
And lookt when all the wondrous Frame would break.
    I trembl'd as the Winds grew high,
And so did many a braver Man than I: 50
For he whose Valour scorns his Sence,
Has chang'd his Courage into Impudence.
    Man may to Man his Valour show,
    And 'tis his Vertue to do so.
But if he's of his Maker not afraid,
He's not courageous then, but mad.

    Soon as I heard the horrid Blast,
    And understood how long 'twould last,
View'd all the Fury of the Element,
    Consider'd well by whom 'twas sent,   60
And *unto whom* for Punishment:

It brought my Hero to my Mind,
William, the Glorious, Great, and Good, and Kind.
    Short Epithets to his Just Memory;
The first he was to all the World, *the last to me*.

The mighty Genius to my Thought appear'd,
    Just in the same Concern he us'd to show,
    When private Tempests us'd to blow,
Storms which the Monarch more than Death or Battel fear'd.
When Party Fury shook his Throne,   70
And made their mighty Malice known,
    I've heard the sighing Monarch say,
    The Publick Peace so near him lay,
    It took the Pleasure of his Crown away.
    It fill'd with Cares his Royal Breast;
Often he has those Cares Prophetickly exprest,
    That when he should the Reins let go,
Heaven would some Token of its Anger show,
    To let the thankless Nation see
How they despis'd their own Felicity.   80
    This robb'd the Hero of his Rest,
Disturb'd the Calm of his serener Breast.

    When to the Queen the Scepter he resign'd,
    With a resolv'd and steady Mind,
Tho' he rejoic'd to lay the Trifle down,
He pity'd Her to whom he left the Crown:
    Foreseeing long and vig'rous Wars,
Foreseeing endless, private, Party Jarrs,
    Would always interrupt Her Rest,
And fill with Anxious Cares Her Royal Breast.   90
    For Storms of Court Ambition rage as high
    Almost as Tempests in the Sky.

    Could I my hasty Doom retrieve,
And once more in the Land of Poets live,
    I'd now the Men of Flags and Fortune greet,
    And write an Elegy upon the Fleet.

First, those that on the Shore were idly found,
Whom other Fate protects, while better Men were drown'd,
They may thank God for being Knaves on Shore,
But sure the Q— will never trust them more.   100

　　They who rid out the Storm, and liv'd,
But saw not whence it was deriv'd,
Sensless of Danger, or the mighty Hand,
That could to cease, as well as blow, command,
　　Let such unthinking Creatures have a Care,
　　For some worse End prepare.
　　Let them look out for some such Day,
When what the Sea would not, *the Gallows may*.

Those that in former Dangers shunn'd the Fight,
But met their Ends in this Disast'rous Night,   110
　　Have left this Caution, tho' too late,
　　That all Events are known to Fate.
Cowards avoid no Danger when they run,
And Courage scapes the Death it would not shun;
　　'Tis Nonsence from our Fate to fly,
All Men must once have Heart enough to die.

　　Those Sons of Plunder are below my Pen,
Because they are below the Names of Men;
Who from the Shores presenting to their Eyes
The Fatal *Goodwin*, where the Wreck of *Navies* Lyes,[2]   120
A thousand dying Saylors talking to the Skies.
From the sad Shores they saw the Wretches walk,
　　By Signals of Distress they talk;
There with one Tide of Life they're vext,
　　For all were sure to die the next.
The Barbarous Shores with Men and Boats abound,
The Men more Barbarous than the Shores are found;
　　Off to the shatter'd Ships they go,
　　And for the Floating Purchase Row.
　　They spare no Hazard, or no Pain,   130
But 'tis to save the Goods, and not the Men.[3]

Within the sinking Supplaints Reach appear,
   As if they'd mock their dying Fear.
Then for some Trifle all their Hopes supplant,
With Cruelty would make a *Turk* relent.

   If I had any *Satyr* left to write,
   Cou'd I with suited Spleen Indite,
My Verse should blast that Fatal Town,
And Drowned Saylors Widows pull it down;
   No Footsteps of it should appear,   140
   And Ships no more Cast Anchor there.
The Barbarous Hated Name of *Deal* shou'd die,
   Or be a Term of Infamy;
And till that's done, the Town will stand
   A just Reproach to all the Land.[4]

   The Ships come next to be my Theme,
The Men's the Loss, I'm not concern'd for them;
   For had they perish'd e'er they went,
   Where to no Purpose they were sent,
   The Ships might ha' been built again,   150
And we had sav'd the Money and the Men.
   There the Mighty Wrecks appear,
Hic Jacent,[5] Useless Things of War.
   Graves of Men, and Tools of State,
There you lye too soon, there you lye too late.
   But O ye Mighty Ships of War!
   What in Winter did you there?
Wild *November* should our Ships restore
   To *Chatham, Portsmouth,* and the *Nore,*[6]
   So it was always heretofore,   160
For Heaven it self is not unkind,
If Winter Storms he'll sometimes send,
   Since 'tis suppos'd the Men of War
   Are all laid up, and left secure.

Nor did our Navy feell alone,
   The dreadful Desolation;

It shook the *Walls of Flesh* as well as Stone,
   And ruffl'd all the Nation.
   The Universal Fright
Made Guilty *H*—[7] expect his Fatal Night;   170
   His harden'd Soul began to doubt,
And Storms grew high within, as they grew high without.

   Flaming Meteors fill'd the Air,
But *Asgil* miss'd his *Fiery Chariot* there;
   Recall'd his black blaspheming Breath,
And trembling paid his Homage unto Death.[8]

   Terror appear'd in every Face,
Even *Vile Blackbourn*[9] felt some shocks of Grace;
Began to feel the Hated Truth appear,
     Began to fear,   180
After *he had Burlesqu'd a God* so long,
   He should at last be in the wrong.
   Some Power he plainly saw,
(And seeing, felt a strange unusual Awe;)
   Some secret Hand he plainly found,
   Was bringing some strange thing to pass,
And he that neither God nor Devil own'd,
   Must needs be at a loss to guess.
   Fain he would not ha' guest the worst,
But Guilt will always be with Terror Curst.   190

   Hell shook, for Devils Dread Almighty Power,
At every Shock they fear'd the Fatal Hour,
   The Adamantine Pillars mov'd,
And Satan's *Pandemonium* trembl'd too;
   The tottering *Seraphs* wildly rov'd,[10]
Doubtful what the Almighty meant to do;
For in the darkest of the black Abode,
There's not a Devil but believes a God.
   Old *Lucifer* has sometimes try'd
    To have himself be Deify'd;   200
But Devils nor Men the Being of God deny'd,

Till Men of late found out New Ways to sin,
And turn'd the Devil out to let the Atheist in.
But when the mighty Element began,
    And Storms the weighty Truth explain,
Almighty Power upon the Whirlwind Rode,
    And every Blast proclaim'd aloud
There is, there is, there is, a God.

Plague, Famine, Pestilence, and War,
    Are in their Causes seen,   210
The true Originals appear
    Before the Effects begin:
But Storms and Tempests are above our Rules,
    Here our Philosophers are Fools.
The *Stagyrite*[11] himself could never show,
    From whence, nor how they blow.
Tis all Sublime, 'tis all a Mystery,
They see no Manner how, nor Reason why;
All Sovereign Being is the amazing Theme,
    'Tis all resolv'd to Power Supreme;   220
    From this First Cause our Tempest came,
And let the Atheists spight of Sense Blaspheme,
    They can no room for Banter find,
Till they produce another Father for the Wind.

Satyr, thy Sense of Sovereign Being Declare,
    He made the Mighty Prince o'th' Air,
And Devils recognize him by their Fear.

    Ancient as Time, and Elder than the Light,
Ere the First Day, or Antecedent Night,
Ere Matter into settl'd Form became,   230
And long before Existence had a Name;
Before th' Expance of indigested Space,
While the vast *No-where* fill'd the Room of Place.
Liv'd *the First Cause* The First Great *Where* and *Why*,
Existing *to and from* Eternity,
Of His Great Self, and *of Necessity*.

This I call God, that One great Word of Fear,
   At whose great sound,
When from his Mighty Breath 'tis eccho'd round,
Nature pays Homage with a trembling bow,   240
And Conscious Men would faintly disallow;

The Secret Trepidation racks the Soul,
And while he says, no God, replies, thou Fool.
   But call it what we will,
First Being it had, does Space and Substance fill.
Eternal Self-existing Power enjoy'd,
And whatsoe'er is so, *That same is God*.

If then it should fall out, as who can tell,
   But that there is a Heaven and Hell,
Mankind had best consider well for fear   250
'T should be too late when their Mistakes appear;
   Such may in vain Reform,
Unless they do't before another Storm.

   They tell us *Scotland* scap'd the Blast;
No Nation else have been without a Taste:
   All *Europe* sure have felt the Mighty Shock,
   'T has been a Universal Stroke.
But Heaven has other Ways to plague the *Scots*,
   As Poverty and Plots.
Her Majesty Confirms it, what She said,   260
   I plainly heard it, tho' I'm dead.

The dangerous Sound has rais'd me from my Sleep,
   I can no longer Silence keep,
Here *Satyr*'s thy Deliverance,
A Plot in *Scotland*, Hatch'd in *France*,
And Liberty the Old Pretence.[12]
   Prelatick Power with Popish join,
The Queens Just Government to undermine;
   This is enough to wake the Dead,

The Call's too loud, it never shall be said   270
    The lazy *Satyr* slept too long,
When all the Nations Danger Claim'd his Song.

Rise *Satyr* from thy sleep of legal Death,
    And reassume Satyrick Breath;
What tho' to Seven Years sleep thou art confin'd,
    Thou well may'st wake with such a Wind.
    Such Blasts as these can seldom blow,
But they're both form'd above and heard below.
Then wake and warn us now the Storms are past,
Lest Heaven return with a severer Blast.   280
    Wake and inform Mankind
    Of Storms that still remain behind.

    If from this Grave thou lift thy Head,
They'll surely mind one risen from the Dead.
Tho' *Moses* and the Prophets can't prevail,
    A Speaking *Satyr* cannot fail.
Tell 'em while secret Discontents appear,
    There'll ne'er be *Peace and Union* here.
    They that for Trifles so contend,
    Have something farther in their End;   290
    But let those hasty People know,
The Storms above reprove the Storms below,
    And 'tis too often known,
The Storms below do Storms above Forerun;

    They say this was a High-Church Storm,[13]
    Sent out the Nation to Reform;
But th' Emblem left the Moral in the Lurch,
For't blew the Steeple down upon the Church.
    From whence we now inform the People,
The danger of the Church is from the Steeple.   300
    And we've had many a bitter stroke,
    From Pinacle and Weather-Cock;
From whence the Learned do relate,

That to secure the Church and State,
   The Time will come when all the Town
   To save the Church, will pull the Steeple down.

   Two Tempests are blown over, now prepare
For Storms of Treason and Intestine War.
   The High-Church Fury to the North extends,
      In haste to ruin all their Friends.   310
      Occasional Conforming led the Way,
And now Occasional Rebellion comes in Play,
      To let the Wond'ring Nation know,
   That High-Church Honesty's an Empty Show,
      A Phantasm of Delusive Air,
   That as Occasion serves can disappear,
      And Loyalty's a sensless Phrase,
An Empty Nothing which our interest sways,
      And as that suffers this decays.

   Who dare the Dangerous Secret tell,   320
      That Church-men can Rebel.
Faction we thought was by the Whigs Engross'd,
And *Forty One* was banter'd till the Jest was lost.
   Bothwel and *Pentland-Hills* were fam'd,
And *Gilly Cranky* hardly nam'd.[14]
   If Living Poets Dare not speak,
   We that are Dead must Silence break;
And boldly let them know the Time's at Hand.
When Ecclesiastick Tempests shake the Land.
Prelatick Treason from the Crown divides,   330
   And now Rebellion changes sides.
Their Volumes with their Loyalty may swell,
   But in their Turns too they Rebel;
      Can Plot, Contrive, Assassinate,
And spight of Passive Laws disturb the State.
Let fair Pretences fill the Mouths of Men,
      No fair Pretence shall blind my Pen;
They that *in such a Reign as this* Rebel
Must needs be in Confederacy with Hell.

    Oppressions, Tyranny and Pride,   340
     May give some Reason to Divide;
But where the Laws with open Justice Rule,
He that Rebels *Must be both Knave and Fool.*
May Heaven the growing Mischief soon prevent,
    And Traytors meet Reward in Punishment.

FINIS.

Notes

THE STORM

Biblical citations in the Notes are taken from the King James Version.

THE PREFACE

1. *Noverint Universi . . . Presents*: Since the Elizabethan era, legal documents, such as title deeds, began with the Latin phrase 'Noverint universi per presentes' ('be it known to all men by these presents that').
2. *Rhodomontades*: Boasts.
3. *Belus . . . Jupiter*: Ancient gods and legendary kings: Belus was an Assyrian god; Nimrod and Nimrus were Babylonian kings; Saturn and Jupiter were powerful ancient Greek divinities.
4. *Deucalion's Time*: Greek myth relates that, in around 1450 BC, Zeus decided to destroy mankind by flood as a punishment for its impieties. Deucalion, the son of Prometheus and Clymene, and his wife Pyrrha, were said to be the only survivors.
5. *Dedalus . . . flying through the Air*: According to myth, Daedalus built a labyrinth for King Minos of Crete, but was himself imprisoned in it after he fell from favour. He and his son Icarus escaped from the island by contriving wings made of feathers and wax, but Icarus flew too near to the sun and was drowned in the Aegean sea. Daedalus made it safely to Sicily.
6. *Samaria . . . ever since*: In Greek myth, Phaeton was the son of the sun-god Helios, who lived and rose in the East. Phaeton made the journey to meet his father and begged for the chance to drive his sun-chariot across the sky. Phaeton was unable to control the powerful horses, however, and his attempt caused fire and

destruction on earth until Zeus struck him down with a thunder-bolt. Samaria, a region of Palestine, often suffered from heatwaves and drought.

7.   *King Arthur . . . and the like*: Legendary British heroes who were the subjects of popular chapbooks, romances and histories such as Geoffrey of Monmouth's *History of the Kings of Great Britain* (*c.* 1136).

8.   *set at such a Main*: To take such a chance.

9.   *If it shou'd . . . Mistakes appear*: Lines from Defoe's *An Essay on the Late Storm*, p. 210.

CHAPTER I
Of the Natural Causes and Original of Winds

1.   *Antiperistasis*: Opposition or resistance.

2.   *Aristotle . . . Bohun of Winds, P. 9*: Defoe apparently quotes Aristotle (*c.* 384–322 BC), *Problems*, Bk 23.2; Seneca (*c.* 3 BC–AD 65), *Naturales Quaestiones*, Bk 5.1.1; Thomas Hobbes (1588–1679), *Dialogus physicus* (London, 1661); Georges Fournier (1595–1643), *Hydrographie* (Paris: Michel Soly, 1643), p. 698; René Descartes (1596–1650), *Les Météores* (1637); and Ralph Bohun (d. 1716), *A Discourse Concerning the Origine and Properties of Wind: With An Historicall Account of Hurricanes, and other Tempestuous Winds* (Oxford: Tho. Bowman, 1671), p. 7. In fact all of Defoe's quotations here are taken directly from Bohun's *Discourse*, pp. 5–9.

3.   *the wisest Philosopher in the dark*: Defoe uses the terms 'Philosophy' and 'Philosopher' throughout *The Storm*, by which was meant natural philosophy, to which we would now refer as science, and natural philosophers, to whom we would now refer as scientists or naturalists.

4.   *Vossius . . . Philosophy*: The Dutch polymath Isaac Vossius (1618–89); the Irish Protestant chemist Robert Boyle (1627–91); the renaissance courtier and explorer Sir Walter Raleigh (1552–1618), to whom Defoe claimed a family connection; the pioneer of empiricism Francis Bacon, later Lord Verulam (1561–1626); and the physician William Harvey (1578–1657) form Defoe's pantheon of respectably Christian scientific thinkers. Hobbes, however, is singled out for rebuke as an atheist.

5.   *hunt Counter*: To search backwards from effect to cause.

6.   *Terra Incognita*: (Latin) Unknown lands.

7.   *Champion Country*: Open fields.

8.   *When I view the Heavens . . . What is Man!*: Psalm 8:3–4.

9. *Johan Remelini . . . Riolanus*: Johann Remmelin (b. 1583), lead-
    ing German-born anatomist, and Jean Riolanus (1580–1657),
    leading French anatomist.

10. *I was fearfully and wonderfully made, &c.*: Psalm 139:14.

11. *The Winds . . . from the middle Region*: Bohun, *Discourse*,
    pp. 9–10. 'Resilition' means recoiling.

12. *as the Lord Verulam . . . Case of his Feathers*: Convection from
    the fire caused suspended feathers to move in the current. Francis
    Bacon described the experiment in *The Naturall and Experi-
    mentall History of Winds, &c.* (London: Humphrey Moseley,
    1653), pp. 92–3.

13. *He holds the Wind in his Hand*: Isaiah 11:15

14. *The Wind blows . . . it cometh*: John 3:8.

15. *Mansones*: Monsoons.

16. *God shall rain upon . . . a horrible Tempest*: Psalm 11:6.

17. *Sodom and Gomorrah on fire*: See Genesis 19:24–5.

CHAPTER II
Of the Opinion of the Ancients

1. *Cambden tells us*: William Camden (1551–1623) in his *Britannia*
    of 1586, translated from the Latin in 1610 as *Britain: or, a
    Chorographical Description of the most flourishing Kingdomes,
    England, Scotland, and Ireland, and the Islands adjoyning, out
    of the depth of Antiquitie* (London: Bishop & Norton, 1610),
    pp. 34–9.

2. *Et Penitus Toto . . . known World*: Virgil, *Eclogues*, Bk I. 66.

3. *Quem Littus . . . Fretum*: 'Lybia's sun-scorched shores and Thule,
    whither no ship can sail': Claudian, *The Third Consulship of
    Honorius*, 53.

4. *Belluosus . . . Britannis*: 'the ocean teeming with monsters, that
    roars around the distant Britons': Horace, *Odes*, Bk IV. xiv. 47–8.

5. *Shooters-Hill in Kent*: In *A Tour thro' the Whole Island of Great
    Britain*, ed. Pat Rogers (Harmondsworth: Penguin Books, 1971),
    p. 118, Defoe points out that Shooters Hill, near Greenwich,
    marks the geographical border between London clay and the
    chalk of the North Downs.

6. *the Danish Fleet came almost up to Hartford*: Defoe had recently
    contemplated the impact of the Danish raids of the tenth and
    eleventh centuries in *The True-Born Englishman*, his verse satire
    of *c.* 1701: 'Danes with Sueno came,/In search of plunder, not
    in search of fame.' See *The True-Born Englishman and Other*

Writings, ed. P. N. Furbank and W. R. Owens (London: Penguin, 1997), p. 31.

7. *Rumney-Marsh*: Much of the Romney Marsh, in Kent and Sussex, was under water until the retreat of the sea in the Middle Ages. The former port of Rye, on the River Rother, now sits three miles inland.

8. *Ely . . . to dislodge them*: Ely, built on a clay island surrounded by marshland, was a centre of Anglo-Saxon resistance to the Norman invasion, holding out for five years until its defeat in 1071.

9. *The Piss-pot of the World*: Defoe is only too happy to offer a meteorological refinement to his general hatred and suspicion of Catholic Ireland.

10. *the Phœnicians*: Inhabitants of Phoenicia, an ancient maritime nation, corresponding to the coastal plains of modern Lebanon and Syria.

11. *And Thule . . . Sails to bear*: Claudian, *The Third Consulship*, 53.

12. *Quanto Delphino . . . major*: 'The British whale exceeds the dolphin': Juvenal, *Satires*, X. 14.

13. *Yarmouth Road . . . them*: In his *Tour* Defoe described the loss of a 200-strong fleet of coal ships off Yarmouth Roads in 1692, branding that stretch of the Norfolk coast 'one of the most dangerous and most fatal to the sailors in all England, I may say in all Britain'. *Tour*, pp. 92–4.

14. *Barbary*: North Africa.

15. *a Lee Shore*: A shore upon which the wind blows.

16. *Sea-room*: An unobstructed sea in which to manoeuvre a ship.

17. *go under a main Course*: Use the main sails on the lower yards of a ship.

18. *the Battle of Actium*: A sea-battle fought off the west coast of Greece in 31 BC, in which Octavian's Roman fleet defeated the combined forces of Antony and Cleopatra.

19. *Julius Cæsar's Fleet . . . Carthage*: Caesar's fleet was hit by a storm in the English Channel in 55 BC (see *The Gallic War*, Bk IV. 29); for Aeneas's storm see Virgil, *Aeneid*, Bk I. 34–123.

20. *Spanish Armada . . . every Shore*: Francis Drake's (*c.* 1540–96) 'Hell Burners', as fireships then were known, were powerful psychological weapons in the battle against the Spanish Armada of August 1588. The storm of 14–15 August drove the Spanish ships into the North Sea, where they dispersed, to the advantage of the victorious British.

21. *the Downs*: The sea off the east Kent coast, bounded by the Goodwin Sands.

CHAPTER III
Of the Storm in General

1. *our Barometers*: Like many of his contemporaries Defoe owned and occasionally consulted an indoor barometer. His tutor at the Newington Green Academy, Charles Morton (1627–98), encouraged his students in natural philosophy and equipped the school laboratory with an impressive array of equipment, including barometers.

2. *directed to the Royal Society . . . as follows*: The Royal Society of London for the Improving of Natural Knowledge was founded in 1660. Its proceedings, the *Philosophical Transactions*, were published from 1665 onwards.

3. *the Reverend Mr. William Derham, F.R.S.*: Derham (1657–1735) was a prominent natural theologian and author of *Physico-Theology: or a Demonstration of the Being and Attributes of God from his Works of Creation* (London: W. Innys, 1713). His letter was published in the *Philosophical Transactions*, vol. 24 (1704–5), pp. 1530–4.

4. *St. Andrews Day*: 30 November.

5. *Richard Townely, Esq*: Richard Towneley (*c.* 1629–1707), of Towneley Hall, Lancashire, was a noted experimental meteorologist.

6. *l.*: Pound: many early meteorologists measured rainfall by weight.

7. *Tunnel*: A funnel leading into a rain gauge.

8. *Nitro-sulphureous . . . Atmosphere*: Francis Bacon had suggested in the 1620s that the presence of nitre (saltpetre, an ingredient of gunpowder) could adversely affect the weather, a belief which remained current until the late eighteenth century.

9. *Mr. Halley*: Edmond Halley (1656–1743), Clerk to the Royal Society. Wind and weather were high on his list of interests.

10. *Ph. Tr. No. 262*: See *Philosophical Transactions*, vol. 22 (1700–1), pp. 527–9.

11. ☿: The chemical symbol for Mercury.

12. *Travail*: Labour.

13. *Out-Parts*: Suburbs.

14. *several Rods*: One rod is equivalent to 16.5 feet (5.029 metres).

15. *Almanacks*: Annually published calendars of information and events.

16. *Damon, Melibæus*: Pastoral characters taken from Virgil's *Eclogues* (*c.* 42–39 BC).

17. *Isis*: The Oxford stretch of the river Thames.

18. *Cherwel's banks*: The River Cherwell, which flows south from Northamptonshire and into the Thames at Oxford.

19. *Orpheus Lyre . . . Amphion's Hand*: In Greek myth Orpheus, son of the Muse Calliope, was able to tame all nature with the beauty of his lyre-playing; Amphion, the son of Jupiter and Antiope, was said to have built the walls of Thebes with the magical sound of his lyre alone.

20. *Neptune*: The Roman god of the sea, corresponding to the Greek Poseidon.

21. *Thetis*: In Greek legend, Thetis was one of the Nereids (minor sea deities) and the mother of Achilles, one of the heroes of the Trojan War.

22. *the Æolian God*: Aeolus, the ancient Greek god of winds and storms.

23. *Charles of Spain's*: Archduke Charles (1685–1740), the second son of the Emperor Leopold of Austria, was waiting to be escorted from Holland to Lisbon, from where he would launch his claim on the Spanish throne as 'Charles III of Spain'. The effort was unsuccessful, but in 1711, at the death of his older brother Joseph, he became Charles VI of Austria.

24. *angry Juno's Hate*: Juno, the jealous wife of Jupiter, was responsible for the storm that drove Aeneas on to the shore at Carthage; see Virgil, *Aeneid*, Bk I. 34–80.

25. *Dardan Prince*: Trojan prince, i.e. Aeneas.

CHAPTER IV
Of the Extent of this Storm

1. *Sir Francis Wheeler . . . Straelsond*: Admiral Sir Francis Wheler (*c.* 1656–94) and 548 of his men drowned in a storm off Gibraltar on 19 February 1694. Straelsond is a small Pomeranian city on the Strelasund, an inlet of the Baltic sea. The church there lost its spire in the storm of 26–7 November 1703.

2. *Sir William Temple*: The diplomat and author Sir William Temple (1628–99) was English ambassador to The Hague from 1668.

3. *the Texel*: An island in the Waddenzee, off the coast of Holland.

4. *I stay'd only a Night . . . lost*: From William Temple, *Memoirs of What Pass'd in Christendom, from the War Begun in 1672, to the Peace Concluded 1679* (London: Samuel Buckley, 1709), pp. 34–5, 105.

5. *Mirabilis Annis*: From *Mirabilis Annus Secundus; or, the Second Year of Prodigies; Being a True and Impartial Collection of Many Strange Signes and Apparitions, which Have This Last Year Been Seen in the Heavens, and in the Earth, and in the Waters* (London, 1662), pp. 54–9.

6. *lest we likewise perish*: Luke 13:3.

7. *Fane*: Weathervane.

8. *Audley-End House . . . Earl of Suffolk*: Audley End House, a vast Jacobean mansion, was built in the early seventeenth century for the Earls of Suffolk. The lighthouse designer Henry Winstanley (1644–1703), who lost his life in the storm, was brought up at Audley End, where his father was head steward.

9. *Hampton-Court*: A Thames-side Tudor palace built in 1516 by Cardinal Thomas Wolsey (*c.* 1475–1530), chief political advisor to Henry VIII. Henry requisitioned the palace and rebuilt it as a royal residence following Wolsey's later fall from favour. It was to be William III's favourite palace.

10. *Sir Edward Harly*: Sir Edward Harley (1624–1700), governor of Dunkirk.

11. *a Pole in Length*: A pole is equivalent to a rod, i.e. 16.5 feet (5.029 metres).

12. *the white Tower*: Part of the Tower of London, built by William the Conqueror in the eleventh century, with four corner cupolas added during the reign of Henry VIII.

13. *the several Triumphant Arches*: James I had seven triumphal arches built along the route of his coronation in 1603.

14. *some of the Heads . . . Westminster-Hall*: The heads of executed traitors were displayed on the outer walls of Westminster Hall.

15. *he only knows . . . the Dust of his Feet*: Nahum 1:3. Defoe cites this passage on the title-page of *The Storm*, and takes it as his text for *The Lay-Man's Sermon upon the Late Storm*.

16. *Meridian*: Greatest.

17. *Leagues*: One league was equivalent to just under three nautical miles (just under five kilometres).

18. *the Nore*: A sandbank in the outer Thames Estuary, which was marked by a warning buoy.

19. *Sir Cloudsly Shovel*: Admiral Sir Cloudesley Shovell (1650–1707), commander of the fleet, who was to die in a shipwreck off the Scilly Isles in October 1707.

20. *the Gunfleet*: A sandbank in the Thames estuary, off Clacton.

21. *Tenders and Victuallers*: Ships carrying fuel, water and food for the fleet.

22. *Admiral Dilks ... Lisbon*: Rear-Admiral Sir Thomas Dilkes (*c.* 1667–1707); for the 'King of Spain' and his trip to Lisbon see note 23 to Ch. III.

23. *Admiral Callenberge*: Vice-Admiral Gerrit van Callenburgh (1642–1722). Defoe questions his abilities in *The Lay-Man's Sermon upon the Late Storm*, p. 195.

24. *Paris Gazetteer*: A French newspaper, founded in the seventeenth century, the contents of which were regularly summarized in the London press.

OF THE EFFECTS OF THE STORM

1. *Fox, Grimston, Holinshead or Stow*: The four long history books mentioned here are: John Fox, *Book of Martyrs*, 2 vols. (London: John Daye, 1570); Sir Harbottle Grimston, *The Reports of Sr George Croke, &c.* (London: R. Hodgkinsonne, 1658); Raphael Holinshed, *The Chronicles of England, Scotlande, and Irelande*, 3 vols. (London: John Harrison, 1577); and John Stow, *A Survey of London* (London: John Wolfe, 1598).

I. Of the Damages in the City of London

1. *Earls of Northampton*: A notable royalist family that included Henry Compton (1632–1713), Bishop of London.

2. *Bills of Mortality*: Parish burial records, which were published on a weekly basis.

3. *Coin of the House*: Corner-stone, also known as coin-stone or quoin.

4. *a Wherry*: A passenger boat.

5. *the Indraft*: Inward flow of air.

6. *Cardinal Woolsey*: Thomas, Cardinal Wolsey (*c.* 1475–1530), chief political advisor to Henry VIII.

II. Of the Damages in the Country

1. *riving*: Tearing or rending.

2. *Circumgyration*: A circular course of movement.

3. *Fell-mongers*: Dealers in animal skins.

4. *Rouses*: Rice, that is, brushwood twigs.

5. *Plummer*: Plumber, a craftsman working in lead.

6. *the dismal Accident of our late Bishop and Lady ... remarkable*: The Bishop of Bath and Wells, Richard Kidder (1633–1703) and

his wife Elizabeth (*c.* 1638–1703) were killed at their home during the storm.

7.   *an Ell*: 45 inches (114 cm).
8.   *Miserere, &c.*: 'Lord have mercy': Psalm 51:1.
9.   *Ashler*: Square hewn stone used in building.
10. *Munnel*: Mullion, a vertical bar dividing the windowpanes.
11. *Trenchard*: Trencher, a plate for serving food.
12. *Loads*: The maximum amount that could be carried by a single horse or cart.
13. *Imprimus*: In the first place.
14. *Stadle*: Platform or base.
15. *Holms*: Holly trees.
16. *Causeth the Vapours . . . remembrance*: Psalm 135:7; Ecclesiasticus 17:9.
17. *Closes*: Enclosed fields.
18. *Deals*: Deal-boards, thin planks made of fir or pine timber.
19. *Perches*: The same as poles and rods, a measure equivalent to 16.5 feet (5.029 metres).
20. *Bed-teaster*: Tester, the canopy over a four-poster bed.
21. *Hoy*: Sea-going passenger sloop.
22. *Pannel of Pales*: Fence-panels.
23. *lights*: Small panes of glass.
24. *Furlongs*: A furlong is one eighth of a mile (220 yards or 201 metres).
25. *Hogsheds*: Large wooden casks that could hold around 52.5 gallons (239 litres) of liquid or other goods.
26. *the Watch*: Night watchmen patrolled the streets of London until the late nineteenth century.
27. *That a Physician . . . therewith*: From *Philosophical Transactions*, vol. 24 (1704–5), p. 1534.
28. *Anthony van Lauwenhoek, F. R. S.*: The Dutch naturalist and microscope-maker Anthony van Leeuwenhoek (1632–1723) was a regular correspondent to the *Philosophical Transactions*. This letter appeared in vol. 24 (1704–5), pp. 1535–7.
29. *Quick-silver*: Mercury.

Of the Damages on the Water

1.   *Negoce*: Commerce.
2.   *Sheet Anchor*: The largest anchor on a ship, used only in emergencies.
3.   *Groundsils, Cap-heads*: Timber foundations, tops of shafts.
4.   *Wood-buss*: A boat or barge carrying wood.

5. *Ruff-cast*: Rough-cast, a lime and gravel wall coating.
6. *Moars*: Roots.
7. *Pink*: A large vessel with a narrow stern.
8. *Shrouds*: Ropes leading down from the head of a mast.
9. *Salt-terns*: Boats laden with salt.
10. *Healing*: Roofing.
11. *the Cob*: The Cobb, Lyme Regis's distinctively curved harbour wall.
12. *Hookers*: One-masted fishing smacks.
13. *the Rear Admiral of the Blew*: The fleet was made up of three squadrons, the red, the white and the blue, each squadron having its own admiral, vice-admiral and rear-admiral.
14. *small Bower Anchor*: One of the two anchors carried at the bows of a vessel.
15. *Kedge Anchor*: Small mooring anchor.
16. *bonet*: Bonnet, an extra piece of canvas laced to the foot of a sail.
17. *Slop-Seller*: A dealer in ready-made clothing for sea-goers.
18. *Boltsprits*: Bowsprits, large spars pointing forwards from the bows of ships.
19. *Watermen*: Ferrymen.
20. *Lighters*: Flat-bottomed barges used for unloading larger ships.
21. *Flambro*: Flamborough Head, East Yorkshire.
22. *advice Boat*: Intelligence, or dispatch, boat.
23. *Ricebank*: A sea-wall made of brushwood.
24. *Sir Stafford Fairborn*: Sir Stafford Fairborne (*c.* 1660–1742), vice-admiral of the red.
25. From Abel Boyer, *The History of the Reign of Queen Anne, Digested into Annals: Year the Second* (London: F. Coggan, 1704), Appendix II, pp. 8–11.
26. *Port*: A shutter covering a porthole.
27. *Gun-Wale*: The timbers running along the top of a ship's sides.
28. *Belle Isle*: Belem, a magnificent harbour town to the west of the Portuguese capital, Lisbon, was known to the British as Belle-Isle.
29. *Privateers*: Privately owned armed vessels authorized to attack enemy merchant and naval shipping.

Of the Damage to the Navy

1. *Mr. Winstanly*: Henry Winstanley (1644–1703), the doomed designer of the Eddystone Lighthouse.

Of the Earthquake

1. *Pharos*: The Lighthouse of Alexandria, built *c.* 290 BC, and one of the Seven Wonders of the Ancient World.

2. *Innocent's Day*: Childermas, the Feast of the Holy Innocents: 28 December.

3. *Mr. Thorsby of Leeds in Yorkshire*: Ralph Thoresby (1658–1725), Yorkshire antiquary and topographer.

4. *December 1703*: See *Philosophical Transactions*, vol. 24 (1704–5), pp. 1555–8.

Of Remarkable Deliverances

1. *as David said to Jonathan ... outward Appearance*: 1 Samuel 20:3.

2. *Reeks*: Ricks.

3. *Clavel*: The lintel over a fireplace.

4. *Funnels*: Flues.

5. *Rother*: Rudder.

6. *shoul Water*: Shallow water.

7. *Hallelujah ... Hallelujah*: See Psalm 148: 1–14.

8. *Ground Tackle*: Ropes and cables used for anchoring.

9. *Haiser*: Hawser, a rope or cable used for mooring.

10. *the Board*: The sides of the ship.

11. *Jury Missen*: Temporary sail attached to the mizzen-mast.

12. *the Brill*: Brielle, a Dutch port served by Harwich packet-boats during the 17th and 18th centuries.

13. *Weather-shore*: A windward shore.

The Conclusion

1. *We receiv'd a Letter ... excuse Us*: Bishop Kidder made many enemies during his career, among the last of whom was the Revd Samuel Hill, Rector of Kilmington, Somerset, who may well have been responsible for the anonymous letter sent from nearby Somerton.

THE LAY-MAN'S SERMON UPON THE LATE STORM

1. *Nineveh*: The capital of the Assyrian Empire, destroyed by Babylonian-led forces in 612 BC.

2. *the Lord is ... acquit the wicked*: Nahum 1:3.

3.   *God is jealous . . . his Enemies*: Nahum 1:2.

4.   *Elija . . . God in Israel*: 1 Kings 18:27–36.

5.   *That if a Nation . . . their King*: 1 Samuel 12:25.

6.   *Miserere Dei*: God have mercy. For the story of the carpenter see *The Storm*, p. 59.

7.   *Jacobites and Non-Jurants*: Jacobites were supporters of the deposed Stuart King James II (1685–8) and his descendants, whom they regarded as their lawful sovereigns; non-jurors were members of the clergy who refused to swear the oath of allegiance to William and Mary, the monarchs who replaced James II in 1689.

8.   *Occasional Conformists*: Some Dissenters practised Occasional Conformity, which involved taking communion once a year in an Anglican church, in order to comply with the Test Act of 1673, while continuing to worship regularly at a Nonconformist chapel. Defoe wrote a number of pamphlets attacking the practice, which he described as 'playing Bo-peep with God Almighty'.

9.   *the late King William*: William, Prince of Orange (1650–1702), crowned William III in 1689, died on 8 March 1702 after falling from his horse while out riding in Hampton Court Park.

10. *the Streights*: The Straits of Gibraltar, the entrance to the Mediterranean, where the English fleet had had a generally unsuccessful campaign during the summer of 1703.

11. *pay so dear for Coals*: In order to pay for the rebuilding of London following the Great Fire of 1666, the tax on coal was raised; many coal-merchants took advantage of this by raising their prices even further, some of them, allegedly, inventing stories of robbery by French privateers in order to justify the increase. See the *Review*, 8 April 1704.

12. *If Mr. Sachaverell . . . Guilty*: Defoe's model for *The Shortest-Way with the Dissenters* was the High Church minister Dr Henry Sacheverell (*c.* 1674–1724), who preached a sermon in Oxford on 2 June 1702 against toleration of the Dissenters, in which he called upon his followers to 'hang out the bloody flag, and banner of defiance'.

13. *If Dr. J—ne . . . not Guilty*: Henry Sacheverell (see above) was the author of *The Character of a Low-Churchman* (1702), while the non-juror Charles Leslie (1650–1722), was author of the *New Association* (*c.* 1700, part II, 1703). In 1685 Louis XIV revoked the Edict of Nantes, which extended religious freedom to the Protestant Huguenots, many of whom fled to England during the ensuing persecution.

14. *If Sir John Friend . . . Repentance*: Sir John Friend (d.1696) and
    Sir William Parkyns (*c.* 1649–1696) were both executed in 1696
    for their part in a conspiracy to assassinate William III in 1695.
    Jeremy Collier (1650–1726), and two other non-juring clergymen
    (Snett and Cook) gave public absolution to the prisoners at the
    gallows, for which they were themselves arrested.

15. *Fuller*: William Fuller (1670–1733), Dissenting pamphleteer,
    who was pilloried and imprisoned in 1703, as was Defoe only a
    few months later.

16. *Father P—, my Lord S—*: Father P—is William Bentinck, first
    Earl of Portland (1649–1709), at one time William III's closest
    friend and advisor; John, Lord Somers (1651–1716), Lord Chan-
    cellor of England, was forced to resign his post in 1699.

17. *the Settlement*: The Act of Settlement of 1701 was a statute
    providing for a Protestant monarch if either William III or Anne
    died without an heir.

18. *Our Observator*: John Tutchin (*c.* 1661–1707), author and editor
    of the Whig newspaper the *Observator*, which he ran from April
    1702 until his death in September 1707.

19. *Sons of Levy*: Priests and clergymen. See Deuteronomy 31:9.

20. *Trimming*: To adjust one's outlook to suit the mood of the times
    (originally a nautical term meaning to adjust a ship's sails to suit
    the prevailing wind).

21. *Prelacy*: A hostile term for episcopacy, the system of church
    government by prelates or lordly bishops.

22. *Thanksgiveing for Victories*: The Duke of Marlborough's success-
    ful military campaign of 1702 was marked by a thanksgiving
    service and a grand procession through London on 12 November
    1702. See also note 24 below.

23. *against it self*: 'And if a kingdom be divided against itself, that
    kingdom cannot stand': Mark 3:24.

24. *The D—of M— . . . Mannagement*: John Churchill, Duke of
    Marlborough (1650–1722), a supporter of William III, was
    created a duke in 1702 at the accession of his wife's friend Anne.
    He was commander-in-chief of the allied forces during the War
    of the Spanish Succession (1702–13).

25. *his hand is Stretched out still*: Isaiah 5:25.

26. *the Persons . . . of this War*: The various admirals of the Anglo-
    Dutch fleet, under the command of Sir George Rooke (1650–
    1709), had had a generally unsuccessful campaign season during
    the summer of 1703.

27. *But David was not the Man . . . Throne*: See 1 Kings 6.

28. *the Bill against Occasional Conformity . . . Lords*: Defoe suggests here that the Tories care more about settling domestic scores against their enemies than in supporting the military campaign in Europe. The Occasional Conformity Bill, an attempt by the Tories to outlaw the practice, was passed by the House of Commons in November 1702, but was turned down by the House of Lords soon after. Landau, a Bavarian town, was captured from the French by the Duke of Marlborough in September 1702, with the aid of troops hired out to him by Charles, Prince of Hesse-Cassel, the first European ruler to put a mercenary army at the disposal of foreign powers; Augsburg, also in Bavaria, was badly damaged during a siege by the Duke of Bavaria, who fought as an ally of France.

AN ESSAY ON THE LATE STORM

1. *Limbus*: In Catholic theology Limbo is the temporary place for souls awaiting Christ's ascendancy into Heaven.

2. *The Fatal Goodwin . . . Lyes*: Goodwin Sands, off the Kent coast, where some 1,800 ships have been lost over the centuries.

3. *But 'tis to save . . . not the Men*: In *The Storm*, p. 134, Defoe records the actions of some of the people of Deal, who were too intent on salvaging goods from the storm-wrecked ships to assist in the saving of lives.

4. *The Barbarous Hated Name of Deal . . . all the Land*: Thomas Horne, the new mayor of Deal, threatened Defoe with a libel action over his damning portrayal of the town.

5. *Hic Jacent*: 'Here lie', a phrase commonly used on tomb inscriptions.

6. *the Nore*: see note 18 to *The Storm*, Chapter IV, 'Of the Extent of this Storm'.

7. *Guilty H—*: John Grubham How (1657–1722), Tory politician, who incurred Defoe's lifelong enmity by making insulting remarks about William III's policies in a notorious parliamentary speech.

8. *But Asgil . . . Homage unto Death*: The eccentric author John Asgill (1659–1738) published a much-mocked book in 1700 which argued that Christians might be 'translated from hence, into eternal life, without passing through death'. Defoe published a refutation of Asgill's thesis in November 1703.

9. *Vile Blackbourn*: John Blackbourne (1683–1741), non-juror,

whose refusal to recognize the Act of Settlement earned him many enemies and harmed his early career.

10. *And Satan's Pandemonium ... Seraphs wildly rov'd*: 'Pandemonium' is Satan's palace. The word was coined by Milton in Book I of *Paradise Lost* (1667). Seraphs are members of the highest order of angels, often depicted as winged childrens' heads.

11. *The Stagyrite*: The Greek philosopher Aristotle (*c.* 384–322 BC), so called because he was born at Stagira, in Macedonia.

12. *Liberty the Old Pretence*: The deposed James II died in exile in September 1701, but Louis XIV gave encouragement to the Jacobites by recognizing James's thirteen-year-old son, 'James III and VIII', as the Pretender to the British throne.

13. *a High-Church Storm*: An ironic opposition to the 'Protestant Wind' of 5 November 1688 which had assisted William of Orange's triumphant landing at Torbay while keeping James II's fleet stranded in the Thames.

14. *Bothwel and Pentland Hills ... nam'd*: The battles of Bothwell Bridge (1679), Rullion Green (1666), which ended the Pentland Rising, and Killiecrankie (1689) were fought to decide the religious destiny of Scotland. Defoe writes later of 'the Bothwell-Bridge Rebellion, and several other little disturbances of the Whigs in those days; for Whigs then were all Presbyterians', *Tour*, p. 617.